THE BALANCE BETWEEN INDUSTRY AND AGRICULTURE IN ECONOMIC DEVELOPMENT
Volume 4: SOCIAL EFFECTS

THE BALANCE BETWEEN INDUSTRY AND AGRICULTURE
IN ECONOMIC DEVELOPMENT

Volume 1 BASIC ISSUES
Kenneth J. Arrow (*editor*)

Volume 2 SECTOR PROPORTIONS
Jeffrey G. Williamson and Vadiraj R. Panchamukhi (*editors*)

Volume 3 MANPOWER AND TRANSFERS
Sukhamoy Chakravarty (*editor*)

Volume 4 SOCIAL EFFECTS
Irma Adelman and Sylvia Lane (*editors*)

Volume 5 FACTORS INFLUENCING CHANGE
Nurul Islam (*editor*)

The Balance between Industry and Agriculture in Economic Development

Proceedings of the Eighth World Congress of the International Economic Association, Delhi, India

Volume 4
SOCIAL EFFECTS

Edited by
Irma Adelman
and
Sylvia Lane

St. Martin's
Press
New York

in association with the
INTERNATIONAL ECONOMIC
ASSOCIATION

© International Economic Association, 1989

First published in the United States of America in 1989

Printed in Hong Kong

ISBN 0–312–02377–4

Library of Congress Cataloging-in-Publication Data
(Revised for vol. 1 & 4)
International Economic Association. World Congress
(8th : 1986 : Delhi, India)
The balance between industry and agriculture in
economic development.
(v. 1,   : International Economic Association
series)
Vol. 2 has imprint: London : Macmillan ;
New York : St. Martin's Press.
Includes indexes.
Contents: v. 1. Basic issues/edited by Kenneth J.
—v. 2. Sector proportions/edited by Jeffrey G.
Williamson and Vadiraj R. Panchamukhi—   —v. 4.
Social effects/edited by Irma Adelman and Sylvia Lane
1. Economic development—Congresses.   2. Agriculture
—Economic aspects—Developing countries—Congresses.
3. Developing countries—Industries—Congresses.
I. Arrow, Kenneth Joseph, 1921— . II. Title.
III. Series.
HD75.I587   1989   338.9   88–6459
ISBN 0–312–02377–4

Contents

Preface   vii

The International Economic Association   ix

Acknowledgements   xi

IEA Programme Committee   xiii

Indian Steering Committee   xiv

List of Authors, Session Organisers, and Rapporteurs   xv

Abbreviations and Acronyms   xvii

Introduction
Irma Adelman and Sylvia Lane   xviii

PART I   SOCIAL JUSTICE AND DEVELOPMENT   1

1   International Co-operation and Global Justice   3
     Paul Streeten

2   Welfare, Positive Freedom and Economic Development   18
     Partha Dasgupta

3   The New Economics of Child Health and Survival   32
     James P. Grant and Richard Jolly

4   Planning Techniques for Social Justice   45
     Erik Thorbecke

Discussion on Part I   72

PART II   AGRICULTURAL DEVELOPMENT AND
POVERTY   79

5   Growth and Equity in Agriculture-led Growth   81
     Alain de Janvry and Elisabeth Sadoulet

**6   Impact of Rural Development Programmes on the Economic
     Structure of Rural Communities**   97
     V. M. Rao

v

7   **What can Agriculture do for the Poorest Rural Groups?**   110
    Hans P. Binswanger and Jaime B. Quizon

Discussion on Part II   136

**PART III   AGRICULTURE AND INDUSTRY UNDER
CAPITALISM**   141

8   **On the Nature and Implications of Intersectoral Resource
    Allocations: Argentina 1913–84**   143
    Domingo Cavallo and Yair Mundlak

9   **The Choice of Tenancy Contract**   161
    Clive Bell

Discussion on Part III   179

**PART IV   AGRICULTURE AND INDUSTRY IN
SOCIALIST EXPERIENCE**   183

10 **Economic and Social Development of Czechoslovak
    Agriculture**   185
    V. Jeniček

11 **Socialist Technically-oriented Production Systems: the Case
    of Hungarian Agriculture**   197
    Aladár Sipos

12 **China's Economic Structural Reform and Agricultural
    Development**   211
    Luo Yuanzheng

13 **Intensification of Land Utilisation**   216
    Tigran Khachaturov

Discussion on Part IV   230

Index   237

Preface

The Eighth World Congress of the International Economic Association was held in Delhi from 1 to 5 December 1986, presided over by Professor Kenneth J. Arrow, President of the IEA from 1983 to 1986, on the subject of 'The Balance between Agriculture and Industry in Economic Development'. It was organised by the Indian Economic Association.

Participation in the Congress was broadly based in terms both of geography and of the types of economy from which participants came; market orientated and centrally planned; developed and developing; mainly agricultural and predominantly industrial. The Congress included a number of plenary sessions, but much of the work of the Congress was undertaken in eighteen specialised meetings. The volume of papers was too large for them all to be published, but the five volumes in this group, together with a volume on the Indian economy being published separately in India, represent the major viewpoints expressed. The volumes generally contain reports on the discussions which took place during the specialised sessions.

The volumes are:
1. *Basic Issues*, edited by Kenneth J. Arrow
2. *Sector Proportions*, edited by Jeffrey G. Williamson and Vadiraj R. Panchamukhi
3. *Manpower and Transfers*, edited by Sukhamoy Chakravarty
4. *Social Effects*, edited by Irma Adelman and Sylvia Lane
5. *Factors Influencing Change*, edited by Nurul Islam

The Indian volume is edited by Dr P. R. Brahmananda and Dr S. Chakravarty under the title *The Indian Economy: Balance between Industry and Agriculture* and will be published by Macmillan India.

This volume contains selected papers from four sessions of the Congress, as follows:

Session 3   Agriculture and Industry in Socialist Experience, organised by Professor Béla Csikós-Nagy

Session 7   The Effects on Social Justice, organised by Professor Irma Adelman

Session 12   Effects of Sectoral Shifts on Social Variables, organised by Professor Amartya K. Sen

Session 14   Economic Organisation in the Rural Areas, organised by Professor Yair Mundlak

The International Economic Association

A non-profit organisation with purely scientific aims, the International Economic Association (IEA) was founded in 1950. It is in fact a federation of national economic associations and presently includes fifty-eight such professional organisations from all parts of the world. Its basic purpose is the development of economics as an intellectual discipline. Its approach recognises a diversity of problems, systems and values in the world and also takes note of methodological diversities.

The IEA has, since its creation, tried to fulfil that purpose by promoting mutual understanding of economists from the West and the East as well as from the North and the South through the organisation of scientific meetings and common research programmes and by means of publications on problems of current importance. During its thirty-seven years of existence, it has organised seventy-nine round-table conferences for specialists on topics ranging from fundamental theories to methods and tools of analysis and major problems of the present-day world. Eight triennial World Congresses have also been held, which have regularly attracted the participation of a great many economists from all over the world. The proceedings of all these meetings are published by Macmillan.

The Association is governed by a Council, composed of representatives of all member associations, and by a fifteen-member Executive Committee which is elected by the Council. The present Executive Committee (1986–89) is composed as follows:

President:	Professor Amartya Sen, India
Vice-President:	Professor Béla Csikós-Nagy, Hungary
Treasurer:	Professor Luis Angel Rojo, Spain
Past President:	Professor Kenneth J. Arrow, USA
Other members:	Professor Edmar Lisboa Bacha, Brazil
	Professor Ragnar Bentzel, Sweden
	Professor Oleg T. Bogomolov, USSR
	Professor Silvio Borner, Switzerland
	Professor P. R. Brahmananda, India
	Professor Phyllis Deane, United Kingdom

	Professor Luo Yuanzheng, China
	Professor Edmond Malinvaud, France
	Professor Luigi Pasinetti, Italy
	Professor Don Patinkin, Israel
	Professor Takashi Shiraishi, Japan
Adviser:	Professor Tigran S. Khachaturov, USSR
Secretary-General:	Professor Jean-Paul Fitoussi, France
General Editor:	Mr Michael Kaser, United Kingdom
Adviser to General Editor:	Professor Sir Austin Robinson, United Kingdom
Conference Editor:	Dr Patricia M. Hillebrandt, United Kingdom

The Association has also been fortunate in having secured the following outstanding economists to serve as President: Gottfried Haberler (1950–53), Howard S. Ellis (1953–56), Erik Lindahl (1956–59), E. A. G. Robinson (1959–62), G. Ugo Papi (1962–65), Paul A. Samuelson (1965–68), Erik Lundberg (1968–71), Fritz Machlup (1971–74), Edmond Malinvaud (1974–77), Shigeto Tsuru (1977–80), Victor L. Urquidi (1980–83), Kenneth J. Arrow (1983–86).

The activities of the Association are mainly funded from the subscriptions of members and grants from a number of organisations, including continuing support from UNESCO.

Acknowledgements

The host for the Eighth World Congress of the International Economic Association was the Indian Economic Association and all Congress participants are in its debt for the organisation of the Congress itself and for the welcome given to economists from all over the world. The preparation for such a gathering, culminating in a week of lectures, discussions and social activities, is an enormous undertaking. The International Economic Association wishes to express its appreciation on behalf of all participants.

Both the Indian and the International Economic Associations are grateful to the large number of institutions and organisations, including many states, banks, business firms, research and trade organisations which provided funds for the Congress. They particularly wish to thank the following Indian Government Departments and other official agencies:

Ministry of Finance
Ministry of External Affairs
The Reserve Bank of India
The State Bank of India
The Industrial Development Bank of India
The Indian Council of Social Science Research
The Industrial Credit and Investment Corporation of India
The Industrial Finance Corporation of India
The National Bank for Agriculture and Rural Development
The Industrial Reconstruction Bank of India
The Punjab National Bank
The Canara Bank
Tata Group of Industries
The Government of Uttar Pradesh
The Government of Karnataka
The Government of Kerala
The Government of Madhya Pradesh

Valuable support was given by the Ford Foundation and the International Development Research Centre. The Research and Information System for Non-aligned and Other Developing Countries and the

Institute of Applied Manpower Research provided valuable assistance
in staffing and in the infrastructure of the Congress.

The social events of the Congress provided a useful opportunity for
informal discussion as well as being a source of great enjoyment. The
hospitality of the Indian Economic Association, the Export Import
Bank of India, the Federation of Indian Chambers of Commerce and
Industry, the Punjab Haryana and Delhi (PHD) Chambers of Commerce and Industry and the DCM Ltd created memorable occasions.
Thanks go to the Indian Council for Cultural Relations who organised
a cultural evening. In addition there were many small social gatherings
which stressed the international flavour of the Congress.

Lastly, and vitally important, was the contribution of the members
of the IEA Organising Committee and the Indian Steering Committee –
in particular, Dr Manmohan Singh, Chairman of the Steering Committee, Professor S. Chakravarty, President of the Indian Economic
Association and then Vice-President of the International Economic
Association, and Dr V. R. Panchamukhi, Convenor of the Steering
Committee; the authors; the discussants; the rapporteurs and the ever-
helpful students. The International Economic Association wishes to
thank them all for the success of the Congress in Delhi in 1986.

Thanks are expressed to the International Social Science Council
under whose auspices the publications programme is carried out, and
to UNESCO for its financial support. (Under the auspices of the
International Social Science Council and with a grant from UNESCO
(1986–87/DG/7.6.2/SUB. 16 (SHS))).

IEA Programme Committee

Irma Adelman
Kenneth J. Arrow
P. R. Brahmananda
Sukhamoy Chakravarty
Béla Csikós-Nagy
Shigeru Ishikawa
Nurul Islam
Bruce Johnston
Paolo Sylos-Labini

Indian Steering Committee

Dr Manmohan Singh (Chairman)
Professor S. Chakravarty (President, Indian Economic Association
   then Vice-President of the International Economic Association)
Dr V. R. Panchamukhi (convenor)

Dr Malcolm S. Adiseshaiah
Dr M. S. Ahluwalia
Dr D. S. Awasthi
Dr Mahesh Bhatt
Professor P. R. Brahmananda
Shri M. Dubey
Professor Alak Ghosh
Professor P. D. Hajela
Dr Bimal Jalan
Professor A. M. Khusro
Professor D. T. Lakdawala

Dr M. Madaiah
Professor Gautam Mathur
Professor M. V. Mathur
Professor Iqbal Narain
Professor D. L. Narayana
Dr D. D. Narula
Professor Kamta Prasad
Dr C. Rangarajan
Dr N. K. Sengupta
Professor Shanmugasundaram
Dr R. K. Sinha

List of Authors, Session Organisers and Rapporteurs

Professor Irma Adelman, Department of Agricultural and Resource Economics, University of California, Berkeley, USA

Professor Clive Bell, Department of Economics and Business Administration, Vanderbilt University, USA

Dr Hans P. Binswanger, The World Bank, Washington DC, USA.

Professor Domingo Cavallo, Instituto de Estudios Economicos Sobre la Realidad Argentina y Latino Americano (IEERAL), Argentina

Professor Béla Csikós-Nagy, Hungarian Economic Association, Budapest, Hungary

Professor Partha Dasgupta, St John's College, Cambridge, UK

Dr James P. Grant, UNICEF, New York, USA

Professor Alain de Janvry, Department of Agricultural and Resource Economics, University of California, Berkeley, USA

Professor V. Jeniček, Economic Research Institute for Agriculture and Food, Prague, Czechoslovakia

Dr Richard Jolly, UNICEF, New York, USA

Academician Tigran Khachaturov, Association of Soviet Economic Scientific Institutions, Moscow, USSR

Professor Yair Mundlak, Hebrew University of Jerusalem, Israel and University of Chicago, USA

Dr Jaime B. Quizon, Chase Econometrics, USA

Professor V. M. Rao, Institute for Social and Economic Change, Bangalore, India

Dr Elizabeth Sadoulet, Department of Agricultural and Resource Economics, University of California, Berkeley, USA

Professor Amartya Sen, Littauer Center, Harvard University, Cambridge, Mass., USA

Professor Aladár Sipos, Institute of Economics, Budapest, Hungary

Professor Paul Streeten, World Development Institute, Boston, Mass., USA

Professor Erik Thorbecke, Cornell University, Ithaca, New York, USA

Professor Luo Yuanzheng, Economics Institute of the Chinese Academy of Social Sciences, Beijing, China

Volume Rapporteur

Professor Sylvia Lane, Department of Agricultural and Resource Economics, University of California, Berkeley, USA

Rapporteurs

Dr Aiyaswammi, Department of Economics, University of Madras, India

Dr Santosh Mehrota, Research and Information System for the Non-aligned and Other Developing Countries, New Delhi, India

Dr G. V. S. N. Murthy, Sardar Patel Institute for Economic and Social Research, Ahmedabad, India

Dr P. R. Panchamukhi, Indian Institute of Education, Pune, India

Mr K. Seetha Prabhu, Department of Economics, University of Bombay, Bombay, India

Dr R. K. Sen, Calcutta, India

Dr Rameswari Varma, Institute of Development Studies, University of Mysore, India

Dr Arvind Vyas, School of International Studies, Jawaharlal Nehru University, New Delhi, India

Dr Vinod Vyasulu, Department of Economics, Indian Institute of Management Studies, Bangalore, India

Abbreviations and Acronyms

AIC	agro-industrial complex
CGE	computable general equilibrium
CPI	consumer price index
CPSU	Communist Party of the Soviet Union
f.o.b.	free on board
GATT	General Agreement on Tariffs and Trade
GNP	gross national product
IEERAL	Instituto de Estudias Economicos sobre la Realidad Argentina y Latino Americano
IFPRI	International Food Policy Research Institute
IMR	infant mortality rate
IRDP	Integrated Rural Development Programme (India)
ISEC	Institute for Social and Economic Change (India)
MEP	Marginal expenditure propensity
mmt	million metric tons
NGO	non-government organisation
OECD	Organisation for Economic Co-operation and Development
OEEC	Organisation for European Economic Co-operation
ORS	oral rehydration salt
ORT	oral rehydration therapy
PHC	Primary Health Care
RLEGP	Rural Landless Employment Guarantee Programme (India)
SAM	social accounting matrix
U-5MR	under-5 mortality rate
UNICEF	United Nations International Children's Emergency Fund
WHO	World Health Organisation

Introduction

Irma Adelman and Sylvia Lane
UNIVERSITY OF CALIFORNIA, BERKELEY

The basic goal of accelerated economic growth should be poverty eradication. Optimally, the pursuit of growth should be so structured that growth offers the systemic conditions for the attainment of the human potential of all. At a minimum, the pursuit of growth should be so structured that growth offers the systemic conditions for basic needs fulfilment for all. The eradication of spiritual and physical poverty cannot be complete in any society. There will always be some who will fall by the wayside for reasons of bad luck, ill health, poor personal choices, or improvidence. This type of 'frictional' poverty should be kept to a minimum and alleviated by means of a safety-net consisting of transfers. What economic development should aim at is the eradication of 'structural' poverty – the poverty that arises from a paucity of assets and income earning opportunities for the poor, and from the low productivity and low returns to the meagre assets held by the poor. Economic growth is an essential component of such a development strategy. But growth by itself will not result in the removal of spiritual and physical deprivation. Indeed, the wrong kind of growth may actually exacerbate poverty. What is required for rapid reductions in 'structural' poverty are strategies and policies leading to efficient labour-intensive growth patterns that stress labour-intensive products and production processes. Two strategies recommend themselves in this regard: agriculture-led industrialisation, or export-led growth.

The present volume is devoted to the consideration of the ethical and strategy issues relating to egalitarian development. In Part I, in which the writings on the relationship between social justice and economic development appear, Professor Streeten discusses required precepts for international co-operation if it is to lead to social justice. Professor Dasgupta comments on the relationships between human welfare, freedom and economic development. Dr Grant and Dr Jolly write about the new economics of child health and child survival noting both costs and benefits. Professor Thorbecke is concerned with planning techniques for social justice. The prevailing concern is whether economic development will lead to social justice and how it may do so.

The next three chapters of the book deal with the role of agriculture in poverty eradication. Agriculture and mass poverty are almost synonymous in developing countries. The poverty population in most LDCs is 60 to 80 per cent rural, and consists mostly of landless labour, and of semi-subsistence farmers. The institutional structure of agriculture, agricultural terms of trade policies, and the nature of agricultural infrastructure and technology therefore have a critical impact on poverty in general and on the rural poor in particular. The rest of the present volume examines different facets of the impact of agricultural institutions and of policies with respect to agriculture on poverty and economic growth in both mixed-enterprise and socialist countries.

The transition process in developing countries transforms the agricultural sector from the mainstay of the economy, absorbing 80 to 90 per cent of the population in low productivity employment and generating 60 to 90 per cent of export revenues, into a high-productivity sector that accounts for less than 20 per cent of employment and for a comparable percentage of exports. But how this transition takes place varies among countries in both speed and timing and the differences have a strong impact on poverty in agriculture and on the growth and development potential of the rest of the economy.

The history of agriculture–industry interactions during the nineteenth century is instructive in this regard. It offers examples of countries in which agricultural and industrial development reinforced each other; countries in which rapid primary export expansion led eventually to widespread economic development; countries in which rapid primary export expansion led to only narrowly-based economic growth; countries in which industrial growth led to dualistic growth which did not diffuse to the agricultural sector and countries in which rapid industrialisation led to the diffusion of economic growth and its benefits into the rural economy. Twentieth century development exhibits a similarly varied pattern of agriculture–industry interactions. One of the striking conclusions of comparative economic history during the nineteenth century is that all countries that achieved economic development before 1914 had a high productivity agriculture with institutions that made for a wide dispersion of the agricultural surplus. Conversely, countries with a backward agricultural sector, or with a dualistic agriculture that combined large-scale commercial enterprises with traditional subsistence farming, did not succeed in developing before 1914.

During the nineteenth century an agricultural surplus above subsistence was crucial to the early phases of development, regardless of the development strategy chosen. Only with a surplus could exports be expanded and food supplies for growing populations increased. The size and distribution of the agricultural surplus were consistently tied to agricultural institutions. Where cultivators had greater control over production decisions, where legal changes established clear cultivator titles to land, and where land holdings were large, staple export growth was faster. However, as growth proceeded, institutional prerequisites for further growth changed. A wide distribution of a subtantial surplus became crucial to the shift from dualistic export expansion or industrialisation to wider growth based on domestic demand. Unless there was peasant farming and peasant farms had a surplus to invest in increased productivity, food production lagged, labour was released only slowly to non-agricultural occupations, continued food imports used up scarce foreign exchange and domestic demand growth was limited to the rate of growth of the 'modern' sector.

Critical to the development of appropriate agricultural institutions was the role and autonomy of the state. Countries in which foreign interests or landed élites dominated the political process did not develop agricultural institutions that made for a wide ownership of land, and failed to invest in transport and rural education. In them, lack of agricultural purchasing power, together with poor transport and illiteracy, interacted greatly to impede further agricultural growth and industrial wage-goods production. As a result, these countries remained at a certain phase of development. By contrast, countries in which the state had a certain degree of autonomy, and in which modernising urban groups of industrialists and workers gained political power, promoted agrarian institutions, giving cultivators rights and incentives to improve productivity, invested in roads, canals and railways linking farmers with markets, and built rural schools. The result was a positive feedback process between agricultural and industrial development.

The papers in Parts II to IV of this volume present a cross-section of thinking concerning agriculture, development and poverty and are suggestive of the degree of parallelism between nineteenth and twentieth century agricultural development. In Part II, entitled Agricultural Development and Poverty, Professor de Janvry and Dr Sadoulet ask whether greater equity in the distribution of income will decrease the growth effect of agriculture on industry and increase that of industry on agriculture. They conclude that an agriculture-led industrialisation strategy can promote both economic growth and equity. Professor Rao, writing on the impact of rural development programmes on the economic structure of rural communities concludes that programmes have helped Indian farmers with small and medium-sized holdings but not labourers or the landless. Drs Binswanger and Quizon ask what agriculture can do for the poorest rural groups and conclude that it is extremely difficult to raise their wages through agricultural development. They therefore emphasise the crucial importance of holding food prices down if the rural low-income groups' welfare is a policy concern.

Part III, entitled Agriculture and Industry under Capitalism, contains Professor Bell's argument that the observed patterns of share and fixed leases and self-cultivation, tenancy and wage employment stem from the absence or imperfection in insurance and other markets and from the structure of enforcement costs. His policy recommendations therefore stress risk-reduction measures. Professors Cavallo and Mundlak study labour and capital allocation between sectors in Argentina over the extended period 1913–84. Their results have important implications for government economic policy.

In Part IV, entitled Agriculture and Industry in Socialist Experience, Professors Jeniček, Sipos and Luo and Academician Khachaturov describe the present state of agricultural development and provide some insights on its relation to industrial development in Czechoslovakia, Hungary, China and the Soviet Union respectively. The parallels between agricultural development and its relationships to industrial development in socialist and non-socialist economies, which can be gleaned from these papers, are of particular interest.

Part I

Social Justice and Development

1 International Co-operation and Global Justice

Paul Streeten

WORLD DEVELOPMENT INSTITUTE, BOSTON UNIVERSITY

1 NATURE OF THE PROBLEMS

Many of the problems in the international relations of interdependence arise from a combination of the free rider problem, Olson's problem,[1] and the prisoners' dilemma. Indeed, the free rider, or contributor's, dilemma is a special case of the prisoners' dilemma. The free rider problem exists because some of the solutions of international difficulties consist in the provision of public goods (Kindleberger, 1978, p. 15 and 1986). A public good is one from the supply of which all those who value the good derive some benefit, irrespective of whether they have contributed to its costs. The concept can readily be extended to cover common goals or common interests, the achievement of which benefits all, irrespective of whether they have contributed to the costs of achieving these goals or interests. The enjoyment of the good or service by one person does not detract from the enjoyment by others. In this sense international co-operation and the prevention of international wars are public goods. So are markets and a working international monetary order, with an international central bank as a lender of last resort and as a provider of liquidity. Scientific research is of this kind. An international income tax or the co-ordination of international fixed investment decisions fall under the same heading. But these public goods will be systematically undersupplied, because any one country will not find it worth its while taking the appropriate action, relying on others to do so, even though the benefits would exceed the costs, were all to contribute. And each country knowing that others act that way, will not have an incentive to be the only one which contributes to something that benefits others. As a result international co-operation, peace, research, international monetary stability, and world develop-

3

ment will be undersupplied. No one contributes and everyone is worse off. The Invisible Hand, which, according to Adam Smith, co-ordinates the independent decisions of a multitude of individuals, could also be applied and has been applied to the unintended co-ordination of the actions of nation states. But this Invisible Hand that is supposed to guide the self-interest of each agent, whether individual or country, to the common good is not to be seen in the cases discussed above.[2]

It is true that free rider problems are not ubiquitous. Individuals may be afraid of the sanctions attached to such behaviour. Or they may avoid free riding because they believe that their contributions will make others contribute. Individuals sometimes do behave according to Kant's categorical imperative, in a manner that can be universalised. Otherwise why should anybody clap after a theatre performance (assuming you don't get pleasure from clapping), or vote in a democratic election? But Kant's categorical imperative, or the notion that we should behave in the way we should want others to behave, may apply less to the actions of nation states than to those of individuals. Leadership, and even hegemony, particularly by a strong superpower, and enlightened self-interest, can contribute to such Kantian behaviour by nation states.

The prisoners' dilemma arises because each country, in promoting its own national interest rationally, contributes to a situation in which all countries are worse off. Just as public goods are undersupplied, public bads are oversupplied. No single actor has an adequate incentive to remove them. This applies to competitive protectionism, beggar-my-neighbour devaluations or deflations, the spread of inflation, investment wars, the arms race, global pollution of the air and the sea, overfishing and excessive exploitation of exhaustible resources to which no property rights are attached, and similar situations. Richard Cooper has likened the situation to a crowd in which each member, wishing to see better a passing parade, rises to his tiptoes, with the result that no one sees better but everyone is more uncomfortable (Cooper, 1968). What is needed is either co-ordination and co-operation, or supranational sanctions that force all countries to act in what will amount to their self-interest. Without such co-ordinated or enforced action, the outcome of nationally rational actions will be irrational damage and mutual impoverishment. For the damaging action is the best, whether other nations act similarly or not.

On the other hand, according to Coase's theorem, if, in the absence of transaction costs, and in the presence of a legal framework and full information, one country inflicts damages on another which are greater than the benefits to the first country, the injured country can enter into a contract and compensate the injuring country for not inflicting the injury and be better off, or the injuring country can compensate the injured country for the damage, and still be better off. Such international compensations or bribes are in fact not common but they point, in principle, to the other extreme from that of the prisoners' dilemma. In such a world Pareto optimal allocations would be achieved, for any deviation would give rise to joint gains, out of which losers could be compensated for accepting them (Lipton, 1985).

The difficulties of reaching Coase-type agreements and the dangers of ending in prisoners' dilemma situations are aggravated by four factors. First, there is no longer a hegemonous power, such as Britain before the First World War and the USA for a quarter of a century after the Second World War, which is prepared to carry a large part of the cost of the public goods and to exercise leadership to make others contribute. Secondly, the proliferation of independent nation states to about 160 makes agreements more difficult than in an age when fewer governments could establish a system of mutual trust or enforcement (Olson's problem). It is, however, true that most of these are quite small and that co-ordination by a few large ones is what matters. Thirdly, the rapid pace of social and technical change makes it more difficult to evolve the stability on which trust can be built. It has been shown that repeated games of prisoners' dilemma in similar situations tend to lead to co-operative solutions. Rapid change of the conditions on which co-operation is based prevents the basis for this to be formed (Axelrod, 1984). And fourthly, the absence of world government and world courts makes it impossible to establish property rights, enforce contracts and set the sanctions against freaking agreements.

As Michael Lipton (1985) has said, if all outcomes were nonco-operative prisoners' dilemmas, no government would be possible. If all were according to Coase's theorem, no government would be needed (except for income redistribution). The actual world is between the two extremes. But the relations of nation states are nearer the prisoners' dilemma end of the spectrum, for the four reasons given above.

2 THREE SYSTEMS OF RESPONSE

In order to set up a framework for a more constructive response to the call of the South for a better world order, Kenneth Boulding's distinction between the exchange system, the threat system and the integrative system is useful. The exchange system is based on the principle: 'I do something good for you if you do something good for me'. It covers the area of mutual interests. The threat system is based on the principle: 'Unless you do something good for me I shall do something horrid to you'. In the integrative or love system the principles of love and duty applied to ourselves and our family are extended to other members of a wider community. We do good neither in the expectation of good in return nor under the threat of harm, from a sense of unity or solidarity or duty. This sense can derive from a common ideology or from a sense of community and obligation. These not only reduce the danger of too many free riders, so that each contributes voluntarily to the common good that also benefits him, but also lead to some sacrifice for the benefits of others: genuine altruism. The three systems correspond roughly to positive sum games, in which all participants benefit, avoiding negative sum games, in which all would lose in the absence of co-ordinated action, and zero sum games, in which one side has to make concessions for the benefit of others.

Systems can, of course, be mixed. What appears to be a genuine sacrifice in the short run may turn out to be beneficial to the sacrificer in the long run. Or the removal of the benefit (such as access to markets) can constitute a threat. Or the division of the joint gains can give rise to conflicts. This, in practice, is a particularly important obstacle to the pursuit of positive sum games. The gains come to be accepted and only the wrangles over their division remain.

It is important to distinguish between doing what is right, and wishing to be seen to be doing right, because this is in the nation's self-interest. The United States is dedicated to a value system, what Myrdal called the American Creed. It adds cohesion to American society and strength to its foreign policy. But it is an entirely different thing to say, as a paragraph in the Kissinger Commission Report on Central America does, that it is in the American national self-interest *to be seen* to be acting right. 'To preserve the moral authority of the United States. To be perceived by others as a nation that does what is right *because* it is right is one of this country's principal assets'. There is all the difference in the world between doing what is right because it is right, and doing it because the USA must be seen to do what is right because it is right. It is in the US national interest to be seen to act in a moral way. The first action is moral, disinterested; the second self-interested.[3]

The distinction between the three systems is useful for a clear analysis, but not for negotiations. There we have an interest in pretending that what is truly a benefit to us is a sacrifice, so that we may get concessions on other fronts.

The exchange system of mutual interests has been much prompted, especially by the Brandt Commission, the OECD and the Overseas Development Council. Trade liberalisation is the most frequently advocated policy. 'Man was born free, but everywhere he is in chains'. Similarly, all economists recommend free(r) trade, but everywhere there is protection.

It might be thought that, by and large, people, groups, and nations are very good in detecting and pursuing their self-interest, and that not much exhortation is needed. But, as we have seen, there can be important divergencies between reaching for and achieving what is in one's interest. In some cases the self-interested action leads to damage to oneself. We have already discussed the prisoners' dilemma and its free rider problem. The first leads to the infliction of mutual harm, the second to the undersupply of public goods and the oversupply of public bads. In addition, the national interest may be damaged for several reasons. There can be conflict between groups with different power, articulateness, and influence, so that the more powerful influence policy more strongly, even if their gains are smaller than the losses of the less powerful, less articulate, less influential. Or there may be conflict between dispersed larger and concentrated smaller gains, or between uncertain larger and certain smaller gains, or between larger future and smaller present gains, or between perceived larger but really smaller gains. The last may be one of the reasons why the general public and policy-makers are not prepared to surrender national sovereignty, even though its surrender would lead to a more effective achievement of self-interested objectives than the formal adherence to full sovereignty, autonomy and control, in the same way in which the acceptance of traffic regulations enlarges our freedom to drive accident-free, while restricting our freedom of choice. Finally, the gains to some may be much larger than the gains to others, who, though gaining a little, resent this. In any case, the distribution of gains presents quite different problems at the international level from those at the national. For any national community, a central government can tax and redistribute gains if this is deemed desirable. But without a world government, this cannot be done at the international level.

In all these cases selfish action may not lead to the achievement of the self-interest, and the achievement of self-interested objectives may involve some sacrifice in unconstrained and uncoordinated selfishness. Moreover, it would only be a fluke of coincidence if the actions dictated by national self-interest were to coincide with our development objectives, whether these are accelerated growth, growth with equity, redistribution with growth, or basic needs. In particular, the poorest groups and the poorest countries will tend to be left out in a strategy based on national self-interest.

Removal of dangers of the threat system, the avoidance of negative-sum games, should have a high priority, for it can lead to mutual impoverishment and even destruction: disarmament, removal of the threat of protection, an end to beggar-my-neighbour deflation and devaluation or inflation, and of 'voluntary' export restraints, are clearly lines of action worth pursuing. They call for international co-ordination and institutional reponses of the kind discussed above and below.

It may be thought that all agreements entered into voluntarily between states must amount to positive-sum games, in which each is better off. But this is not so. Some alliances may be formed with the specific purpose, or with the unintended result, of inflicting costs on outsiders. In this case alliances or pacts can lead to negative-sum games.

One of the reasons why agreements on avoiding negative-sum games, on reducing bads and creating anti-bads, are so difficult, is to be found in the logic of collective action, so well analysed by Mancur Olson (1971). The larger the group, the weaker the incentive for any one member to contribute to the action that benefits all. And we now have about 160 countries in the world. As a result, the public goods are not produced, or are underproduced, even though their value is greater than their costs to the group of countries, the Group of 5 or the Group of 7, may take responsibility for the rest, but they may also act in a way that imposes costs on others.

We can build on areas of common national interests, emphasising mutual benefits to be derived from, for example, resumption of orderly and equitable growth in the world economy, forswearing self-defeating protectionism, exploring ways of increasing the resources in globally scarce supply, etc. But while there is considerable scope for positive sum games in exploring areas of common and mutual interests, and of avoiding self-defeating, mutually destructive policies of the prisoners' dilemma type, there is also a 'higher' interest in a world order that both is, and is seen to be, equitable, that is acceptable and therefore accepted, and that reduces conflict and confrontation.

All societies need for their self-regulation and for social control a basis of moral principles. Individuals are ready to make sacrifices for the communities they live in. This forms the basis of the integrative system. Can this principle stop at the nation state? A belief in the harmony between self-interest and altruism is deep-seated in Anglo-Saxon thought and action. One is reminded of the eighteenth century Bishop Joseph Butler: 'when we sit down in a cool hour, we can neither justify to ourselves this or any other pursuit, till we are convinced that it will be for our happiness ... (Butler, 1718–26, para. 20). The only question is why it appears to be easier to identify, or at least harmonise, individual happiness with the national interest than with that of the world economy. It is odd that a moral, disinterested concern by rich countries with the development of the poor is hardly ever conceded. As hypocrisy is the tribute vice pays to virtue, so professions of national self-interest in the development of poor countries may be the tribute that virtue has to pay vice.

In the present fashion of stressing common and mutual interests, we run the danger of underestimating the power of moral or humanitarian appeals. Holland, Sweden and Norway, which have put international co-operation squarely on a moral basis, have hit the 0.7 per cent aid target. It is the countries in which aid has been sold to the public as in the national self-interest where the effort is lagging.

The common interests must also be defined in terms of different time horizons: the next year, the next five years, the next twenty years. There may be conflicts and trade-offs between these different time spans. For example, concessionary aid to the poorest may involve economic sacrifices in the near future but, by laying the foundations for a world in which all human beings born can fully develop their potential, it contributes to the longer-term interest of mankind.

One difficulty is that in democracies adults have votes, but children and the unborn have no votes. The fight is not only against powerfully organised vested interests, but also against all our own short-term interests, that neglect the interests of future generations.

Any attempt to build co-operation for development on moral principles has to answer three questions. First, do the rich in a community have an obligation to provide social justice (not only charity) to the poor and do the poor have just claim on the rich? Secondly, does mankind constitute a community in the relevant sense or do communities stop at national boundaries? Thirdly, does the existence of national governments not interfere with the discharge of the obligations of the rich, if such obligations exist, to the poor in the world community, if there is such a community?

The first question cannot be answered without an analysis of various theories of moral philosophy. But both utilitarianism and various types of entitlement theory would provide a basis for and obligation of the rich to contribute to improving the lot of the poor in a community. Perhaps more difficult is the case for saying that mankind does constitute a community in the relevant sense. Social contract theories might say that we need not do everything for the world community because the world community does not do anything for us, whereas the state provides protection, security and certain other services. But even if the first two questions were answered in the affirmative the third question presents the difficulty that the discharge of the obligation may take the form of what opponents of aid-giving have called, 'a redistribution of resources from the poor in rich countries to the rich in poor countries'. To meet this difficulty we have to exercise our institutional imagination in finding procedures and institutions that avoid, or at least minimise, this possibility.

The 'higher' interest in an acceptable world order can be defined either in moral terms or in terms of the desire to avoid negative sum games, to avoid breakdown and wars. Whatever the definition and justification, its aim is to transform adversary relationships into co-operation. When interests diverge or conflict, the task of statesmanship is to reconcile them. This is the task quite distinct from, and more important than, that of exploring areas of common or mutual interest. It is in this light that co-operative action to eradicate world poverty and to restructure the international economic order have to be seen.

3 RULES FOR INTERNATIONAL ORDER

What, then, are the requirements of a sensible international order? It will consist of negative rules of what national governments must not do, and agreements on certain positive co-operative actions. The rules of abstention will be intended to prevent negative sum games, and the rules of action to create some public goods and avoid public bads. Ralph Bryant (1980, p. 470) has called these rules 'supranational traffic regulations'. Some critics have accused the developing countries of wishing exemption from some general rules (such as reciprocity in tariff reductions or the banning of preferential trading arrangements) to which the developed countries should adhere. The discussion about appropriate rules for international economic relations has suffered from a long-standing confusion. It is the confusion between *uniform* (sometimes also called *general*) principles or rules (the opposite of specific ones, and therefore necessarily simple) and *universal* principles or rules (which may be highly specific and complicated, provided that they contain no uneliminable reference to individual cases). Further confusion is caused if a third characteristic of rules is added: *inflexibility* over time, and confused with either uniformity or universality. A rule is capable of being *altered*. Though it remains either uniform, i.e., simple, or universal, it may have lots of 'exemptions' written into it. The 'equal' treatment of unequals is not a principle of justice, and a general rule commanding it is an unjust rule. In order to prevent partiality and partisanship, rules have to be universal, i.e., not contain references to individual cases. They may, and indeed should not, be uniform. They should pay attention to the varying characteristics and circumstances of different countries.

Those who charge the developing countries with asking for exemptions from rules are guilty of this confusion betwen *uniform* and *universal* rules. Thus a differentiated system of multi-tier preferences according to the level of development of the exporting countries, may be best and most just for a group of trading countries at different stages of development. A fair system of rules also points to the differentiation in responsibilities and rights according to circumstances. Middle income countries would not have the responsibility to give aid, but neither would they receive it. They would not have to give trade preferences, but neither would they receive them. Even finer differentiation would be possible. A country with a large balance-of-payments surplus might be asked to contribute to loans because of its foreign exchange earnings, and, if its citizens enjoy high incomes, to aid because of its income per head, but might receive trade preferences, if its level of industrialisation is low. The 0.7 per cent aid target would be replaced by a system in which those below a certain income per head are exempted, and the percentage target rises with income per head.

There is, of course, a practical and tactical case for *simple* rules, which might overrule the case in fairness for universal (though complex) rules: they are less open to abuse and easier to police. And there may be a tactical case for uniform rules; they may be easier to negotiate. It is for such pragmatic reasons rather than on theoretical grounds that one may advocate that rules should not be too complex, and should not be changed too often.

Any specific proposals, such as non-reciprocity in trade concessions, or trade preferences would, of course, have to be examined on their merits. But the distinction between 'exemption from rules' and 'drawing up new rules' is logically untenable, to the extent to which the call for exemption is really a call for a set of universal rules that pays attention to the different characteristics and circumstances of different countries, just as income tax allowances for dependents or lower rates on earned than on unearned income, are not 'exceptions' but reflect our notions of fairness.

Those who are concerned with changing the rules of international relations are aiming partly at removing biases in the present rules, partly at the exercise of countervailing power where at present the distribution of power is felt to be unequal, and partly at counteracting biases that arise not from rules but from the nature of economic processes, such as the cumulative nature of gains accruing to those who already have more resources, and the cumulative damage inflicted on those who have initially relatively little.

In so far as the call for new rules is about strictly economic relations, there is scope for positive sum games. But in so far as it is about national power relations between sovereign states with different and conflicting aims, power is by its very nature a *relative* concept, and what is at stake is *zero sum games*. The demand for greater participation in the councils of the world and for corrections by the developing countries in the biases of the international power distribution are bound to diminish the power of the industrialised countries in conditions of conflict.

4   INSTITUTIONS FOR INTERNATIONAL ORDER

In addition to rules there is a need for institutions. Let me give five illustrations of the kind of institutional reform I have in mind. First, there is the creation of an international central bank that would be able to create (and withdraw) international liquidity, both for transactions and for precautionary reason. A panic run on the banks would cause an international financial breakdown unless an institutional arrangement existed that provided the liquidity. The General Arrangements to Borrow do this now to some extent, but a Central Bank would do this on a more solid and reliable basis.

The Central Bank would also be responsible for the growth of global reserves at a pace which gives neither an inflationary nor a deflationary bias to the world economy. In the absence of such a global authority, the competitive actions of nation states will tend to be either too restrictive, transmitting unemployment and unused industrial capacity, as each country scrambles to accumulate scarce reserves, or too expansionary, transmitting inflation throughout the world, as the reserve currency country incurs large balance of payments deficits to pay for economic or military ventures abroad.

Secondly, there is the institution of an international income tax, levied progressively on GNP according to incomes per head, or, better, consumption per head, so as to encourage saving, with a lower exemption limit, collected automatically, but disbursed to developing countries according to agreed criteria. The monitoring of the fulfilment of the criteria should be done either by the developing countries themselves or by a mutually accepted transnational body.

Thirdly, there is an international body to provide information on decisions for fixed, durable investment with long construction periods, so that we avoid the lurches from scarcity to excess capacity in steel, shipbuilding and fertilisers that we are suffering now. It should obviously not be a super-cartel that goes in for market sharing agreements, but a method of co-ordinating investment decisions.

Fourthly, there is an international investment trust that channels the surpluses of the surplus countries in a multilaterally guaranteed scheme to the developing countries. It would have guarantees against inflation and exchange rate losses for the lenders, the loans would be on commercial terms to middle-income countries. At the time of writing, Japan has become the largest lending country with a large surplus in its balance of payments on current account. This surplus is in search of good and safe investment opportunities which call for the creation of appropriate institutions that convert these surpluses into long-term loans to the developing countries. This would be in the interest of Japan, which could continue her export-led growth without having either to reduce her rate of savings or find domestic, lower-yielding alternatives; it would be in the interest of other OECD countries on whose exports some of the loans will be spent; it would be in the interest of the capital-hungry developing countries, whose resources are waiting to be mobilised by such capital flows; and it would be in the interest of the world economy which could maintain its expansionary momentum. An interest-subsidisation scheme could be grafted onto this for the low-income countries.

If this argument is accepted, the general call for Japan to raise its level of consumption or divert investment to the domestic market is seen to be misplaced. Higher consumption should not be applauded in a world that is short of savings and in need of capital. And higher domestic Japanese investment is not desirable if it is subject to declining returns. Instead of calling on Japan to reflate, we should mobilise its excess savings and channel them on acceptable terms, by long-term lending or equity capital, through either the private or the public capital markets to the developing countries.

Fifthly, there should be a better way of dealing with the oil price problem than the erratic zig-zag movements that we have experienced since 1973. Oil-producing and oil-consuming countries would get together and agree on a small, annual increase in the real price of oil, say 2 per cent. This assumes agreement on the best guess as to the real price of oil in twenty years' time. The balance of payments surpluses generated by such an increase could be channelled into the investment trust proposed above. The incentives to explore for more oil, alternatives to oil, and conservation, would be gradual but steady. The incentives for oil-exporting countries to use their revenue for investment in alternative productive assets would be gradual and steady. Incentives to consumers of oil would also permit a foreseeable and gradual adaptation. There would be neither debt crisis nor the sloshing around of large funds in search of remunerative and safe returns. And the world-economy would be spared at least one major source of shocks and instability. Both inflation and unemployment rates would be reduced.

There is also a need for reforming the institutions charged with North–South co-operation. What has the Marshall Plan to teach us for current relations with the South? It is now generally agreed that the Marshall Plan loans to Europe were given on too soft terms, perhaps in too large amounts, but they achieved their objective of rapid European reconstruction. It has also become a platitude to say that the lessons are not applicable to the developing countries because in Europe the human capital existed and to reconstruct with a skilled and well-motivated labour force is a much easier task than developing an underdeveloped society. But one important lesson can still be learned. Critics of both the Left and Right have pointed out numerous faults of aid, and in particular that it has not achieved its intended objectives, whether they are poverty alleviation, redistribution or economic growth. They conclude that we should get rid of aid. A better conclusion might be to get rid of the faults and to evolve mechanisms that ensure that the objectives of the aid donors are achieved. The intervention of donor governments for the purpose of applying performance criteria to development aid has been regarded as inconsistent with national sovereignty, has been dismissed as intrusive, and has bred acrimony. It has also been difficult to separate objectives of accelerating development from objectives in the narrow national interest such as export promotion, gaining votes in the UN, forming political alliances or getting strategic support. Performance criteria imposed in bilateral relations by donor governments have therefore been suspect and counterproductive.

The task is then to evolve institutions that achieve the objectives of the donors and the recipients and are trusted by both sides. It is to resolve the dilemma between avoiding intrusiveness and paying respect to national sovereignty on the one hand, and responsible accounting for taxpayers' money on the other. Here the Marshall Plan has still something to teach. It is not about the speed of development, which, for European reconstruction was much faster than for the structural changes needed for development; nor about the terms of aid, which were too soft compared with today's terms for development aid, but about monitoring procedures. The European powers were encouraged to monitor one another's performance, and the heavy hand of the US government was kept out of it. Each government submitted a plan which was inspected, vetted and monitored by other European governments in the Organisation for European Economic Co-operation (OEEC). Control by peers rather than supervisors is also a principle advocated in business management. A similar procedure could be adopted for groups of developing countries.

There are at least two other options. It would be desirable to create a genuine transnational secretariat whose loyalty would be only to the international community, that would be trusted by both donors and recipients. The staff of the present multilateral agencies does not quite achieve this, partly because the system of country quotas emphasises national origins rather than merit, partly because the organisations are intergovernmental institutions, and partly because the recruitment, training, location, etc. of the staff of these organisations to some extent conflicts with the ethos of a staff serving only the global community. In addition to having technical competence, the staff would be trained to be sensitive to social and political factors.

Finally, we might consider setting up a council of wise men and women whose task it would be to monitor the performance of both donors and recipients, and who again would be trusted by both sides. The existence of national governments that insist on the exercise of their full sovereignty at present interfaces with the moral and enlightened self-interest objectives of development co-operation, and not until this obstacle is overcome can we make progress.

Notes

1. See p.5.
2. Related problems have also been discussed under the concepts of 'tragedy of the common' (each agent, acting in his self-interest, contributes to social losses, such as overgrazing on a common pasture or overpopulating the globe) and 'social traps' (no driver has an incentive to install a gadget that reduces pollution). These, as well as prisoners' dilemma, 'collective action' and Olson's problem are special instances of 'market failure'.
3. The point is made and the quotation cited in an article (Garton Ash, 1984).
4. Of this long-standing confusion between universal and uniform, or general rules, even such a clear-headed thinker as David Hume is guilty. Hume contrasts the highly specific reactions when we are seeking our own self-interest with the 'universal and perfectly inflexible' laws of justice. He seems, like many others (including GATT), not to make a necessary distinction between general principles (the opposite of specific ones and therefore necessarily simple) and universal principles (which may be highly specific and highly complicated, provided that they contain no uneliminable reference to individual cases). Thus, Hume says in one place 'universal and perfectly inflexible', but lower down 'general and inflexible'. And the use of the word 'inflexible' conceals a confusion between a principle being able to be altered (which has nothing to do with its universality or generality) and its having a lot of exceptions written into it (which is consistent with universallity but not with generality). Hume evidently thinks that the rules of justice have to be simple, general ones. He argues that, unless the rules are general, people will be partial in their application of them and 'would take into consideration the characters and circumstances of the persons, as well as the general nature of the question ... the avidity and partiality of men would quickly bring disorder into the world, if not restrained by some general and inflexible principles'. But this is fallacious. In order to prevent people from being partial, the principles have to be universal, that is, not contain references to individuals; they may, and indeed should, not be general; surely our judgements based on them ought to 'take into consideration the characters and circumstances of the persons, as well as the general nature of the question'.

References

Axelrod, R. (1984) *The Evolution of Cooperation* (New York: Basic Books).
Bryant, Ralph (1980) *Money and Monetary Policy in Interdependent Nations* (Washington DC: The Brookings Institution).
Butler, Joseph (1718–26) *Five Sermons Preached at the Rolls Chapel*, Sermon II (New York: Liberal Arts Press, 1950).
Cooper, Richard N. (1968) *The Economics of Interdependence: Economic Policy in the Atlantic Community* (New York: McGraw-Hill for the Council on Foreign Relations), pp. 160–73.

Garton Ash, Timothy (1984) 'Back Yards', in *New York Review of Books*, 22 November.

Kindleberger, C. P. (1978) *Government and International Trade, Essays in International Finance*, no. 129, Princeton University.

Kindleberger, C. P. (1986) 'International Public Goods without International Government', Presidential Address to the Ninety-Eighth Meeting of the American Economic Association, 29 December 1985, New York, *American Economic Review*, vol. 76, March.

Lipton, Michael (1985) 'Prisoners' Dilemma and Coase's Theorem: A Case for Democracy in Less-developed Countries?' in Matthews, R. C. O. (ed.) *Economy and Democracy* (London: Macmillan).

Olson, Mancur (1971) *The Logic of Collective Action*, 2nd edn. (Cambridge, Mass.: Harvard University Press).

2 Welfare, Positive Freedom and Economic Development

Partha Dasgupta

UNIVERSITY OF CAMBRIDGE

1 UTILITY VERSUS WORK CAPACITY

Two aspects of man have successively dominated the thinking of social philosophers over the past two centuries, each relevant in itself but sadly incomplete without the other. One sees him as a socio-biological machine, capable of effort and work for which he requires fuel in the form of nourishment. The other sees him as a seat of 'utility' or 'satisfaction', possessing desires and aspirations which need to be fulfilled. Classical political economy, developed in the early stages of the industrial revolution, emphasised an aspect of the first. The idea of a socially-determined 'minimum subsistence wage' occurs in David Ricardo's writings, just as it does in the writings of Robert Malthus. It is, however, the latter aspect which has dominated social thought over the past hundred years or so. This too is understandable. With rising wealth in the industrialising economies, the basic necessities of life were beginning to be met for a majority of the population. What remained of concern were the 'higher pleasures' (for an illuminating account of this see A. K. Dasgupta, 1985).

A most extreme form of this latter concern, appears in John Maynard Keynes's celebrated 1930 essay, 'Economic Possibilities for our Grandchildren'. As a result Keynes envisages an end to the economic problem for the western world by the year 2030, even with only a 2 per cent rate of growth of the capital stock.

He envisages that the economic problem is not a permanent problem of the human race, for he says that we may be forgiven for not sharing his extreme optimism – and not thinking that this agreeable life is within sight of all, even in the western world. And when one's gaze falls

18

on what is euphemistically called the Third World, the thought rings desperately hollow.

Political economy in this century has for the overwhelming part been thoroughly 'utilitarian' in character. Individuals are seen as having preferences or desires – which, to be sure, are seen as being socially conditioned; they choose from what are available to them, and their choice affects their welfare, their sense of well-being. The point is not that individual choice is necessarily dictated exclusively by preference, or that what is chosen from the available set of options necessarily maximises the individual's sense of well-being, for both, as psychologists have pointed out, would be false claims. Rather, I am making the point that individuals make their appearance in economic thinking as seats of 'utility'; in their capacity to do basic work, to have goals and aspirations and to produce labour power. All this is raw data, unexplained by theory. In the standard model an individual is seen as choosing some combination of consumption goods and leisure in the face of market prices of commodities and work. The study of 'inequality' as a result reduces to a study of the inequality of 'utility' across people or, to have an operational account, a study of the inequality in income and wealth. The theory says nothing about the basic necessities of life and what transpires if food intake falls on the wrong side of required needs. The link between food intake and a person's ability to work, to take decisions, to have desires and aspirations, is for the most part absent in economics.

To locate the link one is tempted to turn to classical political economy. But the picture portrayed there is woefully inadequate. For example, in his famous chapter on wages, David Ricardo begins by saying: 'the natural price of labour is that price which is necessary to enable the labourers, one with another, to *subsist* and to perpetuate their race, without either increase or diminution' (Ricardo, 1911, p. 52; emphasis added).

This suggests a demographic principle, namely that the rate of population growth is dependent on the wage rate and that there is a critical, or threshold, wage, at which population growth is nil. Viewing the matter over the long haul, this threshold is the subsistence wage. Any wage below this spells doom for the labour force. But over the short and medium run the theory says nothing. It does not postulate anything about a *person's* overall capabilities for *being* a person. It is mostly a theory concerning a person's propensity to *breed*.

2 WELFARE AND RIGHTS

Welfare economics has been concerned with the production and distribution of individual welfare, or well-being, where individual welfare is seen as being founded on, among other things, the availability and use of goods and services. This would seem to be incontrovertible. To question this concern would be to suggest that in judging economic states, and thus policies that have them as consequences, we should reach for something other than the human interests and well-being they promote and sustain. It is not difficult to locate such other considerations; excellence, valour, the sense of national identity, all deserve consideration. But it is not at all clear how one may argue for such virtues if not in terms of the human interests they serve and promote.

In fact, of course, much of welfare economic theory – and I want to distinguish this from applied welfare economics and development planning theory – has displayed a greatly narrower moral focus. Thus, for the greater part, social and economic states have been judged solely on the basis of the individual welfare characteristics of these states. This is seen most clearly under utilitarianism, which ranks social states on the basis of the sum of individual utilities, or welfares. If two distinct commodity allocations produce the same utility values and thus the same sum, utilitarianism is indifferent between them. This exclusive concern with the welfare characteristics of social states, labelled 'welfarism' by Sen (1979), has been much scrutinised in the literature on social choice (Arrow, 1951; Guha, 1972; d'Aspremont and Gevers, 1977, and Sen, 1979). But we may have good reasons *not* to be neutral between commodity allocations yielding identical welfare assignments, because the 'non-welfare' characteristics of these states may be morally relevant.

What might such non-welfare characteristics be? Of central relevance, it can be argued, would be the production and distribution of what are sometimes called 'natural-rights goods', (see, e.g., Weitzman, 1977). The most serious non-welfare characteristics of economic states pertain to their assignment of individual rights and thence to their allocation of such goods and services that meet the claims based on such rights. These rights include not only the treatment of individuals meted out by others, but also an access to, and command over, commodities that enable them to realise their humanity [Adelman, 1975). Both pertain to individual liberty, and both have been much discussed.

In his classic essay on liberty, Professor Isaiah Berlin disentangled these two concepts of liberty which, although they had become fused in the literature and in one's thinking, had historically '... developed in divergent directions not always by logically reputable steps, until, in the end, they came into direct conflict with each other' (Berlin, 1969, p. 132). In contrast with *negative freedom*, that is freedom from coercion – including, of course, freedom from state interference – Berlin spoke of *positive freedom*, the ability

> to be somebody, not nobody; a doer – deciding, not being decided for, self-directed ... conceiving goals and policies of [one's] own and realizing them

and of the ability

> to be conscious of [oneself] as a thinking, willing, active being, bearing responsibility for [one's] choices and able to explain them by reference to [one's] own ideas and purposes. (Berlin, 1969, p. 131)

At one level the two concepts amount to the same thing. Both are concerned with the extent of one's feasible set of choices. At another they are, as Berlin elaborated, quite different, for they differ by way of the sources, or agencies, which constrain choice, and which etch the contours of the feasible set.[1] For example, a person may be assetless and, more importantly, chronically malnourished, lacking thereby motivation and physical capabilities necessary to be employable in a freely functioning labour market, his sole means of escape from the bonds of deprivation. He does not enjoy positive freedom. He is unable to be a 'thinking, willing, active being'. Such a man does not have life plans, or projects, or 'own ideas and purposes'. But if he is not prevented by others from seeking and obtaining employment in a freely functioning labour market he is negatively free. In this example, what keeps him in wretchedness, what deprives him systematically of his right to positive freedom, is not the dictates of a person, or an agency, but the way the 'workings of the free-play of market forces impinge upon an initial distribution of endowments.[2]

Positive freedom is concerned, among other things, with the ability of a person to function. And a person's ability to function depends on his personal characteristics, his command over commodities and resources, the commodity and resource-use made by others in his community, and so on. What are often called 'basic needs' (see, for example, Streeten *et al.*, 1981), commodities such as basic food and shelter, medical care and sanitation facilities, are goods that are required in order that a person is capable of functioning. Whatever else he requires or wants to have, he requires these. Within bounds a person can function better, more effectively, with greater availability and use of such goods. There is thus a continuum of possible levels of use: it is not all or nothing. There is evidence, in the case of nutrition, of (approximate) threshold effects, where prolonged restrictions in nutrition-intake can produce severe stress in a person's metabolism (see Dasgupta and Ray, 1986a). There are thus (approximate) minimum needs in this case.

Primary education is also thought of as a basic requirement, but it is of a slightly different variety. It is not much use being literate if all others are illiterate and if there are no books in sight. Primary education offers 'network externalities', in that if a sufficient number of people use it, one's own need for it increases dramatically. This is because other channels previously available to enable a person to function, for example, by being able to keep in touch with others, are effectively foreclosed.

It might seem then that at the most general level an economic state is characterised completely by the production and distribution of goods and services. But this would be incorrect; for in evaluating an economic state one would wish to know of what value the allocation has to the population in question. *Rights-based theories* are concerned exclusively with the allocation of rights associated with commodity distributions. *Welfarism* is concerned exclusively with the welfare characteristics of commodity allocations. *Pluralist* moral theories, of the kind many development economists have espoused, if only implicitly, have their attention on both.

It is as well to formalise these ideas. With N persons and M 'physically' and 'temporally' distinguishable commodities let x_{ij} be the quantity of commodity j $(j = 1, \ldots, M)$, at the disposal of person i $(i = 1, \ldots N)$, and let $\{x_{ij}\}$ denote the MN-vector of these named commodities. We denote by $r_k(\{x_{ij}\})$ the vector of *rights* attained by person k, $(k = 1, \ldots, N)$. Making r_k a function of $\{x_{ij}\}$ means that the attainment of rights depends on commodity allocations. Now let $w_k(\{x_{ij}\})$ denote the welfare of person k when the commodity allocation is $\{x_{ij}\}$. At a general level, then, an economic state is characterised by the array $[\{x_{ij}\}, r_k(\{x_{ij}\}); w_k(\{x_{ij}\}); k = 1, \ldots, N]$. But not all its characteristics are morally relevant. Commodity allocations cannot be evaluated unless we know something of what people achieve with them.

Rights-based theories concentrate their attentions on certain components of the sub-array $[r_k(\{x_{ij}\}); k = 1, \ldots, N]$.[3] Welfarism, on the other hand, evaluates an economic state solely on the basis of its welfare sub-array, $[w_k(\{x_{ij}\}), k = 1, \ldots, N]$. Pluralist doctrines that are sensitive to both rights and welfare evaluate economic states on the basis of the larger sub-array $[r_k(\{x_{ij}\}), w_k(\{x_{ij}\}); k = 1, \ldots, N]$.

I think it is useful to reiterate that rights must be justified by the human interests they serve and promote. If I am thought to have a right to certain basic commodities because without them I cannot function as a 'thinking, willing, active being', my right to an access to these goods presumably arises because my interests are served and promoted by being able to so function.

Rights-based theories are *not* to be confused with paternalistic doctrines. To be sure, there are connections between them for certain categories of persons, such as children, who are thought not to know their own interests. However, once we know what these special cases are, we can for analytical clarity ignore them and treat the theories as distinct. In any event, although rights-based theories and welfarism are contrasting moral theories, rights are founded on individual welfare and interest. If a person is thought to possess a right to protection against 'force, theft and fraud' it is because his interests are promoted by such protection (Nozick, 1974). Likewise, if he is judged to possess a right to a sphere of decision-making, (Hayek, 1960), it is an acknowledgement that economic states which differ solely in terms of the features within the sphere in question ought to be valued in the light of the interests of the person in question (Sen, 1970). Of course, there may not be economic states which differ solely in terms of these features. But this would merely mean that rights clash against one another, and we would have to prepare ourselves for tradeoffs.

Rights are then relationships that people are entitled to have among one another and with goods and services. It is then convenient to interpret in a broad way the idea that a right to negative freedom is a right to certain types of relationship among individuals, and a right to positive freedom a right to certain relationships with goods and services. This is to put matters in a stark way. But stark ways are often a help. They enable us to contrast ideas in a sharp manner.

We noted earlier that pluralist doctrines evaluate social states on the basis of those characteristics which are summarised by the array $[r_k(\{x_{ij}\}), w(\{x_{ij}\}); k = 1, \ldots, N]$. Now there is, in fact, one strand in the literature on economic development which, in sharp contrast with much of welfare economic theory, has pursued this doctrine and attempted to draw out its implications. At a fairly earthy level, the level of project evaluation, the argument that governments ought explicitly to use premia on employment generation – that is, to have employment as a primary, as opposed to a derived, objective (Dasgupta, Marglin and Sen, 1972) – is based on pluralism. At the grandest levels, Irma Adelman's advocacy of what she termed 'depauperization' (Adelman, 1975), Paul Streeten's emphasis on 'basic needs' (Streeten *et al.*, 1981) and, most explicitly, Amartya Sen's formulation of the concept of 'capabilities' (Sen, 1983), were each an insistence that welfarism is limiting; misleadingly so.

And yet one may ask if at an *operational* level, or what men of affairs often call the *practical level*, there is much difference between pluralist doctrines and welfarism. For example, it can be argued that the concept of 'basic needs' can as well be packaged under welfarism covers if one awards very low social value to economic states where individual welfares will be low if 'basic needs' go unfulfilled. So too with 'capabilities'.

There is something in this argument, although it does ignore a good deal of anthropological data. The point is that social conditioning may result in individual welfares *not* being overly low even when 'basic needs' go unfulfilled. I am here thinking of nutrition deprivation in young girls, lack of access to certain resources for lower castes and so forth. It is not that the disadvantaged do not care. They do. But social conditioning can ensure that they do not care *enough*, or anyhow, do not care enough to record serious welfare deprivation for the measuring welfarist. For this reason we would want to know *why* a person's welfare is what it is. Is a person's welfare low because she has been systematically deprived of nourishment or is it because he cannot afford a Honda? Once we ask this we are seeking information about the economic state not captured by welfare and are entering the regime of pluralist moral theories.

But for persons of affairs such distinctions may seem overly fine. Welfarists do not carry welfare metres with them. The person of affairs may not even have heard of welfarism. At a practical level he might all too often think in terms of priorities, such as a priority to the fulfilment of 'basic needs', on the grounds that their fulfilment is imperative. Certainly, some serious implications for resource allocation would follow if the fulfilment of basic needs were to be awarded priority. This much is clear. But do the contrasting moral theories have differing implications for the design of economic organisations?

I think they do, and it is for this reason that such distinctions as I have been drawing can be of great practical importance. Contrast, for example, positive rights theories with welfarism. Earlier we noted that among other things, positive freedom is concerned with the *ability* of a person to function and that it values a person's access to, and command over, certain specific commodities because they are a *means* to this ability. Rights to such commodities, therefore, are in such theories, derived rights. But people differ, and in particular their requirements – in the sense of enabling them to function – for these commodities vary; over time (as a person ages), across regions (because, say, of climatic differences), and by virtue of their physiological differences. It follows that their (derived) rights to these commodities vary. A positive-rights doctrine, that is, a doctrine which emphasises the right to positive freedom would, as noted above, regard the just distribution of these 'positive rights' goods as being determined by requirements. People's welfare indicators for these goods relative to other goods would not count for everything. Now both income and requirements vary across people and, as a matter of incontrovertible fact, governments possess only incomplete information about both requirements and incomes. Suppose the government has at its disposal a certain quantity of a positive rights good, for example, foodgrain, which it wishes to distribute. Two polar distribution mechanisms suggest themselves: in kind or in transferable coupons; or, to put it more grandly, by rations or by the help of the price mechanism based on transferable coupons issued by the government. Elsewhere (see Dasgupta, 1986), I have argued that positive-rights theories would typically advocate distribution in kind (with a prohibition of resale) if the dispersion in income is large compared to the dispersion in requirements, and furthermore, that the price mechanism emanating from a distribution of transferable coupons is better if the dispersion in requirements is large compared to the dispersion in incomes. The point is that if income variability across the population is small, the induced price mechanism is better because people with greater requirements will end up consuming more of it because their incomes are about the same as those with lesser requirements and this is precisely what positive rights advocate. But if income dispersion is large this is no longer so, for people with large requirements and low income will end up consuming less than people with low requirements and high income. It is this possibility which the rationing mechanism prevents.

Contrast this result with the implications of welfarism. If income effects are negligible welfarism would recommend the allocation of this commodity via exchangeable coupons over allocation in kind, for everyone is better off by voluntary exchange. I conclude that the sorts of argument which rights-based theories provide for prohibitions on the sale of the right to vote in the political arena, and the sale of persons in the economic arena, are applicable for certain categories of commodities. I have in mind here such commodities as basic nutrients, general medical facilities, clean water and so forth. Even in what is often called the economic sphere, rights-based theories can assume cutting edge in the sense of being distinguishable from welfarism.

3 EQUITY, EFFICIENCY AND GROWTH

In what follows I shall take it that economic states are evaluated on the basis of the array $[r_k(\{x_{ij}\}), w_k(\{x_{ij}\}); k = 1, \ldots, N]$. Purely for the sake of expositional ease I shall also take it that the doctrine espousing such a method of evaluation allows for tradeoffs among the components of the array. To be sure, certain distinguished consequentialist doctrines, such as that of John Rawls (1972), commend lexicographic orderings – in Rawls's theory the right to equal basic liberties having priority over the right to equal wealth – but nothing of analytical importance will follow from my allowing for smooth tradeoffs.

Efficiency is easy to define, once we have settled on the space into which $r_k(\{x_{ij}\})$ is mapped. Components of $r_k(\{x_{ij}\})$ which pertain to negative freedom concern activities from which individual k can choose. Thus, these components will be sets of activities. As we noted earlier, so too are components of $r_k(\{x_{ij}\})$ which pertain to positive freedom. They are sets of activities from which individual k can choose.

The idea of efficient allocations is then straightforward. A feasible economic state $[r_k(\{x'_{ij}\}), w_k(\{x'_{ij}\}); k = 1, \ldots, N)$ is inefficient if there is a feasible state $[r_k(\{x_{ij}\}), w_k(\{x_{ij}\}); k = 1, \ldots, N]$ which (weakly) dominates it on a component-by-component basis; where (weak) domination, in the case sets, is set-inclusion. One then has the following definition: a feasible economic state $[r_k(\{x_{ij}\}), w_k(\{x_{ij}\}); k = 1, \ldots, N]$ is efficient if it is *not* (weakly) dominated by any feasible state.

As with welfarism, the criterion of efficiency in pluralist theories yields only a partial ordering of economic states. But unlike welfarism, efficiency in pluralist theories cannot easily be argued against. The point is that pluralism engulfs such moral considerations as have been used to argue that welfare efficiency is undefendable; that is, that it ought not even to be regarded as a necessary condition for optimality.[4]

Equality, as usual, is a far more elusive concept. The problem of ranking economic states on the basis of the criterion of equality is compounded here because some of the components of an economic state, specifically $r_k(\{x_{ij}\})$, are themselves sets of activities, not real numbers. In certain distinguished theories of justice, such as that of Rawls, the components of an economic state are lexically ordered. Thus, Rawls's first principle, that 'each person is to have an equal right to the most extensive total system of equal basic liberties compatible with a similar system of liberty for all' (Rawls, 1972, p. 302) means in our terminology that each person is to enjoy the set $\bar{r}$, where r is the intersection of the maximal feasible sets $r_k(\{x_{ij}\})$ for $k = 1, \ldots, N$. In Rawls's account this takes lexical precedence over the second principle, the first part of which is that 'social and economic inequalities are to be arranged so that they are ... to the greatest benefit of the least advantaged ...' (Rawls, 1972, p. 302). Now it will be recalled that there is a major exercise in aggregation in this latter principle; the economic index that concerns Rawls is (income) wealth. Thus, in Rawls's substantive theory, $w_k(\{x_{ij}\})$ is replaced by k's real income (wealth), I_k.

My purpose in alluding to Rawls's work is that it provides me with a convenient route to return to the literature on economic development, in which real income is often seen as the index of welfare. Certainly, most discussions on inequality measures have been conducted on real income distributions, in their most refined forms the incomes in question being some sort of average over persons' lives (for a survey of inequality measures, see, e.g. Fields, 1980). The limitations of this move, to view income as an index of welfare, have been much discussed. It should be noted, however, that in Rawls's work income plays a different role from this, and indeed, there are several strands in the development literature where, as in Rawls's work, real income is seen as an index of a command over goods and services. From this viewpoint real income assumes the role of an indicator of positive freedom, and one can thus see why so much attention has been given to real national income and its distribution among a nation's population. This then leads me to the classic tension in development economics: growth versus equality of real national income.

It should be evident that growth in (per capita) real national income is not to be confused with efficiency. A desire for high growth in per capita income reflects a desire for a particular type of intertemporal distribution of per capita aggregate consumption, one which favours consumption at future dates at the expense of current consumption. The large, and on occasion rich, literature on optimum economic growth addressed the question of what intertemporal distribution of aggregate consumption – and thus of real income – we should seek under a wide variety of circumstances (see, for example, Dasgupta, Marglin and Sen, 1972, for a non-technical discussion). I conclude therefore that the growth-equality tension in the literature on economic development concerns a tension between intertemporal and intratemporal distributions of income and thereby of goods and services. I say 'tension', because it is in such a manner the issues have been presented in much of the literature.

The origins of this tension in its most recent guise may well have been the oft-discussed Kuznets curve; I cannot tell. But one may in any case ask what necessary relevance the curve has for *policy* debates. I do not think a concentration on growth can be defended by an appeal to such curves as that which Kuznets thought he had identified. Rather, a defence has ultimately to be based simultaneously on two observations. The first is the claim that growth in per capita real income 'trickles down' to the poor over time, either through the operations of the market, or through conscious policy to be held in abeyance until such time as income has grown sufficiently. The second is that redistributive policies designed to alleviate poverty today will lower growth rates dramatically because of their detrimental influence on savings and investment, incentives and so forth. One needs the first argument in order to show that growth in income is a viable means to poverty eradication in the future and one needs the second to display the tension between growth and equality for the immediate future. If both are accepted we have an argument for viewing growth in national income as the most potent means for the removal of poverty and undernourishment.

I am conscious that I have shifted my sight from inequality to absolute poverty. The two are related, but are not the same. This shift, however, is understandable. A good deal of the development literature has studied that aspect of inequality which is occasioned by the presence of large and persistent economic deprivation. There are important and subtle issues raised by the idea of equality which are unrelated to absolute poverty. But one can argue that poverty elimination ought to take precedence. This would appear to be an implicit judgement in the literature on development.

The simplest (and crudest) measures of absolute poverty have been headcounts. More specifically, in estimating the prevalence of absolute poverty in a region or country it has been common practice to select a standard for nutrition requirements and to calculate the number of people whose intakes fall short of the standard. The point I want to emphasise here is not whether headcount is an appropriate measure, but that the idea of nutrition requirements, and their links with the incidence of morbidity and, more generally, the ability to *function* as a person, finds direct expression in poverty studies (see Dasgupta and Ray, 1986b), for an extended discussion of the clinical evidence of the effect of undernourishment on a person's work capacity. Irma Adelman's writings on pauperisation, Paul Streeten's insistence on the primacy of the provision of basic needs, and Amartya Sen's identification of basic capabilities as a 'primary good', were each, among other things, a powerful reminder that growth in real national income may take a long while to trickle down. Keynes's optimism was based on a truism. But it was a misleading truism.

With these considerations we come back in a complete circle to the dual view social scientists have held about persons: the biological organism and the seat of utility and aspirations. And it is this dual view which enables us to ask whether what is often seen as a necessary tension between growth in income and reduction in the magnitude of absolute deprivation may not be illusory; whether there may not be patterns of Lorentz improving asset redistributions which enhance growth. The point here is that, for an average person, a little more than half of his daily energy requirements are in the form of 'fixed costs', requirements for maintenance and the repair of tissues. Allied to this is the fact that beyond certain levels of intake the effects on the ability to function are deleterious. It follows as an analytical point that certain patterns of consumption transfers from groups with high income to those with low income will enhance aggregate work capacity and thus possibly aggregate output.[5] I say 'possibly' because the translation from work-potential to work-realisation is not an easy one and depends among other things upon the economic organisation in question. It can be argued that in extreme cases 'unused labour power' is not really unused, it is not as though the labourer finds no reason for working harder or longer. Rather, it is the economic organisation, allied to harsh inequalities in asset ownership, which disenfranchise large fractions of the assetless. In such circumstances the slack labour power is not slack at all: such labourers are not capable of providing the labour power that headcounts of the labouring class might suggest. If nourishment is distinguishable from hunger, it must lie in the fact that an undernourished person is a physically impaired person. His ability to work is restricted as compared to that of one who is not. For this reason I find it perplexing that the literature on 'basic needs' and 'capabilities' has not made analytical use of these notions in questioning the thesis that economic growth and the reduction in poverty and undernourishment are, for the immediate future, in conflict. To be sure, there are forces that make them so. These have been much aired and discussed. On the other side of the coin are the growth-enhancing potentials of redistributive policies (see Dasgupta and Ray, 1986a,b, 1987), potentials which are readily grasped once one views persons not merely as seats of 'utility', but also as biological organisms, capable of effort and work, provided they have adequate nourishment. There is no question that if concepts such as 'basic needs' and 'capabilities' have operational significance – and if one reads the clinical literature on nutrition one can have no doubt that they do – their significance lies in the dependence of work capacity on consumption and thus in the notion of positive freedom obtained from the availability and use of commodities. There is then some form of causal effect of certain types of Lorentz-improving asset redistributions, or consumption transfers, on improved growth capability of an economy. Economic sophistry notwithstanding, the reduction of one of the world's greatest evils may require no more subtle a policy than one of giving assets and food to those who are outcasts.

Notes

1. Positive and negative freedom are but two senses in which the word 'freedom' has been used. Berlin (1969, p. 121) asserts that there are more than two hundred senses in which the word has been used by historians of ideas! The mind boggles at the mere thought.
2. For an analysis of how this may come about, or how it is that the assetless are the most vulnerable, of how they may become utterly disenfranchised from the economic order under the free-play of fully-functioning market forces, see Dasgupta and Ray (1986b, 1987).
3. Thus rights to negative and positive freedom are, as we have seen, different rights and in the text, $r_k(\{x_{ij}\})$ subsumes both.
4. Notice thus, for example, that Rawls's two principles of justice taken together reject welfare efficiency as a necessary condition for justice, but they espouse efficiency in the broader sense defined above. Note as well that Sen's argument (Sen, 1970) against welfare efficiency (or Pareto efficiency) is not directed against the sense in which efficiency has been defined here. Both Rawls and Sen presented lexicographic orderings, whereas I have not. But it is easy to see that such orderings can easily be considered the general framework I am studying here. See text below.
5. Debraj Ray and I have undertaken a detailed study of these links (see Dasgupta and Ray, 1986a, 1987).

References

Adelman, I. (1975) 'Development Economics – A Reassessment of Goals', *American Economic Review*, Papers and Proceedings, vol. 65.

Arrow, K. (1951) *Social Choice and Individual Values* (New York: Wiley).

Berlin, I. (1969) 'Two Concepts of Liberty', in *Four Essays on Liberty* (Oxford University Press).

d'Aspremont, C. and Gevers, L. (1977) 'Equity and the Informational Basis of Collective Choice', *Review of Economic Studies*, vol. 44.

Dasgupta, A. K. (1985) *Epochs of Economic Theory* (Oxford: Basil Blackwell).

Dasgupta, P. (1986) 'Positive Freedom, Markets and the Welfare State', *Oxford Review of Economic Policy*, vol. 2.

Dasgupta, P., Marglin, S. and Sen, A. (1972) *Guidelines for Project Evaluation* (New York: United Nations).

Dasgupta, P. and Ray, D. (1986a) 'Inequality as a Determinant of Malnutrition and Unemployment: Theory', *Economic Journal*, vol. 96, December.

Dasgupta, P. and Ray, D. (1986b) 'Adapting to Undernourishment: The Clinical Evidence and its Implications', mimeo (University of Cambridge).

Dasgupta, P. and Ray, D. (1987) 'Inequality as a Determinant of Malnutrition and Unemployment: Policy', *Economic Journal*, vol. 97, March.

Fields, G. (1980) *Poverty, Inequality and Development* (Cambridge University Press)

Guha, A. (1972) 'Neutrality, Monotonicity and the Right to Veto', *Econometrica*, vol. 40.

Hayek, F. (1960) *The Constitution of Liberty* (London: Routledge & Kegan Paul).

Keynes, J. M. (1930) 'Economic Possibilities for our Grandchildren' reprinted in *The Collected Writings of John Maynard Keynes* (London: Macmillan for the Royal Economic Society) vol. ix(9), pp. 321–32.

Nozick, R. (1974) *Anarchy, State and Utopia* (New York: Basic Books).

Rawls, J. (1972) *A Theory of Justice* (Oxford University Press).

Ricardo, D. (1911) *The Principles of Political Economy and Taxation* (London: Dent & Sons).

Sen, A. (1970) *Collective Choice and Social Welfare* (San Francisco: Holden Day).

Sen, A. (1979) 'Utilitarianism and Welfarism', *Journal of Philosophy*, vol. 76.

Sen, A. (1983) 'Development: Which Way Now', *Economic Journal*, vol. 93.

Streeten, P. *et al.* (1981) *First Things First: Meeting Basic Needs in Developing Countries* (Oxford University Press).

Weitzman, M. L. (1977) 'Is the Price System or Rationing more Effective in Getting a Commodity to Those who Need it Most?' *Bell Journal of Economics* (Autumn) pp. 517–24.

3 The New Economics of Child Health and Survival

James P. Grant and Richard Jolly

UNITED NATIONS CHILDREN'S FUND

1120
9130

1 INTRODUCTION

To make clear what is new, one must first summarise the old – in this case, what one takes to be the 'old economics' of child health and survival. Essentially, the old view rested on three propositions:

First, that child health and survival was closely related with household income, especially family poverty;

Secondly, that improvements in health depended on increases in health services and thus on expenditure on health services.

The above propositions gave rise to a third: that improvements in health for a country depended on increases in income per capita in that country, which in turn would lead to both increases in family incomes and increases in government expenditure. To ensure that some 'trickle-down' took place, one would need to add the condition that increases in income would have to be accompanied by favourable movements in income distribution to ensure that at least some of the benefits accrued to the groups in need, especially to children and other vulnerable groups.

These propositions formed the basis of much of the health and development planning of the 1950s and 1960s, a period when economic growth was relatively rapid, and when important advances took place in health – as indicated, for example, in the reduction of infant mortality rates from 163 deaths per thousand in 1950 to 82 in 1980, and similarly, in the reduction of under-5 mortality rates from 251 per thousand in 1950 to 125 in 1980.

In short, the 'old economics' treated economic growth as a *sine qua non* for improvements in health, while recognising an additional need for attention to how the additional resources were used.

32

There is, of course, much truth in the above propositions. Ill-health *is* linked to poverty; infant and child mortality rates *are* significantly higher in poorer families than in families better off. Broad long-term improvements in child health survival and welfare *will require* reductions in poverty and increases in the incomes of the poor. And, for most developing countries, sustained economic growth is still a condition for achieving lasting increases in the income of the majority of the population.

Nevertheless, these propositions obscure many possibilities for improved child health and survival in the short and medium run which do not depend on increases in income. They are also apt to encourage a complacent expectation that improvements in health will follow automatically from improvements in income, when what is needed is active policies to ensure that they do – and active policies to guard against deterioration in health which, as with environmental pollution or obesity, often accompany rises in income.

2 DEVELOPING COUNTRIES

The basis for the 'new economics' for health and survival, which is particularly relevant for children who are the most vulnerable in society, was officially articulated in 1978 at the Alma Ata Conference of the world health professionals sponsored by the WHO and UNICEF with the active participation of NGOs which articulated the concept of primary health care. There were several basic principles which have since gained increasing acceptance even though most countries have still not yet fully applied them.

The first principle is that the use made of medical knowledge and the efficiency of health protection depends on social organisation. The immediate social problem is to overtake the lag between modern knowledge and its use in the setting of a community. Thus, we have the knowledge of low-cost means to prevent and respond to diarrhoea and its accompanying dehydration, but diarrhoea remains for children in developing countries the single largest cause of morbidity and mortality, taking the lives of some 14,000 children daily. A dramatic developed country example of this lag in the use of medical knowledge is the nearly 1000 persons who die prematurely in the United States each day because of smoking (United Nations Office on Smoking and Health).

A second basic principle is that, important as is the introduction of an effective health system, a vertical medical system cannot be truly effective or even stand by itself, unless it is integrated in other activities in society in a joint attack on the problems of development and social reconstruction. Health is not simply 'a sector', a responsibility of the Health Ministry alone; it must be an explicit goal to be achieved through all sectors with mass citizen participation – through education, through better nutrition, and through national and local leadership. Thus, the medical system alone cannot change the smoking habit, nor can it educate hundreds of millions of parents to use at home the oral rehydration therapy which could prevent several million child deaths each year.

A third principle is that successful organisation implies reliance upon economically practical strategies for serving the entire population rather than just the relatively well off. It is not difficult to find developing country examples of the establishment or expansion of major hospitals whose operational costs led to the curtailment of far more cost effective health clinics and preventive services. Similarly, we often read of the needless competition of hospitals in industrial countries to have tremendously expensive diagnostic equipment. Conversely, we have the recent example of a full multi-year immunisation programme launched in one country in 1983, and already saving the lives of 100,000 children annually, paid for by postponing expenditure on a major urban hospital for five years.

The fourth principle is one of increasing self-reliance. Resources necessary for health at each level must rest primarily within the control of that level – the household, the village, the district and the nation. Of course, there is a role for some outside support in each of these areas, but as a supplement, not the main effort. This means, of course, that the approach, technology and resources required will at each stage match those of the community involved.

While many countries have since Alma Ata paid more than lip service to promoting Primary Health Care (PHC) (e.g., millions of village health workers have been trained) the majority of health resources are still not applied to achieving it. The health sector has been reluctant to seek aggressively the involvement of other sectors in health promotion, or to shift health knowledge from the traditionally conservative health professional to the general public.

Yet the evidence of what can be achieved in developing countries in terms of relatively high levels of child health and welfare with proportionately low levels of per capita income are clear and impressive. Sri Lanka, for example, has made progress in child survival and health that is disproportionate to its relative low income. In 1984, with a per capita GNP of US $330, the infant mortality rate (IMR) was only 38 deaths per thousand and the under-5 mortality rate (U-5MR) was 50, comparable to that of the United States in the 1940s. Another example is China which, in 1984, had a GNP of US $300, an IMR of 36, and an U-5MR of 50 (UNICEF, 1986). The state of Kerala in India is a further example. Its IMR of 31 in 1982 (Bose, 1986), which is the most recent year for which we have figures, was approximately one-third the IMR for the rest of India, while the state per capita income is of no more than the average. These mortality figures are roughly equal to, for instance, United Arab Emirates (IMR = 36 and U-5MR = 45 for 1984), which in 1984 had a per capita GNP of US $22,370. All three of these countries have infant and child mortality rates well under half of Turkey's rates which had a GNP in 1984 of US $1240, almost four times that of the other three countries (UNICEF, 1986).

These examples make clear that there is no necessary correlation between *levels* of national income and child health and welfare. But the recent evidence of *trends* is both clearer and more dramatic. In spite of sharp deteriorations in per capita income in many countries of Africa and Latin America, it has proved possible to achieve major increases in several of the basic and most cost effective areas of child health.

3 ECONOMIC STAGNATION AND DECLINE

In most developing countries the economic context of the last five years is one of recession and severe retrenchment, especially in Africa and Latin America. Clearly stagnation or decline in per capita income has been the dominating pattern. The number of countries registering the negative or negligible growth in per capita income has increased from 25 in 1979 to 55 in 1982 and remained at 49 in 1985. In Africa, the average over the years 1980–86 has been a decline of 15 per cent in per capita income, in Latin America a decline of 9 per cent. In Asia, the situation for some countries has been much more positive, with India and China experiencing positive growth and several of the East Asian newly-industrialised countries growing rapidly. Even in Asia, however, average incomes have declined or stagnated in one-third of the countries.

Stagnation and decline of average per capita income has usually been accompanied by severe deterioration in the incomes and living standards of the population, especially the poorer sections. This has now been documented in a number of studies (Jolly and Cornia, 1984; Cornia *et al.*, Pfeffermann, 1986). In terms of child health and survival, the effects of the income decline have been particularly serious for several reasons:

- With the decline in average income, government expenditure has also declined. As part of this, health budgets have almost invariably been cut significantly in real terms. In about half the countries of Africa and Latin America, the reduction in health budgets has been greater than that of government budgets as a whole.
- In general, children have been more affected than other groups, in part because poorer families who tend to be politically weak have been proportionately more affected than better-off families, and in part because poorer families tend to have greater numbers of children.

In addition to these direct effects on income, there have been shifts in the locus of policy-making, often reinforcing the negative effects on children and other vulnerable groups. As balance of payments and adjustment issues have become more severe, so government power and attention has shifted to those directly involved with financial/economic policy, often leading to a relative neglect of longer-term development issues in general and social policy in particular.

4   POSITIVE MOVEMENTS IN HEALTH DESPITE ECONOMIC TRENDS

Against this background, it would not be surprising if several declines in child health and deterioration in infant and child mortality were the universal norm. The 'old economics' of child health and survival would lead one to expect nothing less. In fact, the position appears to be much more mixed, with an increasing number of countries showing a different pattern. After a long decline of infant and child mortality until 1970 followed by some slowing for another 10 years, action in many countries now appears to be resulting in *improving* infant and child mortality rates and some aspects of child health, in spite of constraints. What explains these dramatic movements against the economic tide? Essentially, positive forces are at work, each demonstrating the economic potential of new approaches to child survival and development when widely applied.

Diarrhoea in 1980 accounted for a further 5 million deaths, primarily from the dehydration associated with it. The application of oral rehydration therapy, rehydration by giving a young child a simple salt/sugar drink, has made possible widespread action to prevent severe dehydration and death. This simple method replaces costly intravenous feeding which was formerly available only in hospitals or clinics. Again there was a 330 per cent increase in the world-wide use of oral rehydration salt (ORS) packets between 1983 and 1985. The growing application of ORT prevented an additional 500,000 child deaths in 1985.

With the further expansion of these actions since 1985, UNICEF now estimates that some one and a half million child deaths have been prevented in 1986.

One major theme that emerges in the context of improved child health despite a harsh economic environment is that existing resources with important potentials for health, many of which, such as widespread availability of radio and television as a result of recent development progress, are often grossly underused, even in the context of a recession. There is considerable scope for better use of existing:

(a) human resources and human potential;
(b) communications, especially radio, television and school systems;
(c) organisations, public and private, which can play a critical part in social mobilisation.

A second force that appears to have been vital to this process is closely related to better utilisation of resources. By social mobilisation approaches, and far greater use of existing means of communication, changes in *consumer behaviour* can be achieved, including awareness of available health measures – plus the motivation to use them, in general. This shifts more responsibility and initiative for health from the health services to the family, the mother, the individual. UNICEF refers to this as the 'demand' approach, as opposed to a 'supply' approach. It has many parallels with an old argument of Hirschman (1958) in *The Strategy of Economic Development* – this very creation of bottlenecks often stimulates the initiative and motivation to solve the problems they present. In the context of recessions, despair and disillusion over cutbacks can often be remedied by a conscious challenge to do more with less.

Thirdly, the application of the above themes to a number of new or improved but grossly underutilised technologies to tackle directly some of the major causes of child illness and mortality have had noteworthy impact. Nearly 5 million children under five were dying each year around 1980 from diseases preventible with the use of US 50 cents worth of vaccines: measles in particular, which accounted for some one half of these deaths; tetanus, which took another million lives; pertussis (whooping cough), polio, diphtheria, and tuberculosis. The expansion of immunisation over the 1980s – and a threefold increase in world vaccine use between 1983 and 1985 – was by 1985 preventing the deaths of an estimated 800,000 children under five.

To interpret what is happening in many countries, one needs an activist's view of government and non-government social leadership. It is from this vantage that one can stimulate and make aware millions of families as to the action they are capable of, and ought to take, in order to protect the health of their children. In part this is a matter of political leadership, in part of improved management, and it is true in the public health sector as well as outside. In total, it adds up to a process of national mobilisation.

How should one interpret these developments in economic terms? Overall, they provide clear examples of action which is possible, even in the context of declining average incomes and increasing poverty. Such action is clearly not sufficient – poverty itself must be more generally tackled. To this end a resumption of economic growth and an increase of incomes is needed. But this remarkable advance in child health and survival against the downward trend of economics focuses attention on other critical features which are also significant for improved child health.

Examples of countries that are beginning to take advantage of these newly-evolving possibilities are emerging. Colombia, for instance, has been a forerunner in demonstrating the viability of these approaches and their combined effect in support of primary health care. The then-President Betancur in 1984 began a major initiative to raise the proportion of the country's immunised children from about half to near universal coverage, with considerable success. Through three national immunisation days, a nation mobilised to immunise the great majority of its children against five major diseases then killing and crippling tens of thousands of Colombian children each year. There were more than 10,000 TV spots; virtually every parish priest devoted three sermons to the importance of families immunising their children, and every school teacher was involved. President Betancur and other leaders personally immunised children.

The campaign began in June 1984. By the end of that August more than three-quarters of the under-5s had been fully immunised.

Repeated again last fall with particular emphasis on the most vulnerable under-2s, the total rose to over 80 per cent, which is approaching the levels required to provide 'herd' immunisation against the biggest killer, measles. The accelerated effort was able to bolster significantly the on-going Primary Health Care infrastructures. This commitment to improved health care has been maintained when President Betancur was succeeded this August by President Barco, of another party. The new government has embraced the National Child Survival and Development Plan, and is now engaged in further broadening and strengthening it.

Similar techniques are beginning to evolve in many other countries, with each nation tailoring the approach to fit the particular structures and cultures of its people.

Turkey is an example, consciously using these new approaches to reduce its relatively high infant and child mortality rates. Turkey launched its 'Child Survival Revolution' just over a year ago with a national immunisation week for 5 million children under 5 years old. The campaign focused on the six diseases which in 1984 took the lives of more than 30,000 Turkish children, and crippled tens of thousands more. With more than 50,000 Moslem imams taking the lead from their mosques (just as Colombian priests had in their churches), and with the active participation of 95,000 village teachers (who returned from summer vacation two weeks early for the purpose), some 85 per cent of all young Turks were fully immunised against these dread diseases. This spring, this social mobilisation approach was extended to encompass oral rehydration therapy, means for coping with acute respiratory infections, and family planning.

A similar acceleration of primary health care activities has taken place in Burkina Faso, one of the poorest countries of the world, with a per capita income of about US $200 per year, high infant mortality, and a health system which, like other public services, was weak and chronically underfunded. A major immunisation effort was undertaken in late 1984, with broad popular participation and the involvement of nearly all branches of government and the private sector. Immunisation coverage levels were raised from under 20 per cent to over 75 per cent for the three diseases included, preventing thousands of cases and deaths and averting the impact of a measles epidemic. More important, the expansion of immunisation was instrumental to the subsequent development of a community-based primary health care network in which local workers and health posts have been placed in over 7000 of the country's 7500 villages during the past year.

These examples, and others, of countries in vastly different economic circumstances, demonstrate the viability of a primary health strategy based on low-cost interventions and social mobilisation. By the latest count, some 70 developing countries have serious plans towards universal child immunisation by 1990; nearly as many have embarked on rapid expansion of oral rehydration therapy. In many countries massive new efforts are beginning. In India, where more than 1 million children died, and a nearly comparable number were crippled last year as a consequence of not being immunised, a programme is now under way to achieve universal immunisation of Indian children by 1990 as a 'living memorial' to the late Prime Minister Indira Gandhi.

This primary health care approach has equal validity in a wealthy country like the United States, as in a poor country like Burkina Faso. Better health today in all countries depends far more on what individuals can do for themselves than for what capital-intensive hospitals do for them. For example, in the United States, the Center for Disease Control in Atlanta has estimated that it would require additional expenditures of tens of billions of dollars to increase the life expectancy of adult American males by one year relying on improvements in existing hospital approaches. In contrast, 10 years could be added to the life expectancy of the American male in the United States by four changes in individual behaviour:

- by stopping smoking;
- by reducing alcohol consumption from excess to moderation;
- by changing food habits to reduce quantity and to improve the quality of food intake to achieve a better diet, especially less fat and sugar consumption;
- by reasonable exercise.

These four changes would, in most respects, involve less consumption rather than more, and certainly require changes in consumption and consumer behaviour. None is obviously related to increases in income per capita or hospital expenditures; however, a major social mobilisation and expansion of public health information would be needed if these new behavioural patterns gradually being adopted by better educated and higher income Americans are to be adopted by the majority of Americans, including those most in need, in the next decade.

What we are seeing in both developing and industrial countries is a major frontier for progress in difficult economic conditions through far greater use of social mobilisation and existing means of communication to educate and empower individuals to do more to help themselves whether in health or in food production.

5 CONCLUSIONS

What are the lessons for economics – and for economists? There are many, especially for those who follow that school of economics that is concerned to influence events and not merely to contribute to higher mathematics!

First, there is need for a clearer focus on the human objectives of development. For policy-making, it will require a clear focus on human progress as a direct objective, not as a by-product of economic growth. These points have long been made in the development literature but too often are forgotten when formulating national or international economic policies. In this context I recall with pleasure the positive outcome of the recent Summit of the South Asian Association for Regional Cooperation on 19 November:

> The Heads of state or government recognized that the meeting of the needs of all children was the principal means of human resources development. Children should therefore be given the highest priority in national development planning. The Heads of state or government underlined the importance of enhancing public consciousness and building a national political consensus on the rights of the children.

Secondly, the experiences presented in this paper make it clear that policy-making must relate more specifically to the cost effective technologies and approaches available. Unless one focuses on these, many opportunities will be missed. Yet again, experience shows that the technologies already available are often unknown or inadequately known, even by those responsible for health policy, let alone by those responsible for economic planning. In my own experience in the last three years, I have met at least one Minister of Health who had never heard of oral rehydration therapy. This technology in his country would have made possible the treatment of the single most important cause of child death at 1/500th of the cost of intravenous hospital-based technology, and at the same time make possible the use of unskilled instead of skilled personnel. One wonders how much the heavy expenditures on hospitals by governments and aid institutions reflects gross ignorance rather than vested interests. I suspect that if the relative cost-effectiveness of treating basic diseases in different ways were better known, many politicians who currently support a hospital approach would find it in their political interest to switch their attention to low-cost techniques of mass application.

Thirdly, the need for better information about the cost-effectiveness of different health approaches underlines directly the need for more relevant economic research on health-related issues. When one glances at the *American Economic Review*, one must wonder how much human progress could be enhanced if one-tenth of existing economic effort were turned from blackboard abstractions to these practical empirical problems of child health and survival in developing countries. How many graduate students, many from developing countries writing their theses in the United States or Europe, spend their time refining abstract algebraic models with barely a glimpse at reality. Yet one knows from experience in UNICEF how difficult it is to find basic empirical studies on the costs or cost-effectiveness of different approaches to health, education, water or other projects directed to basic child survival and development in almost any country. If economics is the study of the better allocation of resources, economics itself is in danger of becoming the most monumental example of misplaced effort.

Fourthly, concentrated attention on the supply side needs to be supplemented by much more attention to the demand side, especially in relation to health and child survival and development. No doubt this will take economists into more complex multi-disciplinary areas of individual behaviour and public decision-making. As explained earlier, it will also take them into cost-effective approaches from which to influence behaviour and decision-making in ways that enhance human welfare. But those of us interested in affecting policy are already concerned with these issues. What we need is the professional support and analysis of economists and other social scientists to improve the process.

Fifthly, and of the utmost importance in many developing countries at the moment, these broader perspectives of child survival and development need to be brought home to everyone concerned with the making of economic adjustment policy. As UNICEF has argued elsewhere, for most countries in Africa and Latin America today, the making of adjustment policy has virtually replaced development planning, as the short-term imperatives of economic survival squeeze out resources and concern for longer-term economic and social goals. The result, as described earlier, is too often a tragic deterioration in nutrition and human welfare, which in the long run will prove an economic folly as well as a human tragedy. Yet the examples given in this paper make clear that policy alternatives exist. As an increasing number of countries are showing, it is possible to support and accelerate basic child health and survival actions, even in the context of severe economic constraint. The challenge is to make these possibilities more widely known and to extend their application from these initial measurements of primary health care to the full range of actions required to protect basic human needs. This should become second nature to all concerned with making adjustment policy. They should be part of economic orthodoxy. In the last few months we have seen the acceptance of these ideas by the Managing Director of the IMF, by the World Bank and by a number of key governments, in both developing and developed countries. This beginning of a new approach needs further to be carried through into the every-day actions of those agencies and of all countries concerned. And economists need to be in the lead in explaining how this could be done and the rationale for making this part of economic orthodoxy.

Sixthly, economists need to support in all countries the development of a more appropriate monitoring and statistical system, to direct attention to these realities, not divert attention from them. In the early 1970s there was increasing recognition that economic growth alone was insufficient and that specific efforts were needed to direct attention to increasing human welfare, reducing poverty and ensuring a better distribution of income. One reason why attention slipped is that statistical systems never fully caught up with the shift in development thinking. The world was left relying on data focused on GNP, when routines should have been established regularly that provided a more rounded set of economic and social indicators with which to plan development and to assess its progress. In fact, the final resolution of the World Employment Programme in 1976 called for precisely this – but somehow its implementation got lost in the subsequent months. In recent years UNICEF has sought to direct far more attention to consideration of the infant mortality rate, and more recently to the under-5 mortality rate, as key indicators to be considered along with per capita GNP.

44   *Social Justice and Development*

References

Bose, A. B. (1986) *Monitoring Survival and Development of a Young Child*, National Institute of Public Cooperation and Child Development (New Delhi: Hanz Khas).

Cornia, G., Jolly, R. and Steward, F. (1987) *Adjustment with a Human Face: Protecting the Vulnerable and Promoting Growth* (Oxford: Oxford University Press).

Hirschman, A. O. (1958) *The Strategy of Economic Development* (New Haven: Yale University Press).

Jolly, R. and Cornia, G. (1984) *The Impact of World Recession on Children* (Oxford, New York, Toronto, Sydney, Paris, Frankfurt: Pergamon Press).

Pfeffermann, G. (1986) *Poverty in Latin America: The Impact of Depression* (Washington DC: World Books).

UNICEF (1986) *Statistics on Children in UNICEF Assisted Countries* (New York: United Nations).

4 Planning Techniques for Social Justice

Erik Thorbecke*

CORNELL UNIVERSITY, ITHACA, NEW YORK

1 INTRODUCTION

As broad and ambitious a title as that of the present paper needs to be appropriately circumscribed. In Section 2 social justice is equated with poverty alleviation as estimated by a class of poverty measures sensitive to a (variable) relative deprivation concept of poverty. Given the degree of poverty aversion specified exogenously by the policy-maker, budgetary rules for poverty alleviation are presented which show how a given budget should be allocated among different socioeconomic groups – assuming a static framework and no economic interaction among groups.

In Section 3 budgetary rules for poverty alleviation are derived within an interactive and interdependent framework as represented by the social accounting matrix (SAM). It is shown that allowing for interaction among socioeconomic groups and macroeconomic interdependence, the budgetary rules have to be modified. The budget should be allocated among these groups differently than in the non-interactive case.

Finally, in Section 4 structural path analysis is offered as a possible planning technique for social justice. Its usefulness from a policy standpoint is that it identifies the whole network of paths through which influence is transmitted within a disaggregated socioeconomic system. An illustrative example based on the Indonesian SAM explores some of the major paths through which the impact of a budgetary allocation to a given socioeconomic group affects the incomes of other groups.

2 SOCIAL JUSTICE, POVERTY MEASURES, AND BUDGETARY RULES FOR POVERTY ALLEVIATION WITHIN A STATIC NON-INTERACTIVE FRAMEWORK

Social justice is an elusive and essentially normative concept. Looking at it from the vantage point of an economist, the prevalence of very uneven income and asset (physical and human capital) distributions – accompanied by widespread poverty – is the most patent symptom and manifestation of social injustice. For this reason economists and planners alike have increasingly focused on the alleviation of absolute poverty as a fundamental objective of socioeconomic development.[1]

For planning purposes poverty alleviation has to be precisely defined. A specific poverty measure has to be selected which incorporates and reflects the degree of poverty aversion particular to each society, or *faute de mieux*, the policy-makers who presumably represent it. Recently a class of poverty measures has been proposed by Foster, Greer and Thorbecke (1984) (denoted by FGT) which (i) is sensitive to a relative deprivation concept of poverty through the parameter value, α, in (1), (ii) can satisfy the major theoretical requirements of such measures such as the monotonicity, transfer, and transfer sensitivity axioms for appropriate values of α, and (iii) is additively decomposable among population subgroups.

The FGT poverty measure, P_α, is defined as

$$P_\alpha = \frac{1}{n} \sum_{j=1}^{q} \left(\frac{z - y_j}{z} \right)^\alpha \tag{1}$$

where

n is the total number of individuals
q is the predetermined poverty line
y_j is the income of the jth poor individual, and
α is a parameter reflecting the degree of poverty aversion.

The parameter value α can be specified exogenously by the policy-maker. For $\alpha = 0$, the measure becomes the headcount ratio, i.e., the proportion of poor in the total population,

$$P_0 = \frac{q}{n} \tag{2}$$

Adopting P_0 as an objective implies a complete insensitivity to the degree of poverty since the headcount ratio would be reduced by the same amount whether one picks a person just below the poverty line or the poorest individual and brings him or her up to the poverty line. Using P_0 as a policy objective also implies that a fixed budget would be allocated so that the first dollars would go to the individual just below the poverty line, then to the next poorest, and so on (i.e., minimising P_0 favours the least poor). When $\alpha = 1$, the measure becomes the ratio of (a), the total income shortfall necessary to bring everybody up to at least the poverty line to (b), the aggregate income obtaining if each member of the population (n) received exactly the poverty line income (z), that is,

$$P_1 = \frac{\sum_{j=1}^{q} (z - y_j)}{nz} \tag{3}$$

For P_1 it does matter whether someone just slightly poor or someone very poor is brought above the poverty line income. In the latter case the poverty measure will be reduced more. However, for a fixed dollar amount of benefits, it does not matter which of the poor is subsidised, a dollar reduction in the income gap has the same impact on P_1 whether it accrues to the poorest individual or someone less poor. Figure 4.1 illustrates graphically both the headcount and the P_1 measure.

Finally, for $\alpha > 1$, the welfare weights assigned to the poor individuals increase with the income shortfall. In the special case where $\alpha = 2$, each of the poor is assigned a weight exactly equal to his or her shortfall from the poverty line, that is,

$$P_2 = \frac{\sum_{j=1}^{q} (z - y_j)^2}{nz^2} \tag{4}$$

In the limit, as α becomes very large, P_α approaches a Rawlsian measure which considers only the position of the poorest person. Thus the parameter can be viewed as a measure of poverty aversion to be selected by the policy-maker consistent with societal values and norms.

If it is assumed that the planner's objective is a movement towards greater social justice as reflected by a reduction in P_α, and that he uses a 'poverty alleviation' budget for this purpose then, in principle, this

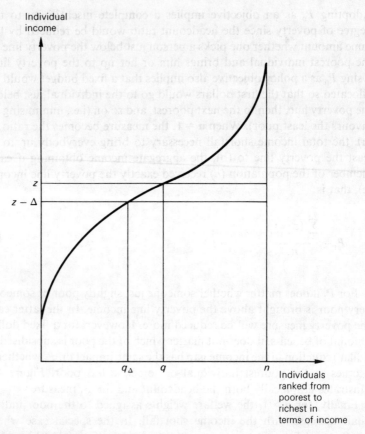

Figure 4.1 Income order function and effect of additional budgetary allocation per capita (Δ)

n is the total number of individuals
q is the total number of poor
q_Δ is the total number of poor after budgetary allocation Δ
z is the poverty line income
Δ is the per capita budgetary allocation received by all n individuals

budget could be allocated in such a way as to minimise P_α. If perfect targeting of benefits on an individual basis were possible, then the policy-maker having chosen, for instance, a poverty aversion parameter $\alpha > 1$ would allocate the first amount of benefits to the poorest individual until this person's income had become equal to that of the next poorest individual and so on until the budget was exhausted. In fact, such perfect identification of the poorest and targeting of benefits is often either administratively impossible, or extremely costly, since poverty is likely to be pervasive and spread among different regions and socioeconomic groups. Consequently in most cases the policy-maker's only realistic alternative is to direct expenditures towards broadly defined socioeconomic groups. Because many of these groups – including the ones with the lowest average income – are likely to contain some individuals with incomes below the poverty line and some above it, leakages will result from targeting benefits to a group rather than to individuals *per se*.

An additional property of the P_α measure is that it is additively decomposable among population subgroups, allowing a quantitative, as well as a qualitative, assessment of the effects of changes in subgroup poverty on total poverty. This means that the effects of benefits directed to a specific socioeconomic group, g, can be estimated both in terms of its impact on poverty alleviation within that group ($P_{g,\alpha}$) *and* on overall poverty alleviation (P_α). P_α is equal to the weighted average of each group poverty measure, $P_{g,\alpha}$, with the population shares (n_g/n) as weights, that is,

$$P_\alpha = \sum_{g=1}^{k} \frac{n_g}{n} P_{g,\alpha} \quad \text{and} \quad \sum_{g=1}^{k} n_g = n \tag{5}$$

Recently Kanbur (1986) devised a set of budgetary decision rules applying to the above case. He showed that if the objective is the minimisation of P_α and the policy-maker could allocate a total budget B with each individual receiving an equal additive per capita amount $\Delta = B/n$, the post-expenditure poverty index, denoted by $P_\alpha(B)$, becomes

$$P_\alpha(B) = \int_{\underline{y}}^{z-\Delta} \left(\frac{z-y-\Delta}{z} \right)^\alpha f(y) dy \tag{6}$$

where $f(y)$ is the income density function and $\underline{y}$ is the income of the poorest person, while all other terms are as previously defined. Figure 4.1 illustrates the impact of an amount Δ accruing to each individual. It is equivalent to reducing the poverty line to an income level $(z - \Delta)$ and the number of poor falls from q to q_Δ. The total budget $B = \Delta \cdot n$ is shown graphically by the rectangle of width Δ and length n in Figure 4.1. This rectangle consists of two parts – (i), the area to the left of the income order function which represents the contribution to poverty alleviation *per se*, and (ii), the area to the right of the same function which represents the 'unavoidable' leakage of not being able to target expenditures on an individual basis.

Kanbur addressed the following question: assuming that the minimisation of P_α is the objective, how should the policy-maker allocate a given budget B among distinct mutually exclusive groups? He showed that in the additive absorption case (where each member of the group would receive the same per capita amount of benefits) the appropriate indicator to use for allocation of benefits is the $(\alpha - 1)$th order poverty index for each group – budget increments should be directed towards the group for which $P_{\alpha-1}$ is greatest. This means, for example, that if the objective is P_1, i.e., minimising the income gap, then the appropriate indicator for budgetary allocation is P_0, the headcount ratio.[2] In this case the policy-maker would allocate to the group with the highest headcount ratio (q_g/n_g) until this proportion was reduced to that prevailing in the group with the second highest proportion of poor at which time both groups would receive benefits and so on until B was exhausted.

The beauty of Kanbur budgetary rules is their simplicity; once the planner has selected his poverty aversion parameter α, and the amount to be budgeted for poverty alleviation purposes, the allocation to groups follows automatically using $P_{\alpha-1}$ as the indicator. The limitation of these rules, on the other hand, is that they are purely static, abstracting from the indirect effects which a budgetary allocation to one group can have on other groups through the interdependence prevailing within a socioeconomic system. If people in one group receive benefits they will spend a high proportion of them. Some of the additional purchases involve sales and production from members of their own group – implying that the group's income may increase by more than the initial subsidy. Furthermore, the group receiving the initial benefits will spend on goods and services produced and sold by members of other groups. In this way other groups are positively affected as well.

The purpose of the next section is to derive budgetary rules which take the effects of interaction within and between groups into account. This requires having information on how groups relate to one another through their production, distribution, and consumption activities. The social accounting matrix (SAM) provides a framework for identifying and analysing just this type of interaction. It will be seen that the simple Kanbur budgetary decision rules have to be appropriately modified to incorporate interactive effects.

3   BUDGETARY RULES FOR POVERTY ALLEVIATION WITHIN A SOCIAL ACCOUNTING MATRIX INTERACTIVE FRAMEWORK

Under certain assumptions, such as excess capacity and fixed prices, the SAM can be used as a basis for simple modelling. In essence, the effects of exogenous injections (such as government expenditures directed to certain socioeconomic groups for poverty alleviation purposes in the present context) on the whole economic system can be explored using multiplier analysis. This requires partitioning the SAM into endogenous and exogenous accounts. Typically the former include (i) factors, (ii) institutions (i.e., distinct socioeconomic groups of households and companies), and (iii) production activities, while the exogenous accounts consist of (iv) government, (v) capital, and (vi) rest of the world. Table 4.1 shows this partition and the transformations (matrices) involving the three endogenous accounts. These matrices are, respectively, T_{13} which allocates the value added generated by the various production activities into income accruing to the factors of production, T_{33} which gives the intermediate input requirements (i.e., the input–output transactions matrix), T_{21} maps the factorial income distribution into the household income distribution (where households are distinguished according to socioeconomic characteristics), T_{22} captures the income transfers within and among household groups and, finally, T_{32} reflects the expenditure pattern of the various institutions (mainly the household groups) for the different commodities (production activities) which they consume. Figure 4.2 shows this same triangular interdependence graphically using the same notation as in Table 4.1.

A coefficient matrix of marginal expenditure propensities (C_n) for the endogenous transactions of Table 4.1 can be computed[3] given the initial transactions matrix and additional information about such parameters as income and expenditure elasticities of the different agents. It has been shown that the change in endogenous income (dy_n) associated with an exogenous injection (dx) is

$$dy_n = [I - C_n]^{-1} dx = M_c dx \tag{7}$$

where M_c has been coined the fixed-price multiplier matrix (see Pyatt and Round, 1979; Defourny and Thorbecke, 1984).

After this short excursion into the SAM methodology, one can

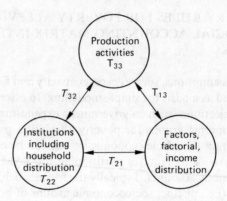

Figure 4.2 Simplified interrelationship among principal SAM accounts (production activities, factors, and institutions). *T* (with a subscript) stands for the corresponding matrix in the simplified SAM which appears on Table 4.1. Thus, for example, T_{13} refers to the matrix which appears at the intersection of row 1 (account 1), i.e. 'factors' and column 3 (account 3), i.e. 'production activities'.

return to the question at hand and show how government expenditures (or subsidies) accruing to one socioeconomic group affect the incomes of other socioeconomic groups, and thereby their relative poverty as well. Let us again assume that the policy-maker chooses to minimise P_α for the society as a whole, starts with a budget *B*, and wants to find out the total effects of allocating increments of *B*, not only on the incomes of the group receiving the subsidy, but also on the incomes of all other groups. Given this knowledge the policy-maker can assess the direct and indirect consequences on poverty alleviation of any given budgetary allocation.[4] In other words, a budgetary allocation received by group *j* in an interdependent system is likely to affect the incomes and poverty status not only of group *j* but all other groups as well.[5]

Let dB_j be the incremental budgetary allocation to group *j* which is taken as the exogenous injection. The impact on the various groups' incomes is given by

$$dy_g^j = M_{c_{gj}} dB_j, \quad g = 1,2,...,k \quad j = 1,2,...,k \tag{8}$$

where

$M_{c_{gi}}$ is the submatrix of M_c giving the fixed-price multipliers of an injection into group *j* on the income of group *g*,[6] and

Table 4.1 Simplified schematic social accounting matrix

			Expenditures			
			Endogenous accounts			Exog.	
			Factors	Households	Production activities	Sum of other accounts	Totals
			1	2	3	4	5
Receipts	Endogenous accounts	Factors	1	0	0	T_{13}	x_1	y_1
		Households	2	T_{21}	T_{22}	0	x_2	y_2
		Production activities	3	0	T_{32}	T_{33}	x_3	y_3
	Exog.	Sum of other accounts	4	l_1	l_2	l_3	t	y_x
		Totals	5	y_1	y_2	y_3	y_x	

dy_g^j is the change in income of group g associated with an injection into group j.

To add some realism to this picture, Table 4.2 gives the actual values of the fixed-price multipliers corresponding to $M_{c_{gj}}$ which obtained in the 1975 SAM for Indonesia.[7] In the breakdown appearing in Table 4.2, the total Indonesian population is divided into ten distinct household groups mainly according to landownership in agriculture and the occupational status of the head of the household in rural non-agriculture and the urban areas.[8] Reading down a column of Table 4.2 gives the impact of dB_j on dy_g^j; thus, for example, an increment of 1 billion rupiahs in subsidies received by 'Agricultural employees' would increase, directly and indirectly, the total income of this group by 1.122 billion rupiahs, and that of the small farmers ('Farm size I') by 259 million rupiahs, and so on.[9]

In order to obtain the effects of dB_j on the per capita income of socioeconomic group (Δ_g^j) the total income impact, as given above, has to be divided by the population size of each socioeconomic group, that is,

$$\Delta_g^j = \frac{dy_g^j}{n_g} = \frac{M_{c_{gi}}}{n_g} \tag{9}$$

where n_g is the population size of each group.

Table 4.3 gives the Δ_g^js for illustrative purposes. Again, one example is sufficient to convey the meaning of these values. An incremental expenditure of 1 billion rupiahs by the policy-maker benefiting, say, agricultural employees (dB_j) would give rise to an increase in the per capita income of the same group of 76.3 rupiahs and of that of the small farmers of 9 rupiahs, respectively (the Δ_gs, in this instance, are read off from column 2).

We can now ask how the poverty alleviation budgetary decision rules as derived by Kanbur, for instance, should be modified to take into account the indirect (interactive) effects of government expenditures (subsidies) targeted to some specific groups. This will be shown, first, in the two groups case before generalising it to the k-group case.

Let the exogenous incremental budget which the policy-maker has earmarked for poverty alleviation be equal to dB. There are two socioeconomic groups $g = 1,2$ with populations n_1 and n_2, respectively ($n_1 + n_2 = n$). The policy-maker can allocate dB to group 1 (i.e. dB_1) or to group 2 (dB_2). In this instance,

Table 4.2 Indonesia: submatrix of fixed-price multipliers $M_{c\bar{x}f}^{1}$ yielding impact of change in injection received by socioeconomic groups on change in incomes of socioeconomic household groups

	Agricultural employees[2] 1	Farm size I[3] 2	Farm size II[4] 3	Farm size III[5] 4	Rural lower 5	Rural middle 6	Rural higher 7	Urban lower 8	Urban middle 9	Urban higher 10
1. Agricultural employees[2]	1.122	0.125	0.110	0.076	0.110	0.113	0.089	0.089	0.098	0.066
2. Farm size I[3]	0.259	1.264	0.231	0.159	0.231	0.236	0.186	0.184	0.202	0.136
3. Farm size II[4]	0.190	0.194	1.170	0.117	0.169	0.173	0.136	0.133	0.145	0.098
4. Farm size III[5]	0.329	0.337	0.295	1.203	0.292	0.299	0.235	0.228	0.248	0.167
5. Rural lower	0.211	0.210	0.181	0.135	1.196	0.203	0.168	0.178	0.199	0.141
6. Rural middle	0.048	0.049	0.045	0.051	0.052	1.043	0.057	0.037	0.040	0.030
7. Rural higher	0.099	0.099	0.087	0.065	0.093	0.099	1.083	0.088	0.100	0.073
8. Urban lower	0.268	0.273	0.243	0.181	0.256	0.275	0.226	1.249	0.281	0.202
9. Urban middle	0.042	0.043	0.039	0.029	0.041	0.042	0.030	0.071	1.044	0.076
10. Urban higher	0.254	0.256	0.227	0.171	0.241	0.261	0.218	0.236	0.271	1.199

Notes:

1. See equation (8) in text.
2. Landless and near landless.
3. Farmers owning between 0 and 0.5 ha.
4. Farmers owning between 0.5 and 1 ha.
5. Farmers owning more than 1 ha.

Source: Khan and Thorbecke, 1986, Table 11.6.

Table 4.3 Effect on per capita income of group g of an additional injection of 1 billion rupiahs into group j (i.e. $\Delta_g^j = dy_g^j/n_g$)

Change in per capita income of group g	Population size (in million) (n_g)	Exogenous expenditure on, or subsidies to, group j									
		Agricultural employees 1	Farm size I 2	Farm size II 3	Farm size III 4	Rural lower 5	Rural middle 6	Rural higher 7	Urban lower 8	Urban middle 9	Urban higher 10
1. Agricultural employees	14.7	76.3	8.5	7.5	5.2	7.5	7.7	6.1	6.1	6.7	4.5
2. Farm size I	29.1	9.0	43.4	7.9	5.5	7.9	8.1	6.4	6.3	6.9	4.7
3. Farm size II	15.7	12.1	12.4	74.5	7.5	10.8	11.0	8.7	8.5	9.2	6.2
4. Farm size III	18.0	18.3	18.7	16.4	66.8	15.1	16.6	13.1	12.7	13.8	9.3
5. Rural lower	19.3	10.9	10.9	9.4	7.0	62.0	10.5	8.7	9.2	10.3	7.3
6. Rural middle	3.8	12.6	12.9	11.8	13.4	13.7	274.5	15.0	9.7	10.5	7.9
7. Rural higher	7.7	12.9	12.9	11.3	8.4	12.1	12.9	140.6	11.4	13.0	9.5
8. Urban lower	12.1	22.2	22.6	20.1	15.0	21.2	22.7	18.7	103.2	23.2	16.7
9. Urban middle	2.0	21.0	21.5	19.5	14.5	20.5	21.0	15.0	35.5	522.0	38.0
10. Urban higher	8.0	31.8	32.0	28.4	21.4	30.2	32.6	27.3	29.5	33.9	149.9

Source: Derived from Table 4.2.

$$M_{c_{gj}} = \begin{bmatrix} m_{11} & m_{12} \\ m_{21} & m_{22} \end{bmatrix} \quad \begin{matrix} g = 1,2 \\ i = 1,2 \end{matrix} \tag{10}$$

What will be the effects of (a) ($dB_1 > 0$ and $dB_2 = 0$), and (b) ($dB_2 > 0$ and $dB_1 = 0$), respectively, on the per capita incomes of each group and, ultimately on the P_a measure? If we start with an injection dB_1 to group 1 the associated increase in per capita incomes of the two groups will be (from (8) and (9))

$$\Delta_1^1 = \frac{m_{11}dB_1}{n_1} \quad \text{and} \quad \Delta_2^1 = \frac{m_{21}dB_1}{n_2} \tag{11}[10]$$

It follows from (5) and (11) that the post-expenditure poverty measure for group 1, associated with an injection into this same group is

$$
\begin{aligned}
P_{1,a}^1 &= \int_{y_1}^{z-\Delta_1^1} \left(\frac{z - \Delta_1^1 - y_1}{z} \right)^a f_1(y_1)dy_1 \\
&= \int_{y_1}^{z-\Delta_1^1} \left(\frac{z - m_{11}dB_1/n_1 - y_1}{z} \right) f_1(y_1)dy_1
\end{aligned}
\tag{12}
$$

Likewise, the impact on poverty in group 2 of a budgetary allocation to group 1 becomes,

$$P_{2,a}^1 = \int_{y_2}^{z-\Delta_2^1} \left(\frac{z - m_{12}dB_1/n_2 - y_2}{z} \right) f_2(y_2)dy_2 \tag{13}$$

The P_a^1 measure for the society overall is obtained from (6) as the weighted average of the above two terms

$$P_a^1 = \frac{n_1}{n} P_{1,a}^1 + \frac{n_2}{n} P_{2,a}^1 \tag{14}$$

Differentiating with respect to B_1, we obtain

$$\frac{\partial P_a^1}{\partial B_1} = -\frac{a}{nz} [m_{11} P_{1,a-1}^1 + m_{21} P_{2,a-1}^1] \tag{15}$$

We can, next, proceed with the same derivation consequent to a budgetary allocation to group 2, $dB_2 > 0$, $dB_1 = 0$. Noting that, in this case,

$$\Delta_1^2 = \frac{m_{12}dB_2}{n_1} \quad \text{and} \quad \Delta_2^2 = -\frac{m_{22}dB_2}{n_2} \tag{16}$$

we get the following expression,

$$\frac{\partial P_a^2}{\partial B_2} = -\frac{\alpha}{nz}[m_{12}P_{1,a-1}^2 + m_{22}P_{2,a-1}^2] \tag{17}$$

The group which should receive the incremental budgetary allocation if the objective is to minimise P_a depends now on the four
multiplier values and the four *ex post* poverty indicators $P_{g,a-1}^j$ appearing in the two expressions in brackets in equations (15) and (17),
respectively. If the expression in brackets is larger in (15) than in (17)
then the injection should be directed to the first group and vice versa. It
is apparent that the Kanbur budgetary decision rules no longer depend
simply on the $P_{g,a-1}$ indicators. They depend not only on which group
receives the initial injection but also on the fixed-price multipliers
which, in turn, capture the direct and indirect effects on the incomes of
the various groups. The initial budgetary allocation (the exogenous
injection) leads to an increase in the recipient group's income. This
additional income is spent on a variety of goods and services which
leads to a corresponding increase in the production of these goods. This
requires, in turn, the employment of additional factors of production.
The value added going to these factors is fed back as incomes to the
various socioeconomic groups and the triangular interrelation among
households, production activities, and factor accounts (depicted in
Figure 4.1) can be repeated. As will be shown in the next section,
structural path analysis provides the complete network of paths
through which the influence of budgetary injection is transmitted
throughout the socioeconomic system.

The budgetary decision rule derived above in the two groups case in
(15) and (17) can be generalised in the multigroup case, that is,

$$\frac{\partial P_a^j}{\partial B_j} = -\frac{\alpha}{nz}\left[\sum_{g=1}^{k} m_{gj}P_{g,a-1}^j\right] \quad g = 1,2...k \quad j = 1,2...k \tag{18}$$

Again, if the policy-maker's objective were poverty alleviation as
reflected by the minimisation of P_a, then the g groups would have to be
ranked according to the expression in brackets in (18). Budgetary
allocation would be made to the jth group with the highest value of this
expression until it were equal to that of the next highest group, at which

time the next allocation would be directed to both of these groups, and so on. This process requires recalculating $P^j_{g,\alpha-1}$ *ex post* each time group j receives an injection, since the term depends on the size of the increase in the per capita income, Δ^j_g consequent to an initial injection as can be verified from (12) and (13).

It is reasonable to wonder whether this concern for interactive effects really makes much difference on policy recommendations and anticipated outcomes of poverty alleviation efforts. Clearly the budget allocation rules that involve the fixed-price multipliers (18) appear different from those derived by Kanbur which assume no interaction among groups, but how significant is this difference?[11] To explore this question an example involving three groups was constructed so that differences in 'optimal' poverty budget allocations and in levels of poverty reduction could be compared between situations that took interactive effects into account and those that did not. Although the example is an artificial construct intended only for illustrative purposes, an effort was made to keep the example 'realistic'.

A society of 1000 persons is divided into three mutually exclusive groups A, B, and C.[12] The assumed income distributions and characteristics of each group are shown in Figure 4.3a.[13] Groups A, B, and C are the three household categories within a SAM framework. The marginal expenditure propensities between the factors of production, households, and productive activities are assumed to be as shown in Table 4.4a. This is the matrix C_n that appears in equation (7) above. The portion of the associated fixed-price multiplier matrix that shows the interactions between groups A, B, and C is given in Table 4.4b.

A total poverty budget of 30,000 units is exogenously provided to this society to reduce poverty, where poverty is measured by P_α with $\alpha = 2$. As in the analysis above it is assumed that it is not feasible to distinguish the poor from the non-poor individuals within groups, and thus when an incremental subsidy is allocated to a given group every person within that group will receive an equal share. The total budget is allocated in 1000-unit increments (this makes per capita benefits from each increment less than 2 per cent of mean per capita income of any group). To accomplish the allocation one calculates the post-expenditure $P_{g,\alpha-1}$ for each group, $g = $ A, B, C, and the bracketed expression in (18). Comparing the latter among the three groups, one looks for the largest corresponding value – this assures that the reduction in P_α for the society as a whole will be the largest. The 'winner' in this comparison gets allocated the 1000-unit budgetary increment which leads to slight changes in the three income distributions. Then, starting

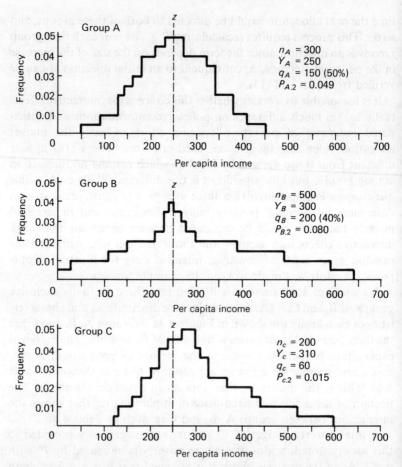

Figure 4.3a Hypothetical income distributions for three socioeconomic groups

from the new income distributions for the groups, this process of calculation, comparison, and allocation is repeated until budget increments add up to the total poverty budget available.

Figure 4.3b shows the results of allocating 30,000 units among the three groups A, B, and C both when interactive effects are considered, and when they are not.[14] This example suggests that the incorporation of interactive effects appears important in judging the effectiveness of poverty alleviation subsidies both for individual groups and for the society as a whole. In the absence of interactive effects overall poverty,

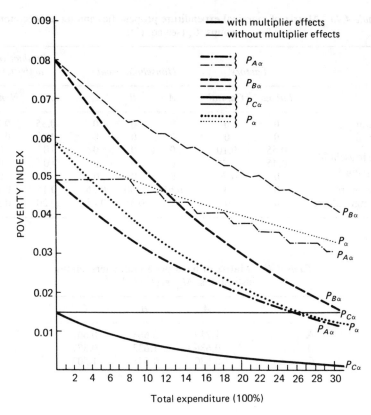

Figure 4.3b Impact on poverty alleviation (P_a) with and without interactive effects

P_a, declines from 0.058 to 0.032, a 45 per cent drop. Also, since group C receives no direct allocation, its poverty measure, $P_{c,a}$ remains unchanged. However, when interactive effects are considered, one sees that overall poverty drops from 0.058 to 0.012 (a 79 per cent reduction), and while group C does not receive a direct allocation, it benefits substantially from re-expenditure of benefits by groups A and B (its poverty measure declines 94 per cent). Additionally there are significant differences for 'optimal' allocations of the budget. Without interactive effects 7000 units would be allocated to group A and 23,000 units would be allocated to group B, while with interactive effects considered all 30,000 units would go to group B.[15]

Table 4.4a Matrix of marginal expenditure propensities among socioeconomic groups, C_n (see eq. (7))

	Factors		Household groups			Productive activities	
	Labour	Capital	A	B	C	Ag.	Non-ag
Labour	0	0	0	0	0	0.35	0.20
Capital	0	0	0	0	0	0.20	0.20
A Household	0.55	0.10	0	0	0	0	0
B groups	0.45	0.20	0	0	0	0	0
C	0	0.70	0	0	0	0	0
Agriculture	0	0	0.65	0.50	0.35	0.15	0.10
Non-agriculture	0	0	0.25	0.35	0.45	0.20	0.30

Table 4.4b Matrix of fixed-price multipliers among institutions, $M_{c_{gj}} = [I - C_n]^{-1}$

	A	B	C
A	1.719	0.668	0.602
B	0.686	1.632	0.577
C	0.580	0.541	1.502

While this example is only illustrative, it does point out the potential importance of incorporating information on the economic inter-relationship of groups when developing budgetary strategies for poverty alleviation and estimating benefits associated with government allocations.

Even more crucial than knowing the magnitude of the interactions is to understand better the underlying mechanisms. Section 4 which follows outlines the contributions which structural path analysis based on a SAM framework can make to such an understanding.

4 STRUCTURAL PATH ANALYSIS AS A PLANNING TECHNIQUE FOR SOCIAL JUSTICE

The global (direct and indirect) effects of injections from exogenous variables on the endogenous variables are captured under certain conditions, by the fixed-price multipliers provided by the reduced form of the SAM model. In the present context the injections consist of budgetary transfers to given household groups while the set of endogenous variables which is focused on is the incomes of the different socioeconomic groups and, ultimately, social justice as reflected by some agreed measure of poverty alleviation. These multipliers, as given in Table 4.2, do not clarify the 'black box', i.e., the structural and behavioural mechanisms responsible for the final (reduced form) solution. The application of structural path analysis to the SAM framework (see Defourny and Thorbecke, 1984), based on the concept of economic influence and its transmission among the agents (sectors or poles) of the structure, reveals explicitly the endogenous interaction process. Structural path analysis shows how influence is diffused from a given pole of origin (which in our specific case would be that household group receiving the initial budgetary transfer), through which specific paths it is transmitted and the extent to which it is amplified by the circuits adjacent to these paths, to ultimately affect the poles of destination (e.g., incomes of the other various socioeconomic groups).

Fixed-price multipliers (reflecting global influence) can be decomposed into total influences carried along the respective elementary paths spanning two given poles.[16] This decomposition – which is illustrated by a concrete example subsequently – allows the policy-maker to identify the specific channels through which influence is transmitted in a disaggregated macro socioeconomic system and thereby contributes to the quality of policy decision.

In the specific context of this paper, structural path analysis is useful in capturing the various paths through which a budgetary allocation enjoyed by any one given group affects the incomes of other groups. For illustrative purposes, let us return to the Indonesian SAM and explore some of the paths through which the impact of a budgetary transfer of dB_j directed, say, to 'agricultural employees' ultimately affects the incomes of three other socioeconomic groups, i.e., small farmers, medium farmers, and 'urban high', respectively. The global influence of this injection on the total incomes of these last three groups is given by the corresponding fixed-price multipliers appearing in column 1 of Table 4.2. The m_{gj} elements from (8) show the impact of an injection received by group j on the incomes of group g. Using the numbering scheme in Table 4.2 where the household group of 'agricultural employees' is denoted by 1, small farmers (2), medium farmers (3), and 'urban high' (10), respectively – the corresponding multipliers are

$$m_{21} = 0.259; \quad m_{31} = 0.190; \quad \text{and} \quad m_{10,1} = 0.254 \qquad (19)$$

These values – although providing important information – looked at from the standpoint of the planner appear to come out of a black box. The policy-maker wants to know something about the underlying structural and behavioural mechanisms yielding these multiplier values. Structural path analysis by decomposing global influence into the whole network of paths through which the impact of policy measures (in the present instance a budgetary allocation to a given group) affect the socioeconomic system helps to open up the black box.

Figure 4.4 identifies some of the major paths through which an initial exogenous allocation to agricultural employees affects the incomes of the other three groups just mentioned. It should be noted that the triangular interrelationship of the endogenous structure of the SAM means that an elementary path must always proceed in the triangular direction as shown in Figure 4.1. Since in the present example the injection occurs in one socioeconomic group (i.e., agricultural employees) all elementary paths originate with that group. This initial injection is transmitted through the increased consumption of that group to production activities and through the induced demand for factors ultimately returns back to the various socioeconomic groups in the form of value added.

The top part of Figure 4.4 shows a number of elementary paths through which a budgetary allocation to agricultural employees (as the pole of origin) affect the incomes of small farmers (as the pole of destination). It should be noted in interpreting the diagram that next to the origin of each arc (arrow) the corresponding MEP (the c_{ij} element from matrix C_n in (7)) is specifically indicated. Likewise, the product of two or more consecutive arcs along any elementary path (i.e., the direct influence) is also given at the end of each relevant arc. A few additional observations should be made about the diagram in Figure 4.4 before discussing it. First, only some of the paths connecting the pole of origin (agricultural employees) to the pole of destination (e.g., small farmers) are explicitly shown. Secondly, the direct influence transmitted through the path we have just described (or any of the other paths appearing in the figure) is amplified through the effects of adjacent feedback circuits which are left out in the diagram.[17] The only feedback which appears is that linking 'agricultural employees' to 'food crops' to 'agricultural paid labour' back to 'agricultural employees'.

One example suffices to illustrate the type of information conveyed by this figure. Let us ask the following question – what is the magnitude of the direct influence from agricultural employees to small farmers travelling along the path Agricultural employees → Food crops → Ag-

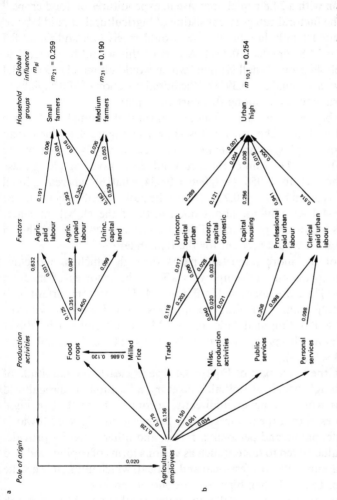

Figure 4.4 Structural network illustrating effects of budgetary injection received by agricultural employees on incomes of small farmers, medium farmers, and urban high group[a]

a For explanation, see text. All the values of the MEPs appearing in the arcs (arrows) above are based on the 1975 Indonesia SAM (see Khan and Thorbecke (1986), Table 11.5).

b Restaurants and prepared food, realty and housing, Kretek cigarettes.

ricultural unpaid labour → Small farmers? This direct influence would be equal to the corresponding product of the corresponding MEPs, i.e., a budgetary increment of 100 rupiahs allocated to agricultural employees would be associated through consumption-cum-increased production with a 24.8 rupiah increase in expenditures on food crops.[18] In turn, the factoral category consisting of 'agricultural unpaid labour' (i.e., imputed family labour income) would receive an additional 8.7 rupiahs (= 24.8 rupiahs × 0.351). A part of this would be directed to the household group 'small farmers' which would ultimately receive 3.4 rupiahs (= 8.7 rupiahs × 0.393) of the initial injection of 100 rupiahs to agricultural employees along this particular path.

It can be seen that the influence transmitted through the above discussed path and the other paths shown in Figure 4.4 which span agricultural employees and small farmers explain only a part of the global influence. The sum of the direct influence travelling along these paths amounts to 0.056 (= 0.006 + 0.034 + 0.016) whereas global influence as given by $m_{21} = 0.259$. Hence the paths specifically identified in Figure 4.4 account for about one-fourth of the global influence. Other less important paths in addition to feedback systems not shown in the diagram would account for the remainder.

Some of the more important paths through which a budgetary allocation to agricultural employees affects the incomes of medium farmers are, likewise, identified in Figure 4.4. The most important path is that going from Agricultural employees → Food crops → Unincorporated capital (imputed land rent) → Medium farmers (the direct influence along this path amounts to 28 per cent of the global influence, i.e., 0.053 ÷ 0.190).

Finally, the lower part of Figure 4.4 reveals clearly the multitude of paths through which an initial budgetary allocation to agricultural employees would influence, indirectly, incomes of the 'Urban high' group. In essence, expenditures by the former group directed towards retail trade, public and personal services, and other activities provide, in turn, value added to factors such as various forms of capital, and two types of labour skills (professional and clerical) which ultimately accrue as incomes to the 'Urban high' socioeconomic groups.

In a general sense, structural path analysis within a SAM framework can be used as a key planning technique. Having determined the policy objectives, t e planner can follow through the quantitative impact of exogenous policy measures (instruments) on policy targets throughout the whole socioeconomic system. In the context of this paper the instruments consist of budgetary allocations to socioeconomic groups and the target is poverty alleviation. However, the policy scope of this approach is much broader.[19] Hence, the effects of budgetary allocations on a variety of potential policy objectives, not just poverty alleviation, can be assessed.

In reality the behavioural and technical mechanisms underlying the operation and performance of an economy over time are much more complex than those implicit in SAM-type analysis and related structural path analysis. A major limitation of the fixed-price multipliers is the assumption of the existence of excess capacity which made it possible to ignore possible supply constraints and consequent changes in prices. There is some evidence in a number of developing countries of the presence of excess capacity in a number of sectors and also of excess supply of labour, with the possible exception of higher skilled workers. In those instances, the comparative static exercises relying on the SAM framework can be defended as reasonably valid in the short run. However, any serious attempt at predicting the macroeconomic effects of budgetary allocations and other policies affecting directly the supply side and the conditions under which production takes place in the medium and long run requires a dynamic model. Such a model should be, at least partially, price endogenous, i.e., be able to determine the new or future sets of prices.

There is a class of computable general equilibrium (CGE) model which, in theory, starting from a given initial SAM (presumed to reflect the initial conditions), can derive endogenously the SAM likely to prevail at some future date.[20] It is clear that this class of models can potentially capture in a more sophisticated way than multiplier analysis the interaction prevailing among economic agents, socioeconomic groups, and accounts. By now there are a number of CGE models which have been constructed to address similar issues to those constituting the focus of this paper, such as the differential impact of different types of food policies (e.g., specific subsidies, general subsidies, two-price policies) on growth and income distribution by socioeconomic groups (see de Janvry and Subramanian, 1986).

There is no reason, in principle, why the analysis which has been presented in this paper and, in particular, the budgetary rules in the interactive case, could not be applied and tailored to such CGE models. It would only require replacing the SAM-multiplier 'black box' by an appropriate CGE model and applying the P_α measure to determine the optimal budgetary decision rules. In this instance, the whole question could be examined within a dynamic growth setting rather than exclusively in a comparative static setting. In any case, as long as the

CGE model is built on the basis of a SAM, structural path analysis –
albeit in a somewhat modified form – can be used as a planning
technique for social justice.

Notes

*   The author gratefully acknowleges the excellent research assistance of
    David Berrian.
1. Social injustice is related to the variance and higher moments of the
    income distribution and to the incidence and extent of absolute poverty.
    Thus, one can conceive of a society characterised by a highly uneven and
    skewed distribution, yet with every individual above the poverty line
    income. In this exercise we ignore this last case and equate social justice
    with the alleviation of absolute poverty.
2. Thus, as Kanbur points out, even if P_0 is rejected as a poverty measure in
    comparison with P_1, the former still has a role in guiding budgetary rules
    for poverty alleviation (Kanbur, 1986).
3. Each c_{ij} element of the C_n matrix gives the marginal expenditure
    propensity relative to the corresponding column sum, y_j where the
    subscript n, in this case, stands for the endogenous variables, that is, the
    various factors, socioeconomic groups, and production activities, res-
    pectively.
4. In Section 4 a detailed specific example based on the SAM for Indonesia
    is presented, but, at this stage, the intuition should be clear. Assume that
    the planner benefits the group of agricultural employees (mainly landless
    and near landless) through a subsidy or income transfer. This group is
    likely to spend a relatively high proportion of this additional income on
    staple foods which, in turn, means additional indirect incomes for those
    socioeconomic groups (such as small and medium-sized farmers) pro-
    ducing these foods.
5. In the next Section (4) the actual mechanism is presented through which
    the influence of a given budgetary injection received by a specific group is
    transmitted throughout the whole socioeconomic system (as represented
    by an actual SAM for Indonesia), to affect ultimately the incomes of
    other groups.
6. $M_{c_{gi}}$ is the submatrix which would correspond to M_{22} in Table 4.1 using
    the notation in that table where the account for households is
    numbered 2.
7. The Indonesian SAM was built by the Indonesian Central Bureau for
    Statistics with technical help from a team of experts from the Institute of
    Social Studies in The Hague and Cornell University. Until a few months
    ago when the 1980 SAM was completed, it was the most ambitious and
    detailed SAM available. The complete M_c matrix (including the $M_{c_{gi}}$
    submatrix) is given in Table 11.6 in Khan and Thorbecke (1986).
8. For example, the socioeconomic group 'rural lower' consists mainly of
    unskilled workers, while the 'urban higher' group consists mainly of

professionals, civil servants, and the military. It should be noted that in the original SAM a much more disaggregated breakdown of household groups is available.

9. Note that the diagonal elements in Table 4.2 are larger than unity since they incorporate the indirect effects on income of an injection into the same group.

10. Note that the jth group receiving the budgetary injection is identified by a superscript, while the ultimate income or poverty impact on group g is indicated by a subscript.

11. Although Kanbur's budget allocation rules appear different from those developed above, it can be shown that they are only a special case of (18); namely, if the fixed-price multiplier is taken to be an identity matrix, then Kanbur's rules result.

12. One could interpret the groupings as three broad socioeconomic groups (for example, A = agricultural employees, B = non-agricultural employees, C = non-employees (capitalists and self-employed).

13. Group A has the lowest mean income and largest proportion of its population below the poverty line, where the poverty line has been set at 250 units per capita. Group B, on the other hand, contains the largest number of persons below the poverty line and more who are very poor. Thirty per cent of group C are in poverty, but as a group it is better off than A or B.

14. Consideration of interactive effects means utilising the fixed-price multipliers of Table 4.4a and the budgetary rules based on (18). Neglect of interactive effects means using a multiplier matrix which is equal to an identity matrix.

15. The reason there is this difference is that when a unit of benefit goes to group B, group B members spend this unit in such a way that group A members experience a total increase in income of 0.67 unit and group C members gain by 0.54 unit.

16. The structural path methodology is developed formally in Defourny and Thorbecke (1984). In essence, the starting point is to equate the notion of expenditure to that of 'influence'. Graphically this means that each marginal expenditure propensity c_{ji} of an 'arc' (i,j) linking two poles of the structure and oriented in the direction of the expenditure is to be interpreted as the magnitude of the influence transmitted from pole i to pole j.

$$c_{ji}$$
$$i \longrightarrow j$$

The marginal expenditure propensity c_{ji} (that is, an element of C_n in equation (7)) reflects the intensity of arc (i,j). A path which does not pass more than one time through the same pole is called an 'elementary path', while a 'circuit' is a path for which the first pole (pole of origin) coincides with the last one (pole of destination).

The concept of influence can be given three different quantitative interpretations, namely, (1) direct influence, (2) total influence, and (3) global influence, which are discussed below. The direct influence transmitted along a given elementary path $p = (i,...,j)$ with origin i and destination j, is equal to the product of the intensities of the arcs constituting the path. The total influence is the influence transmitted from i to j along the elementary path p including all indirect effects within the structure imputable to that path. Thus, total influence cumulates, for a given elementary path p, the direct influence transmitted along the latter and the indirect effects induced by the circuits adjacent to that same path (that is, these circuits which have one or more poles in common with path p). Finally, global influence from pole i to pole j simply measures the total effects on income or output of pole j consequent to an injection of one unit of output or income in pole i. The global influence is captured by the reduced form of the SAM model derived previously in equation (7).

$$dy_n = [I - C_n]^{-1} dx = M_c dx$$

Let m_{cji} be the (j,i)th element of the matrix of fixed-price multipliers M_c then, as was seen previously, it captures the full effects of an exogenous injection dx_i on the endogenous variable dy_j. Global influence cumulates all induced and feedback effects resulting from the existence of circuits in the graph and is equal to the sum of the total influence of all elementary paths spanning pole i and pole j. A specific example is included in the main text.

17. It would have been practically impossible to represent in Figure 4.4 all the paths and adjacent circuits and feedback systems spanning the pole of origin of the injection (agricultural employees) and the poles of destination (the three groups under consideration).

18. Note that, in fact, we are adding the consumption of paddy as an input into milled rice and of other food crops (that is, $0.248 = 0.128 + 0.120$).

19. For instance, a recent study applied structural path analysis to explore the effects of alternative technologies in a number of key sectors on different objectives (that is, income distribution by socioeconomic groups, employment by labour skills, output of the various production activities, energy requirements, and the balance of payments) (see Khan and Thorbecke, 1986).

20. For an excellent and comprehensive survey of SAM based on CGE models, see Robinson (1986).

References

Defourny, J. and Thorbecke, E. (1984) 'Structural Path Analysis and Multiplier Decomposition within a Social Accounting Matrix Framework', *Economic Journal*, vol. 94, pp. 111–36.

Foster, J., Greer, J. and Thorbecke, E. (1984) 'A Class of Decomposable Poverty Measures', *Econometrica*, vol. 52, no. 3, pp. 761–66.

Janvry, A. de and Subramanian, S. (1986) 'The Politics and Economics of Food and Nutrition Policies and Programs: An Interpretation', University of California, Berkeley.

Kanbur, S. M. R. (1986) 'Budgetary Rules for Poverty Alleviation', Department of Economics, University of Essex and Woodrow Wilson School, Princeton University.

Khan, H. A. and Thorbecke, E. (1986) 'Macroeconomic Effects and Diffusion of Alternative Technologies within a Social Accounting Matrix Framework: The Case of Indonesia', paper prepared under the auspices of the Technology and Employment Branch of the World Employment Programme of the International Labour Office.

Pyatt, G. and Round, J. I. (1979) 'Accounting and Fixed-Price Multipliers in a Social Accounting Matrix Framework', *Economic Journal*, vol. 89, pp. 850–73.

Robinson, S. (1986) 'Multisectoral Models of Developing Countries: A Survey', Working Paper no. 401, Division of Agriculture and Natural Resources, University of California, Berkeley.

Discussion on Part I

PAPER BY PAUL STREETEN

'International Co-operation and Global Justice'

Professor Edmond S. Phelps, the invited discussant, noted that, under the Coase theorem, when nations imposed costs on one another and found resource allocations non-optimal, they could enter contractual arrangements compensating one another so that marginal costs were made equal to marginal benefits. Typically, however, the prisoners' dilemma model was the one that applies. Countries did not reach a compatible agreement and, therefore, there were spillover costs. He agreed with the reasons posited by Professor Streeten as to why such agreements could not be reached and added one more to the list, the difficulties encountered in the implementation of contracts and agreements and in prosecuting defaulters. He continued, the problem in applying the Coase theory lay in the uncertainties and probabilities involved in estimating the marginal social benefits and the marginal social costs and in estimating the extent of the externalities that affect countries other than the ones directly involved. At best, these were subjective estimates. At worst, they were a lie. From the perspective of economic theory, the prisoners' dilemma model was the more relevant.

Regarding the second part of the paper, Professor Phelps complained that the author did not fully discuss Rawls's views concerning global justice. Streeten, he maintained, was talking about utilitarianism – aid from rich to poor countries. Foreign aid could be a division of income from the poor of the rich country largely to the rich of the poorer country. When foreign aid was given by one country to another, Streeten worries, it was possible that the sum of their utiities may be reduced. For a Rawlsian, what was decisive was the life of the poor in the poorer country.

Rawlsian justice in a two-country world required that the better-off country hand back gains from trade to the worse-off country until the poor in the worse-off country were brought to the level of the poor in the better-off country. But such bilateral justice in a many-country world might create chaos because many poor countries might want to become partners. Multilateral trade in a Rawlsian justice context would mean each of the better-off countries putting the gains from trade into a pot until each of them reached the level of the next worse off. If there were no constraints, this would have led to equal wage rates for the working poor everywhere in the world at the level of those of the poor in the rich countries.

Then Phelps noted a question sometimes asked, 'How can we expect such international equalisation when huge domestic inequality is seen to be inevitable?' We could not. Rawlsian justice, he adduced, was 'structuralist' rather then 'welfarist'. It required sharing the fruits of collaboration and trade. Like Rawls, Edgeworth was a 'structuralist'. Edgeworth utilitarianism and the contact curve led to no person being worse off than before. Where inequalities were great, international transfers resulted in reaching the Edgeworth–Rawls constraint before equality was achieved. Hence Rawlsian justice might stop short of international as well as domestic equality. There was a difference between being a Good Samaritan and a good Rawlsian.

Professor Streeten replied that the concept of international interdependence induced not merely trade and aid but all forms of mutually-related transactions, including migration, monetary flows, capital movements, educational assistance, cultural impulses, and so on. There were three main questions related to international justice: (1) Do the rich in a community have any obligation towards the poor, and do the poor have any claims? (2) Does the world constitute a community? (3) Does the existence of the state not interfere with the discharge of this duty? Streeten answered all three question in the affirmative.

He then observed that if we believed in the prisoners' dilemma outcome, government was impossible. In the Coase outcome, no government was needed. The real world was that in between. Could we not have international institutions that could intervene in international transfers to avoid prisoners' dilemmas, and if so, how could this be achieved?

One discussant asked about the non-economic exchange resulting in the loss of billions of dollars on the part of developing countries, and what could be said about disarmament as an important source of aid to developing countries. Another commented that the paper relied on both a theoretical framework which was neo-classical, and an institutional framework (the latter for the policy aspects). Joining the two was difficult since the institutional framework varied in different nations. In regard to international co-operation and justice, it might be better to consider groups of nations, that is, regional agglomerations. Such groups might be in a better position to perceive, monitor, control and bargain in terms of social costs and social benefits. Finally, with

74   *Social Justice and Development*

regional units, one could integrate the acquisition of various levels of international public goods. Such goods had to be provided on a scale in which their ubiquity and their feasibility had been considered. Intra-regional efforts could be steps towards global efforts in a global structure in which social justice was considered.

Streeten replied that if we went step by step in providing some public goods, there was a possibility of whole regions and some groups being left out and receiving no aid (for example, South Asia). There was also the danger of fragmentation and of smaller groups becoming exclusive, trade-diverting groups.

PAPER BY PARTHA DASGUPTA

'Welfare, Positive Freedom and Economic Development'

The invited discussant, Professor Sylvia Lane, pointed out that the paper stressed rights-based theories having a bearing upon welfare and utility. Labourers need nutrients to work and, in this paper, the policy was examined in the context of meeting nutritional requirements. But many of the poor, because of disability, ill health, or being elderly, were unemployable, and food would not make them more productive. Food was essential, but if cash were distributed, food *per se* need not be provided. Which assets were to be redistributed, and how, was as important as the amount in the reduction of poverty. Food programmes had to be combined with health programmes, and assets building human and productive capital made available if productivity were to be increased and poverty reduced. Cash could be distributed more cheaply than food and, if given to the very poor, might not produce immoderate increases in food prices.

A questioner asked if there was necessarily a conflict between growth and equity, especially when there was a growth strategy which recorded nutrition towards those population groups whose nutritional levels were initially low and which would raise productivity and growth.

This led to a comment that absolute poverty had been defined in terms of caloric requirement of an individual. The correct approach would be to take into account all the minimum requirements which enabled an individual to function in the society, deprivation of which in any measure would place him in the category of the absolute poor. In a society this would mean a minimum of clothing and shelter requirements, and should also be added to caloric requirements to draw the poverty line. It was said that the poor were unemployable. But unemployability was a result of poverty itself. And therefore one should not feel lost because of the unemployability of the poor. The vicious circle – poverty leading to unemployment to poverty – should be pin-pricked by poverty-alleviation measures which proved effective. Growth with justice or equity required simultaneous recognition of absolute and relative poverty. The top priority needed to go to the guaranteed minimum to every citizen so that society eradicated absolute poverty and was left with relative poverty alone. This type of poverty could be tackled by fiscal measures, expenditure policies etc. and over time, at the point where a rise in real per capita income trickled down to the poor. The trickling-down process could be accelerated once absolute poverty had been eradicated.

Questions and comments that followed concerned whether we could explain inequality of utility across people as stemming from the problem of inequality of income and wealth.

Rights-based theories and welfare-based theories meshed together to explain the welfare level of the household. Rights could be asserted or not asserted. Allocation of commodities or distributions within the family could be explained as the consequence of the right to give up rights. The female members of the family allocate less for themselves and more for the working males and children. The family welfare function was kept even though the individual welfare functions of a few members were lowered. This, in a way, accounted for the perpetuation of poverty of the family and hence of the economy. The rights theories had significance in the explanation not only of welfare improvement, but welfare impairment in the long run, particularly with regard to development of women in terms of their wealth, status, nutritional level, education and employment opportunities; and the policies that had relevance for short-term versus long-term implementation.

The author in responding to the discussion pointed out that the motivation of the paper was to fuse welfare with development economics. Traditional economics had, he said, for the most part shown exclusive concern for utility allocations among members of a society. Commodity allocations in this approach were judged solely by their resulting utility, or welfare, allocations. This was the identifying feature of welfarism. Now it took only a small step to embrace Paretianism if one was already a welfarist; for if one was concerned exclusively with utility allocations the suggestion that an allocation in which all members of society enjoyed higher utility was that welfare, or utility, was only one aspect of a person's quality of life, his well-being. There are many other aspects; extents to which he enjoys certain types of positive freedom were one such aspect. Now, one could try and arrive at a super-aggregate index of his well-being, capturing in it his utility, the extent of positive freedom he enjoys, and so forth, and define a social evaluation function directly, and exclusively, on individual well-being functions. Alternatively, one could, as the author had done, keep his utility index separate from other indices of his state of being, and define a social evaluation function on a larger space of indices, the space of utility indices being only a subspace of this larger space. Either way, you were pretty much forced to eschew Paretianism. One might of course find it compelling to have the social evaluation function subsume efficiency in this larger space, but that was not the same as Paretianism. This much was pretty obvious, but perhaps not widely appreciated and so the first part of the paper addressed these issues. The question remained whether all this was so much classificatory exercise, or whether there was substantive economics that emerged from these considerations. The second part of the paper was designed to show that there were important policy implications for this broader, and ethically correct, approach. For example, the enlarged framework allowed one to provide an account of why the outright prohibition of trade in some commodities (e.g. health care, slavery, etc.) could be justified without recourse to the kind of forced justification that traditional welfare economics employed. Distribution of certain commodities in kind, rather than through coupons, was one example.

PAPER BY JAMES P. GRANT AND RICHARD JOLLY

'The New Economics of Child Health and Survival'

Professor Irma Adelman. from the Chair, noted that when income increased, the numbers of those in poor health might also increase. Both growth and development were required if the health status of the population were to improve. Land reform was needed for growth and poverty alleviation in low-income developing countries. The countries mentioned in this paper had achieved a relatively better combination of income distribution, development and growth. We now needed a research base to understand better how to disentangle the three.

The cost-effective technologies to reduce infant mortality were labour intensive. During harvest time, infant mortality was high because women did not have time to take care of their children. Boiling water was important for the cost-effective technology, but it, and the fuel gathering generally entailed, were time consuming. What happened to the cost effectiveness of these methods if the opportunity cost of the women's time was taken into account?

Discussants then raised questions concerning costs of effective information dissemination and communication, whether better health resulted in more production, and whether health information dissemination programmes were bankable projects. One discussant suggested that a clear focus on human development was important but was not considered important in policy formulation, adding that there was a need for a cradle-to-grave concept of human development for planning purposes. Costs and benefits must be considered in total.

Dr Grant replied that he had analysed infant mortality data. Programmes he described were relatively recent, but thus far immunisation costs were low, that is, $6–7 per child in Turkey. Programme costs there of US $2.5 million received from UNICEF, US $1.5 million from the Ministry of Health, and the cost of 'free' television time and other publicity, might be compared to a potential loss of US $29 million – the economic value of the children's lives. Economically, the programme could be justified. It also provided for a 'felt' need. Governments considered these programmes (immunisation programmes, rehydration programmes, etc.), good politics, and in five to ten years there was now the possibility of a new world ethic emerging on child mortality which no longer accepted high rates of child mortality as inevitable or acceptable. The new cost-effective technologies were female-labour intensive, but improvement in children's health was a key factor in development. In some developing countries mothers spent an average of about 160 days a year caring for sick children. A reduction in children's deaths would lead to increased incomes and fewer births. About three-fourths of the effects of malnutrition on mortality could be reversed with immunisations. Mothers who knew what they could do to save children's lives and knew sick children would survive gained confidence and changed their attitudess about desired family size. Increased child survival rates would affect family planning and result in a reduction in the size of the population, but this revolutionary child survival movement required popular mobilisation and political leadership.

PAPER BY ERIK THORBECKE

'Planning Techniques for Social Justice'

The invited discussant, Dr Bhagwan Dahyia, noted that in almost all developing countries we had a three-tier planning process; one-year plans, five-year plans and prospective plans. Both the periods and the horizon keep changing and we had not been able to construct dynamic planning models.

He also observed that Thorbecke assumed distinction within socio-economic groups was possible and therefore perfect targeting was possible.

Thorbecke replied that perfect targeting might be possible but it would be an expensive exercise. It was not necessarily true that leakages were not desirable. These leakages received by non-needy households might induce the latter to support politically the notion of subsidies benefiting the poor. The present analysis could be extended over time in comparative dynamic models.

A second discussant noted that it might be difficult to distinguish between the poor and the non-poor. There were leakages in the system insofar as subsidies are concerned but it might be possible to stop these leakages if information were available. As for the non-poor, they were not necessarily rural. The entire cross section might have to be considered.

Thorbecke replied that the illustration in the paper was meant only to serve as an example. The social accounting matrix would provide information concerning all socio-economic groups (rural and urban) and the analysis could be extended to urban groups as well.

In response to a question, Thorbecke said that even if one knew the distribution of poverty within a group, one might still not be able to target poverty alleviation programmes because of the administrative difficulties of reaching the poor directly. Concerning decomposability, if one was not capable of giving different subsidies within a group, decomposing larger groups into smaller groups might be of help in achieving appropriate targeting. Particular allocations, however, might not be politically desirable.

Another discussant commented on the possibility of having many different strata among the poor, the small proportion currently benefiting from anti-poverty measures in India, and the need for detailed classification of measures taken to alleviate poverty were to be individually specific.

Part II

Agricultural Development and Poverty

5 Growth and Equity in Agriculture-led Growth

Alain de Janvry and Elisabeth Sadoulet
UNIVERSITY OF CALIFORNIA, BERKELEY

1120
7100

1 BACKGROUND

The role of agriculture in inducing industrial growth has been widely recognised by economists. Among economic historians, this includes the seminal studies of Bairoch (1973) on Europe, Ohkawa and Rosovsky (1964) on Japan, Dobb (1966) on the Soviet Union, and Johnston and Kilby (1975) on Taiwan and South Korea. Among economic theorists, fundamental contributions were made by Lewis (1958), Jorgenson (1969), Fei and Ranis (1964), Lele and Mellor (1981), and Adelman (1984), each stressing different aspects of the relationship between agriculture and industry. In a separate stream of thought, agricultural economists have addressed the issue of the sources of agricultural growth. Prominent are the studies of technological change by Hayami and Ruttan (1985), land tenure by Dorner (1972), and price policy by the World Bank (1986). Rarely have these two streams of thought been integrated in the sense of tracing the feedback between industrial development and sustained sources of agricultural growth. Missing, in particular, is knowledge of how shifts in demand for agricultural products allow protection of the level of agricultural prices and the profitability of investment in agriculture in spite of rapid agricultural growth and a generally inelastic demand. In a closed economy, or in an economy with non-tradable agricultural commodity sectors, the distribution of income may thus be an essential determinant of a sustained process of agriculture-led growth based on the inducement to adopt a continuous flow of land-saving technological innovations. While greater equity in the distribution of income may decrease the growth effect of agriculture on industry, it is likely to increase that of industry on agriculture. It is this asymmetry – in the way in which equity affects intersectoral growth effects – that creates a necessary balance between growth and equity in agriculture-led development strategies. The objective of this paper is to analyse this relationship, and to explore policy instruments that create a balance between growth and equity that enables sustained agriculture-led growth over time.

We approach this problem through both intercountry econometric analysis and policy simulation in archetype dynamic general equilibrium models.

2 INTERCOUNTRY ANALYSIS OF THE RELATIONSHIP BETWEEN AGRICULTURAL AND INDUSTRIAL GROWTH

Different forms of the contribution of technological change in agriculture to industrial growth have been singled out in different intersectoral growth models. In Jorgenson's dual-economy model, technological change in agriculture increases the marketed surplus per rural worker which allows the release of labour for employment in industry. With full employment in all sectors, the migration of agricultural labour to the cities is the way in which agriculture contributes to industrial growth. Fei and Ranis, and Lele and Mellor, stress the key role of technological change in agriculture in lowering the level of food prices. With surplus labour in all sectors of the economy (Fei and Ranis), falling prices lead to falling nominal wages and rising industrial output. With surplus labour in agriculture, full employment in industry, and income sharing in agriculture (Lele and Mellor), falling prices lead to rising real wages and falling nominal wages while inducing a higher level of industrial output.

In the model constructed by de Janvry and Sadoulet (1986), technological change in agriculture increases foreign exchange availability generated by agricultural exports or by import substitution. This increase leads to the importing of capital goods for industry which are imperfect substitutes for domestic capital goods in production. Hirschman (1977) stressed the importance of intersectoral linkages in multiplying the growth effects of investment in agriculture. A variety of computable general equilibrium models capture this type of multiplier effect. The intermediate linkages of agriculture in less-developed countries are, however, acknowledged to be weak relative to those of industry. Finally, Adelman has evidenced the importance of market expansion for industry through rising agricultural income and final-demand effects, inducing 'agricultural demand-led industrialization'. This is due to the fact that agricultural consumption includes a larger share of labour-intensive products with strong linkage effects and fewer external leakages than urban consumption.

To evidence econometrically the relative importance of these four effects – labour, price, foreign exchange, and demand – we proceed in two steps. We first show that there indeed exists a short-run causal link between agricultural and industrial growth. To do this, we use time-series data between 1960 and 1981 for the 42 countries for which complete information is available in the World Bank Tape of Economic Indicators. The estimated equation is between the logarithm of manufacturing output as the dependent variable and the logarithms of agricultural and mining ouputs lagged one year as the predetermined variables. The results show that 76 per cent of the countries have a significantly positive elasticity of manufacturing output with respect to lagged agricultural production. Among these, the average value of this elasticity is 1.38.

Secondly, we use calculated average annual growth rates for 60 developing countries between 1970 and 1980 to estimate an econometric model that decomposes the sources of manufacturing and industrial growth into the four effects mentioned above (Table 5.1).

The labour effect is measured in equation (1) by explaining urban population growth. This effect is significant but has a negative elasticity of -0.11, indicating that successful agricultural growth helps slow down urban migration and does not accelerate the release of labour for urban employment. The price effect is captured in equation (2) by explaining the growth rate of the gross domestic product deflator, excluding two countries with hyperinflation exceeding 100 per cent. It shows that agricultural growth is indeed important in lowering the price level with an elasticity of -1.01. The foreign exchange effect in equation (3) is also highly significant with an elasticity of 1.03. In equation (4) the growth in agricultural exports is seen to explain, on the average, 52 per cent of the growth in total export earnings. Both intermediate and final demand effects of agricultural growth can be expected to be proportional to agricultural growth. In equations (5) and (6), manufacturing and industrial growth are, thus, broken down into labour, price, foreign exchange, and demand effects – the latter being represented by agricultural growth. Except for the labour effect, the other three are highly significant, particularly on manufacturing growth. The industrial sector includes mining in addition to manufacturing, a sector which is not strongly affected by the growth performance of agriculture.

Taking the partial derivative of manufacturing and industrial growth

Table 5.1 Determinants of industrial and agricultural growth

(1) Urb = 2.32 − 0.11 AgGr + 1.33 PopGr − 0.0013 GNP76 $R^2 = 0.53$
        (3.66) (−1.92)   (5.96)   (−3.90)

(2) Inflat = 16.65 − 1.01 AgGr − 0.26 AgImpGr + 0.008 GNP76 $R^2 = 0.18$ (excl. inflat > 100)
        (5.54) (−2.29)   (−1.41)   (2.94)

(3) AgExpGr = 7.50 + 1.03 AgGr + 0.036 AgEinE $R^2 = 0.25$
         (4.73) (3.92)   (1.56)

(4) ExpGr = 2.46 + 0.52 AgExpGr − 0.051 AginGDP $R^2 = 0.30$
      (−1.23) (4.34)   (−1.47)

(5) ManfGr = 3.04 − 0.02 UrbGr − 0.053 Inflat + 0.41 ExpGr + 0.82 AgGr $R^2 = 0.64$
        (1.63) (0.07)   (−2.90)   (4.42)   (3.70)

(6) IndGr = 2.86 + 0.15 UrbGr − 0.047 Inflat + 0.49 ExpGr + 0.37 AgGr $R^2 = 0.58$
      (1.65) (0.50)   (−2.75)   (6.35)   (1.99)

(7) log (LifeExp) = 3.46 + 0.118 log(GNP76) − 0.041 UrbGr $R^2 = 0.71$
          (27.49) (7.12)   (4.88)

(8) AgGr = −6.35 + 0.67 PopGr + 0.33 ManfGr + 4.78 Eres + 0.0111 AgEinE $R^2 = 0.55$
      (−2.11) (1.71)   (6.91)   (1.92)   (1.31)

(9) AgGr = −7.46 + 0.75 PopGr + 0.26 IndGr + 6.08 Eres + 0.008 AgEinE $R^2 = 0.33$
      (−2.14) (1.60)   (4.22)   (2.10)   (0.84)

with respect to agricultural growth in equations (1) to (6), we obtain the decomposition of the four effects mentioned above. It shows that the demand effect dominates the transmission of agricultural growth into manufacturing (74.8 per cent) and industrial (55.9 per cent) growth. The foreign exchange effect is also important (20.1 and 39.6 per cent, respectively) while the price effect is small (4.9 and 7.1 per cent). The labour effect is irrelevant.

Assuming that untapped technological change opportunities exist in agriculture, which is generally the case, the main difficulty with an agriculture-led growth strategy is to maintain profitability in agriculture in spite of an inelastic domestic demand for food. If the domestic demand for food does not shift sufficiently through income effects, if export opportunities are not available, if government minimum price interventions do not exist, or if strong demand multiplier effects in the non-tradable sector do not result, the growth strategy will rapidly exhaust itself as the incentive for continued productivity growth in agriculture vanishes. Export demand and progressive domestic income distribution should then be important determinants of the long-run growth effect of manufacturing and industry on agriculture.

We develop an income distribution index by using the residuals in a double logarithmic fit of life expectancy on GNP per capita in equation (7). The antilog transformation of these residuals gives the variable Eres used for income distribution in equations (8) and (9). The results show that manufacturing and industrial growth, population growth, and income distribution are important determinants of the long-run growth of agriculture. Thus, while income distribution may mediate negatively the relation between agricultural and industrial growth, it mediates positively the relation between industrial and agricultural growth. The result is that a trade-off does not appear to exist between growth and distribution in agriculture-led development strategies. The distribution of income, and the generation of effective demand for agriculture, are essential to the reproduction of this growth strategy over time.

3 IMPACT OF TECHNOLOGICAL CHANGE IN AGRICULTURE ON GROWTH AND EQUITY

3.1. General Equilibrium Models

To explore further the relationship between agricultural growth and overall growth and equity in the economy, the temporal dimension must be added and the role of specific technological and structural parameters identified. To do this, a dynamic three-sector model is constructed, and the impact of land-saving technological change in agriculture is simulated. The equations of the model are given in Table 5.2. Two alternative cases are considered with respect to the relation of agriculture to international trade: (1) an agricultural sector with perfectly tradable products in a food importing country, and (2) a closed economy in which the agricultural balance of trade is kept at its initial exogenous level. The closed-economy model draws heavily on Lele and Mellor in which the causal linkage from agricultural productivity growth to non-agricultural growth runs through lower food prices and lower nominal wages. In the open-economy model, these linkages occur through foreign exchange savings and higher imports of capital goods for the industrial tradable products sector. In both cases a non-tradables labour-intensive sector offers the opportunity for employment programmes, which can enhance the effective demand creation induced by income growth.

The agricultural sector produces with two inputs, land and labour, with land in fixed quantity. The non-agricultural labour-intensive non-tradables sector produces with capital and labour. There is surplus labour, and employment in these two sectors is determined by equating marginal productivity with fixed real wages. Unemployment or underemployment in the economy is equally located in these two sectors, and the income earned by employed workers is shared in the two populations. Per capita income is thus a direct function of the rate of employment.

Inputs in the non-agricultural tradables sector are labour and an aggregate capital stock made of imperfectly substitutable domestic and imported capital goods. Imported capital goods are more productive than domestic capital goods, and the productivity of the stock of capital increases with its size. Workers are employed at a wage rate which differs from per capita income in agriculture by an additive constant.

Consumption behaviour is specified for each of the four social classes (workers of the three sectors and capitalists) by a linear expenditure system where parameters are based on income shares, income elasticities, and Frisch parameters.

Supply and demand are equalised through international trade in the tradable sectors and through price flexibility in the non-tradable sector.

The dynamics of the model is confined to the only impact of an annual technological change in agriculture. Therefore, the dynamic

---

Table 5.2 Model equations

[For $i, j, k = A, T, NT$ (agricultural and non-agricultural tradables and non-agricultural non-tradables sectors)]

Static Relations *(time argument omitted)*

Production:	$X_i = f(L_i, t_{KT}K_i, \lambda_i, \sigma_i)$ with $f = CD$ or CES	(1)
Capital aggregation:	$K_T = CES(KM, KD, \lambda_K, \sigma_K)$	(2)
Capital productivity in tradable sector:	$t_{KT} = t_0 K_T^\epsilon$	(3)
Labour demand:	$\partial X_i / \partial L_i = w_i / p_i$	(4)
Wages:	$w_r = \bar{w}_r^* P_r$ for $r = A, NT$	(5)
	$w_T / P_T = y_A / P_A + \delta$	(6)
Income:	$y_i = w_i L_i / Pop_i$ for workers of sector i (per capita)	(7)
	$YK_i = p_i X_i - w_i L_i$ for capitalists of sector i	(8)
Population distribution:	$Pop_T = L_T$	(9)
	$Pop_k = (Pop - Pop_T)L_k / (L_A + L_{NT})$ for $k = A, NT$	(10)
Demand:	$CW_{ij} = Pop_i LES(y_i, p_k, \alpha_{ik}, \eta_{ik}, \varphi_i)$ by workers of sector i	(11)
	$CK_{ij} = LES(YK_i, p_k, \alpha K_{ik}, \eta K_{ik}, \varphi K_i)$ by capitalists of sector i	(12)
Agricultural imports:	$M_A = \Sigma_i (CW_{iA} + CK_{iA}) - X_A$	(13)
Capital goods imports:	$M_{KM} = eX_T - M_A$	(14)
Numeraire:	$P_T = 1$	(15)
Agricultural price:	$P_A = \bar{P}_A$	(16)
Consumer price indices:	$P_i = (\Sigma_k CW_{ik} p_k) / (\Sigma_k CW_{ik})$	(17)
Market equilibrium for NT sector:	$X_{NT} = \Sigma_i (CW_i, NT + CK_{i,NT})$	(18)

Dynamic Relations (t = *time argument*)

Imported capital accumulation:	$KM(t + 1) = KM(t) + M_{KM}(t)$	(19)
Land productivity:	$t_{KA}(t) = (1 + z)^t$	(20)

Closed Economy

Variables KM and M_{KM} are dropped and equations (16), (2), (14), and (19) replaced by (16') and (19')

Market equilibrium for agricultural sector:	$M_A = \bar{M}_A$ (167.5) (5.02.5)	(16')
Capital accumulation in tradable sector:	$K(t + 1) = K(t) + s[YK_T(t) - YK_T(t - 1)]$	(19')

Table 5.2 (continued)

List of Symbols

CD, CES	Cobb-Douglas and Constant Elasticity of Substitution production functions
LES	Linear Expenditure System

Parameters Derived From Initial-Year Values

λ_i	Labour share parameters in production function
λ_K	Foreign capital share parameter in capital aggregation derived from $\partial K_T / \partial KM = \pi \partial K_{il} / \partial KD$ in initial year
e	Share of tradable production exported to cover agricultural goods imports derived from $M_{KM} = 0$ in initial year
δ	Difference between tradables sector workers' wage and agricultural income per capita
t_0	Parameter of capital productivity derived from $t_{KT} = 1$ in initial year

Parameters Defined in Table 5.3

σ_i, σ_k	Elasticities of substitution of production function and capital aggregation
π	Relative productivity of imported capital compared to domestic capital
α_{ik}, η_{ik}	Income shares and elasticities for consumption of good k by workers of sector i
αK_{ik}, ηK_{ik}	Income shares and elasticities for consumption of good k by capitalists of sector i
φ_i, φK_i	Frisch parameter for workers and capitalists of sector i
ε	Elasticity of capital productivity with respect to the stock of capital in tradable sector
s	Marginal propensity to save from capital income
z	Annual growth rate of land productivity

Exogenous Variables

KD	Domestic capital in tradables sector
K_{NT}	Capital in non-tradables sector
t_K, NT	Capital productivity in non-tradables sector ($= 1$)
$\bar{w}_A^*, \bar{w}_{NT}^*$	Real wage in agricultural and non-tradables sector
$\bar{P}_A^t$	Exogenous agricultural price ($= 1$)
$\bar{M}_A^t$	Exogenous agricultural imports equal to initial year value
Pop	Total population of workers

Endogenous Variables

X_i	Production in sector i
L_i	Employment in sector i
K_A, K_T	Land in agricultural sector; capital in tradables sector
KM	Imported capital in tradables sector
w_i	Nominal wage in sector i
y_i	Per capita income of workers of sector i
Pop_i	Population in sector i
YK_i	Capitalists' income in sector i
p_i	Price of good i
P_i	Consumer price index for workers of sector i
CW_{ij}	Consumption of good j by workers of sector i
CK_{ij}	Consumption of good j by capitalists of sector i
M_A, M_{KM}	Imports of agricultural and capital goods
t_{kA}	Land productivity
t_{kT}	Capital productivity in tradables sector

path it generates should be compared to a steady-state reference path in which the base-year situation is repeated throughout the years. In the open-economy model, land productivity and, thus, also agricultural production, increase every year. The foreign exchange saved in each period after satisfying the demand for agricultural imports is used to import capital goods that increase the stock of capital in the non-agricultural tradables sector in the next period. This use of foreign exchange savings is based on the assumption that, of the two gaps (foreign exchange and domestic savings) which potentially constrain economic growth, the former is the effective one.

In the closed-economy model, no distinction is made between domestic and foreign capital goods. Capital accumulation in the non-agricultural sector is based on the savings from the increase on the return to capital generated by the induced growth.

Empirical values in the model typify a low-income economy which corresponds to the higher half of the World Bank low-income group with a GNP per capita of US $250 to US $400 in 1983 and includes India, China, Sri Lanka, Pakistan, Kenya, and the Sudan. The structural characteristics and parameter values are given in Table 5.3. They are derived as much as possible from average observed values for this group of countries. Empirical evidence on relative productivity of foreign capital and increasing productivity of capital is given in Chenery, Robinson, and Syrquin (1986). Estimates of the Frisch parameters are reported in Lluch, Powell, and Williams (1977).

3.2 Simulation Results

Indicators of growth, profitability, poverty, and equity associated with the simulation of an annual 3 per cent increase in land productivity over 10 years under different structural conditions appear in Table 5.4. In the first group of experiments, the agricultural sector commodities are tradable and the country is a food-deficit economy, while in the second group the economy is closed with respect to its agricultural products.

In a food-deficit open economy, agricultural production growth reduces the need for food imports and releases foreign exchange for the import of essential capital goods for the non-agricultural tradables (T) sector. Key parameters for the magnitude of the induced growth of the T sector are the relative size of the two sectors, the capital intensity of the T sector (experiment 3 with the capital output ratio decreased by 50

Table 5.3 Parameter for archetype low economy

	Sectors		
	Agriculture (A)	Tradable (T)	Non-tradable (NT)
Production: X_i	330	300	370
Employment: L_i	176	80	230
Wages: w_i	1.125	1.5	1.125
Capital: K_i	660	670	550
Population: Pop_i	264	80	345
Consumption Parameters			
Consumption shares: α and αK			
A workers	0.49	0.18	0.33
T workers	0.36	0.27	0.37
NT workers	0.49	0.18	0.33
Capitalists	0.25	0.34	0.41
Income elasticities: η and ηK			
A and NT workers	0.83	1.25	1.12
T workers	0.75	1.15	1.13
Capitalists	0.55	1.10	1.19
Frisch parameters: φ and φK			
A and NT workers (-5.0)			
T workers (-4.0)			
Capitalists (-1.6)			
Capital in Tradable Sector			
Imported capital (KM); domestic capital (KD)		(167.5)	(502.5)
Elasticity of substitution between KM and KD: α_K	(0.4)		
Relative productivity of KM: π	(4)		
Elasticity of capital productivity: ε		(0.2)	
Saving rate: s		(1)	

per cent), and the relative productivity of foreign to domestic capital (experiment 4, with $\Pi = 5$). Rising incomes in the two tradables sectors generate demand for non-tradable goods. Depending on the supply elasticity of commodities in this sector, this results in a price increase (the Dutch disease phenomenon) when low, or in production growth when high. In the base run, the NT price increases by 13.1 per cent and the production increases by 20.6 per cent. With a higher substitutability between capital and labour in that sector, representing an employment strategy to capitalise on the creation of effective demand, growth is enhanced and real income and equity improved substantially (experiment 2, with $\sigma_{NT} = 5$).

Table 5.4 Simulation results: impact of a 3 per cent annual growth of land productivity over a 10-year period[a]

	Growth						Poverty			Profitability								Equity[b]
		Production			Employment		Workers' real income per capita			Prices		Land rent and capital income deflated by						Ratio of workers' to capitalists' real income
												CPI			Investment price index[c]			
	GNP	A	T	NT	T	NT	A. NT	T	All	A	NT	A	T	NT	A	T	NT	
							cumulated growth rates (per cent)											
Tradable Agriculture																		
1. Base run	22.5	26.1	20.9	20.6	1.7	30.8	26.8	13.4	24.2	0	13.1	19.7	14.7	29.4	18.4	20.9	28.0	1.41
2. Employment strategy in NT	28.5	32.4	22.0	30.3	1.2	43.7	38.5	19.2	34.6	0	3.0	30.8	20.5	7.3	30.5	22.0	7.0	1.53
3. Low capital intensity in T	23.6	25.8	23.6	21.6	3.4	32.2	27.7	13.8	25.1	0	13.7	19.1	17.0	30.8	17.7	23.6	29.4	1.41
4. High productivity of imported capital in T	23.3	25.9	23.0	21.4	3.0	31.9	27.4	13.7	24.9	0	13.5	19.2	16.5	30.5	17.9	23.0	29.0	1.41
5. Peasant agriculture	21.1	26.6	17.1	19.4	-7.1	28.9	24.6	20.5	22.7	0	12.3	19.8	10.9	27.1	19.2	17.1	26.4	2.55
Non-tradable Agriculture																		
6. Base run	11.5	16.1	4.1	13.5	8.5	19.8	14.8	7.4	14.1	-21.2	-8.3	0.2	14.0	14.0	-4.6	4.1	8.6	1.42
7. Employment strategy in NT	14.5	19.2	4.2	18.6	8.8	26.8	20.9	10.5	19.7	-22.1	-14.5	4.9	17.7	0	0.1	4.2	-4.6	1.50
8. Employment strategy in T	12.7	17.2	5.9	14.1	14.3	20.8	17.0	8.5	16.7	-19.2	-6.3	2.3	9.6	15.5	-2.2	1.5	10.4	1.46
9. Peasant agriculture	10.4	15.7	1.2	13.2	2.4	12.4	13.4	11.2	11.6	-21.8	-8.9	0	11.7	13.9	-5.3	1.2	7.9	2.41

Notes

a. A = agricultural, T = non-agricultural tradables, and NT = non-agricultural non-tradables sectors.
b. Initial value for the equity indicator is 1.36 with a capitalist agriculture and 2.43 with a peasant agriculture.
c. Investment composition is 100 per cent of T commodities in the T sector and 50 per cent of NT and T commodities in the A and NT sectors.

The same technological change generates a somewhat lower growth when implemented in a peasant economy with no land rent (experiment 5). The main difference comes from the cost of labour in the tradables sector. Since peasant income is much higher than the workers' wage in a capitalist agriculture and only marginally lower than the wage of the tradables sector workers, the cost of labour to the tradables sector increases at a rate comparable to that of the peasants' income.

In a closed economy (experiment 6), increasing the supply of agricultural products with an inelastic demand precipitates a dramatic fall in prices. The relative cost of labour thus increases for the agricultural sector, and very little employment is created to match the increase in land productivity. Consequently, at equilibrium, the overall agricultural growth reaches only 1 per cent the first year and 11.5 per cent cumulated over 10 years – a much lower level than in an open economy – while food prices fall by 21 per cent. At the same time, the benefit of this food price drop through decreasing labour cost is fairly low in the two other sectors, since consumer price indices, and nominal wages, decrease much less than food prices. In addition, any employment creation generates a countervailing force by reducing unemployment, increasing income in the agricultural sector, and thus increasing the real wage in the industrial tradables sector. After 10 years nominal wages and thus relative cost of the T sector workers have fallen only by 4 per cent. This induces an 8.5 per cent increase in employment and a 4 per cent increase in production. For the NT sector, similar effects occur with its own price decrease dampening further the benefits of the food price decrease. Employment generation in the more highly paid T sector and a fall in food prices combine to substantially increase real incomes of the workers and equity in the economy.

A major problem with an agricultural-led growth strategy in a closed economy lies in the falling profitability of the agricultural sector which challenges the very sustainability of efforts to improve land productivity. With agricultural prices falling by more than production increases, nominal land rent decreases by 8.6 per cent in 10 years in the base run. However, the real purchasing power of this land rent is partially or totally protected by falling prices, depending upon the use made of rent income. If this income is consumed, deflating the rents by the landlords' *CPI* shows that the real rent remains about constant (a 0.2 per cent increase in 10 years). If this income is invested, deflating the rent by an index of investment goods that includes 50 per cent tradable industrial goods and 50 per cent non-tradable goods indicates a loss in real rent of 4.6 per cent.

    Growth, poverty alleviation, and particularly equity are all increased
by implementation of employment strategies in the two non-agricul-
tural sectors (experiment 7 with $\sigma_{NT} = 5$ and experiment 8 with $\sigma_T = 5$).
In experiment 7, with higher elasticities of employment creation with
respect to labour cost, overall growth over 10 years reaches 14.5 per
cent (which is only half of the growth in the corresponding employment
strategy in the open economy); but equity improves to a comparable
level. *NT* sector prices fall sharply, and this allows the maintenance of
the real rent in agriculture even when it is used for investment
purposes – to the detriment of profitability of the *NT* sector. Experiment 8 shows that an employment strategy in the *T* sector is less
effective in terms of growth and equity and that it increases the
profitability of the *NT* sector relative to that of the other sectors.
    In a peasant economy (experiment 9), falling profitability is sup-
ported by the peasants themselves, while the capitalist class owns only
the more profitable sectors; this creates increasing inequity in the
economy. Similar to what happens in an open economy, the real wages
of *T* workers increase in direct relation to the increase in real income of
peasants and more than with a capitalist agriculture. The tradables
sector employment and production growth are thus lower. A higher
unemployment rate means lower income, lower food demand, and a
higher drop in food prices.
    Technological change in agriculture creates a net social gain in the
economy but may lead to a fall in real rents in agriculture if rent income
is used for investment purposes. In this case, a compensation scheme
could be implemented to shelter land rents and induce farmers to adopt
technological change. In the base run of a closed economy, the transfer
to farmers in year 10 would represent about 6 per cent of the real GNP
gain created by technological change. While the exact amount and
implications of this transfer depend upon the implementation mechanism and general equilibrium second-order effects, this approximate
calculation shows an order of magnitude that is small and definitely
worth implementing if it allows an agriculture-led development strategy to be sustained over time.

4 CONCLUSION

Econometric decomposition of the different mechanisms through
which agricultural growth induces industrial growth showed that the
demand effect dominates over the foreign exchange effect which also

dominates over the food price effect. Simulation in dynamic general equilibrium models also showed that, with non-tradable agricultural commodities, growth of the *NT* sector (demand effect) largely dominates over that of the *T* sector (price effect). With tradable agricultural commodities, growth of the *NT* sector (demand effect) is equal to that of the *T* sector (foreign exchange effect). The labour contribution of agriculture was dismissed econometrically, and we specified correspondingly a general equilibrium model with surplus labour in agriculture.

An agriculture-led growth strategy is able to promote simultaneously growth and equity when agricultural products are both tradable and non-tradable, with stronger induced growth in the first case since the foreign exchange effect dominates over price effect. This is due to the fact that this strategy mobilises two idle sources: a technological change potential in agriculture and surplus labour in the *NT* sector.

With an inelastic demand for food when agricultural products are not traded, there exists the possibility that falling prices will collapse the profitability of agriculture, provide disincentives to the further adoption of technological change, and choke the strategy of agriculture-led growth. This is indeed the argument which is commonly derived from partial equilibrium analysis of technological change in agriculture since it indicates a falling producer surplus. In general equilibrium analysis we find, by contrast, that even though nominal rents do fall sharply, real rents may or may not fall according to the use made of rent income. If rent income is consumed, real rents increase in spite of falling prices. If rent income is invested, real rents, however, may well fall. Strategies that favour greater equity in the economy through employment programmes in the *NT* sector both protect real rents in agriculture and enhance economic growth. If real rents cannot be sheltered by this type of intervention, then compensation schemes that tax part of the net social gains created by technological change to transfer income to landowners may be needed to sustain an agricultural-led growth strategy. The tax burden necessary to create Pareto optimality appears to be a small percentage of the net social gains from technological change and may well worsen the initiative.

References

Adelman, I. (1984) 'Beyond Export-Led Growth', *World Development*, vol. 12, no. 9, pp. 937–49.
Bairoch, P. (1973) 'Agriculture and the Industrial Revolution, 1700–1914', in Cipolla, C. (ed.), *Fontana Economic History of Europe* (London: Fontana).

Chenery, H., Robinson, S., and Syrquin, M. (1986) *Industrialization and Growth: A Comparative Study* (Oxford: Oxford University Press).

Dobb, M. (1966) *Soviet Economic Development Since 1917* (London: Routledge & Kegan Paul).

Dorner, P. (1972) *Land Reform and Economic Development* (Baltimore: Penguin Books).

Fei, J. and Ranis, G. (1964) *Development of the Labor Surplus Economy* (Homewood, Ill.: Irwin).

Hayami, Y. and Ruttan, V. (1985) *Agricultural Development: An International Perspective* (Baltimore: Johns Hopkins Press).

Hirschman, A. (1977) 'A General Linkage Approach to Development, with Special Reference to Staples', *Economic Development and Cultural Change*, vol. 25, supp., pp. 67–98.

Janvry, A. de and Sadoulet, E. (1986) 'Agricultural Growth in Developing Countries and Agricultural Imports: Econometric and General Equilibrium Analyses', University of California, Department of Agricultural and Resource Economics, Working Paper no. 424, Berkeley (August).

Johnston, B. and Kilby, P. (1975) *Agriculture and Structural Transformation* (Oxford University Press).

Jorgenson, D. (1969) 'The Role of Agriculture in Economic Development: Classical Versus Neo-Classical Models of Growth', in Wharton, C. (ed.), *Subsistence Agriculture and Economic Development* (Chicago: Aline).

Lele, U. and Mellor, J. (1981) 'Technological Change, Distributive Bias, and Labor Transfer in a Two-Sector Economy', *Oxford Economic Papers*, vol. 33, pp. 426–41.

Lewis, A. (1958) 'Economic Development with Unlimited Supplies of Labor', in Agarwala, A. and Singh, S. (eds.), *The Economics of Underdevelopment* (New York: Oxford University Press).

Lluch, C., Powell, A., and Williams, R. (1977) *Patterns of Household Demand and Saving* (Oxford University Press).

Ohkawa, K. and Rosovsky, H. (1964) 'The Role of Agriculture in Modern Japanese Economic Development', in Eicher, C. and Witt, L. (eds.), *Agriculture in Economic Development* (New York: McGraw-Hill).

World Bank (1986) *World Development Report, 1986* (New York: Oxford University Press).

6 The Impact of Rural Development Programmes on the Economic Structure of Rural Communities

India
1120
7180

V. M. Rao

INSTITUTE FOR SOCIAL AND ECONOMIC CHANGE, BANGALORE

1 INTRODUCTION

Intervention by the state in the development of the rural economy in India is an important factor in the prevailing processes of rural change. The purpose of this chapter is to bring together a number of observations obtained during the Institute for Social and Economic Change (ISEC) field investigations in the Karnataka villages. Intervention by the state seems to set in motion a series of initially modest modifications in the relationships among the different strata forming the village community and the extent to which these strata are outward oriented in their economic activities.

It is hoped that this account will be of some use to two groups of economists – those seeking models for local-level rural systems and policy analysts interested in feasible planning systems for small areas like mandals and taluks.

Karnataka is rainfed and drought-prone, with a far weaker rural economy than in the high-agricultural-growth areas of northern India – usually described as the 'green revolution' areas. It would be plausible to assume that rural development in Karnataka would need more state initiative and intervention and would bring about more pronounced changes in the economic structure of the rural communities than the case is in the green revolution areas. At the same time, the rural socioeconomic structure in Karnataka is unlike the structure prevailing in the 'semi-feudalism' areas of eastern India where the problems of rural stagnation and exploitation are, possibly, too chronic and deep-seated to yield to the types of interventions available to the state. Thus, the rural situation in Karnataka is particularly suitable for study.

The scheme of this paper is as follows. Section 2 enumerates the features of the rural context in Karnataka which need to be kept in mind when considering the scope for, and limits of, state intervention for rural development. The interventions of critical importance are those focused on promotion of agricultural production, employment generation for the rural poor, and rural diversification. Sections 3 to 5 describe the likely impact of these three types of interventions. A synthetic scenario of the combined effects of these impacts is presented in the last section of the paper.

2   THE RURAL CONTEXT

The rural economy of Karnataka rests on the precarious base of drought-prone agriculture, which is a developmental handicap in two ways. In such a setting achievement of sustained increases in agricultural growth rates becomes difficult and, secondly, the economy has to keep itself in readiness to cope with scarcities of extreme severity which disrupt the rhythms of rural economy, deplete rural assets, and divert the attention of all concerned from the long-term developmental issues to the day-to-day problems of crisis management.[1] Hence, a major priority area for state intervention in Karnataka is the generation and spread of new technologies for dry-land agriculture.

The economic environment associated with drought-prone agriculture is far from congenial to the development of rural manufacturing and service activities outside agriculture. The Institute for Social and Economic Change (ISEC) has recently conducted a large-scale socio-economic survey in a drought-prone district covering over 30,000 households residing in a statistically-selected sample of 245 villages. It has observed that less than 4 per cent of these households were production or service artisans by their main occupation. Also, and more interesting, only a third of the young adult males (ages 16 to 35) in these households were seen to have taken up the household artisan activity as their main occupation (Rao, 1983a).

The rural communities in the study area seem to be in a state of disorientation brought on by their inability to cope with the transition from the traditional local-area-based neighbourhood economies of which they were constituents for a long time, to the large and urbanised national economies. One indicator of the disruption caused by this transition is, precisely, the very low extent of the artisan occupations noted above (Rao, 1983b). The survey data provided extensive evidence of the sharp rural disparities brought about by the varying ability of the different rural strata and locations to make viable adjustments to the changing conditions.

This setting places the strategy for state intervention for rural development in a paradoxical position. On the one hand it is difficult to see the processes of rural development being activated without substantial and sustained state intervention. On the other it is equally difficult to accept as credible the scenarios of rural development offered by the official documents, particularly the targets for reduction of poverty envisaged in these documents.[2] It seems that state intervention is opening up the rural economy and society to a number of potentially important and fundamental changes without being able to complete the tasks of restructuring entirely with its own initiative and thrust.

3 PROMOTION OF AGRICULTURE

The next few decades are likely to witness a breakthrough in India's dry-land agriculture.[3] Its impact on production could be of a modest order but, on the credit side, the technologies providing the breakthrough would have a better chance of being within the reach of the small and medium cultivators as compared to the 'green revolution' technologies. In Karnataka the state has registered some improvements in the yield of typical dry-land crops which have remained neglected in the country as a whole (see Table 6.1). These improvements can be attributed to the Karnataka's agricultural research and extension system operating through the University of Agricultural Sciences, its research centres and projects and the state Directorate of Agriculture.

This breakthrough in dry-land agriculture may enable the small and medium cultivators in Karnataka to look beyond the problems of precarious subsistence, and acquire a measure of capacity to invest resources and efforts in the development opportunities arising on the farm and in the enterprises supplementary to the farm. This implies the growing contact and rapport of the cultivator with the development

Table 6.1 Improvements in yields of coarse cereals and
pulses – comparison of Karnataka and India

Crop	Karnataka (1955–56 to 1980–81)	India (1949–50 to 1983–84)
Coarse Cereals		
Ragi	1.9	1.5
Jowar	3.8	1.5
Bajra	2.9	1.8
Maize	6.3	0.8
Pulses		
Gram	1.9	0.6
Tur	3.1	– 0.4

Sources: 1. Agricultural Situation in India, March 1985,
p. 901.
2. Season and Crop Reports for the Karnataka
State.

agencies, and improvements in his information and perspective on the
range of economic opportunities available in his village and its neighbourhood.

There are two features of the Karnataka situation which make such a
development plausible. First, the distribution of land in the state, while
unequal, still leaves a substantial portion of land in the hands of small
and medium holdings, as may be seen from Table 6.2. It seems that this
structure of land distribution would be conducive to the relatively
smooth adoption of technological change by the masses of cultivators
as compared to the prospects for technological change in situations
with polarised structures of land distribution. Secondly, and more
important, we often find in the field that the delivery system handling
the rural development inputs has a good reach in the state encompass-
ing the lower strata of cultivators. For example, in a recent field-
investigation conducted in a drought-prone district in connection with
an evaluation of loans given for digging irrigation wells, it was found
that 44 per cent of beneficiaries had holdings below 2 hectares, and
another 29 per cent had holdings between 2 hectares and 4 hectares;
thus, nearly three-quarters of beneficiaries were cultivators with modest
size holdings.

A study in progress in ISEC on the likely impact of technological
change in ragi (the staple foodgrain in the southern parts of Karnataka

Table 6.2   Distribution of holdings by size (1976–77)

Size of holdings (in hectares)	Per cent of total Holdings	Area
Up to 1	33	6
1 to 2	23	11
2 to 4	22	20
4 to 10	17	34
10 and above	5	29
	100	100

Source: Agricultural Census of Karnataka State, 1976–77.

and a major dry-land crop in the state) shows that the increased ragi production is likely to fall short of the level needed to meet the nutritional norm and, also, that the labour absorption in ragi production would not be much of a help in relieving the problem of surplus labour in agriculture.[4] A specific implication of these prospects is that the state intervention for promotion of dry-land agriculture may provide negligible direct benefits to labourers. This would also be true of the smallest size-group of holdings appearing in Table 6.2, containing a third of all cultivators, having holdings which are, possibly, too small ever to become viable in dry-land agriculture.

4   EMPLOYMENT GENERATION

India has a long tradition of organised programmes for provision of employment and relief during periods of acute scarcity like famines. The recent attempts to devise development strategies appropriate to the rural poor – labourers and similar groups – have had the effect of bringing into prominence the notion that the employment programmes should move beyond being *ad hoc* relief programmes to provide guaranteed employment to all those seeking wage employment for a minimum number of days in a year. Karnataka has had its own employment guarantee programme for about a decade and in addition, there are a number of central government schemes for provision of employment to the rural poor.

Two features of these programmes are of particular interest. First, the official machinery has shown commendable capacity to organise the employment programmes on a wide enough scale. It can be seen from Table 6.3 that over the period 1982–83 to 1985–86 (which were years of scarcity) there was an almost threefold increase in the number of works taken up and mandays of employment provided. With the creation of Mandal Panchayats (organisation at the level of clusters of villages to promote and institutionalise participation by the rural people in governance and development planning) and decentralised planning, it should become possible to put the employment programmes on a more secure foundation by integrating them with the long-term area development plans.

Table 6.3   Employment generated in scarcity relief works in Karnataka

Year	Number of works taken up	Peak level employ-ment reached (in lakhs labourers)	Employment generated (in lakh mandays)
1982–83	16,463	2.0	333
1983–84	17,998	2.5	512
1984–85	39,125	4.1	923
1985–86 (up to Feb. 1986)	46,691	6.2	948

Note: A lakh = 100,000 rupees
Source: *The Hindu*, 12 April 1986.

Secondly, and more heartening, it is a consistent finding in our field investigations that the employment programmes belong to that limited range of schemes – the other components in the range being community drinking water wells, small low-cost houses for the rural poor, and the distribution of staple foodgrains at subsidised prices – which show a good capacity to reach and benefit the lowest rural strata. A reason could be that the nature and benefit of these schemes are not attractive enough to induce the rural rich and powerful either to try to corner the schemes for themselves or to prevent the rural poor from receiving the schemes.

The employment programmes are important enough for their impact on incomes of the rural poor to become noticeable in our field data. Consider, for example, the findings presented in Table 6.4, which were obtained in a recent ISEC study on the Rural Landless Employment

Table 6.4 Extent of poverty among landless agricultural labour households

		% below poverty line
(i)	Before RLEGP	75
(ii)	After RLEGP	57
(iii)	If RLEGP covers fully the gap between actual employment and full employment	30
(iv)	If RLEGP offers full employment and increased wage rate of Rs 10 per day	13

Source: M. Vivekananda, RLEGP in Karnataka – An Evaluation, ISEC, February 1986.

Guarantee Programme (RLEGP). The study covered samples of landless agricultural labour households from the four main regions in Karnataka. While Table 6.4 shows a modest measure of reduction in poverty brought about by RLEGP, what is even more significant is the indication available in the table that the expanded scale of employment programmes and modest increases in the wage rates paid by the programmes have the potential to make a substantial contribution to poverty alleviation among the lowest rural strata, namely, the landless agricultural labour households.

It is interesting to speculate on the likely changes in the rural community structure due to the effective state intervention to support the income and employment of the households in the lowest rural strata. First, these households are usually the principal victims of the exploitative relationships and transactions resting on arrangements with deep roots in the rural society. Would the state intervention weaken these roots and create conditions favourable for the coming together of the rural poor against the rural rich and élite? Secondly, perceiving the palpable benefits of state intervention, would not the rural poor, in the next step, begin to exert pressure on the state for more room in the rural economy, and a greater say in the formulation of rural policies and programmes? In our field investigations we do encounter incidents indicative of the new perceptions and mood among the agricultural labourers and the apprehensive reactions of the rural élite to these changes.[5]

It is necessary to take a balanced view of the scope for state intervention. A critical factor is the adequate availability of viable opportunities for the formation of rural assets through employment programmes. We see substantial scope in Karnataka villages for new roads, schools, public buildings and better rural housing. But doubts begin to creep in when one considers the returns obtained from the economic assets created by employment programmes. For example, a recent ISEC study on the construction of village tanks for irrigation purposes – a typical activity in employment programmes – has brought out the weak economic case of such tanks compared to other modes of irrigation, as well as alternative ways of generating income for the rural poor (see Rao and Chandrakant, 1984). The point is that rural situations of chronic pressure of population on resources, and extensive penetration by market forces, are unlikely to have an abundance of viable economic opportunities capable of being exploited through employment programmes. In such situations, employment programmes would be akin to a holding operation designed for interim support to the rural poor until stable and remunerative occupations are created for them in the rural economy.

5 DIVERSIFICATION OF RURAL ECONOMY

How successful are the attempts to build up such occupations in rural Karnataka? Presented in this section are some findings of the ISEC's current evaluation of the Integrated Rural Development Programme (IRDP) in Karnataka. The main thrust of IRDP is on creating self-employment opportunities for the rural poor by building up small-scale household activities based on local resources and serving local markets.

A persistent criticism of the IRD Programme in India has been of the leakage of its benefits to the rural rich. In the ISEC's Concurrent Evaluation, the IRDP beneficiaries have been grouped into three categories (a) the landless persons belonging to the lowest rural strata, (b) the cultivators with weak economic viability, and (c) the rural rich. It can be seen from Table 6.5 that the rich form only 6 per cent of total beneficiaries and, obviously, leakage does not seem to be a serious problem in Karnataka. However, it should also be clear from Table 6.5, column (2), that the IRDP does not find it possible to work exclusively for the lowest rural strata since, excluding the rich, the IRDP beneficiaries are equally divided among the labourers and the cultivators. Table 6.6 contains a plausible explanation for this feature of the IRDP. It is observed in Table 6.6 that nearly 70 per cent of beneficiaries

Table 6.5 Distribution of beneficiaries by their economic status and abandonment of schemes

	% of total beneficiaries (1)	% of beneficiaries in each category who abandoned the IRDP scheme within the first two years (2)
Landless labourers	47	36
Cultivators	47	28
Rich	6	—
All categories	100	31

Source: Concurrent Evaluation of IRDP, ISEC, 1986.

Table 6.6 Distribution of beneficiaries by schemes and reduction in poverty

Scheme	% of total beneficiaries (1)	% of poor who crossed the poverty line (2)
Dairy	53	35
Animal husbandry		58
Trading (petty shops, tea stalls, etc.)	18	56
Agriculture (pair of bullocks etc.)	16	52
Village industries	9	23
Services	4	20
Total	100	41

Source: Concurrent Evaluation of IRDP, ISEC, 1986.

received schemes falling in the land-linked sectors of animal husbandry and agriculture. Village industries and services accounted for only 13 per cent of beneficiaries. It may come as a surprise to many that trading activities like petty shops, tea stalls, etc. absorbed more beneficiaries than village industries, but a fuller analysis of the structure of rural economy and its relationships with the larger economy would show that this is inevitable, given the prevailing severe constraints on rural diversification. A clue to these constraints is provided by column 2 of Table 6.6, which indicates that the reduction in the extent of poverty was the least among those taking up village industries and services as compared to the beneficiaries taking up other activities.

The IRD programme is too recent to evaluate its lasting impact on the rural community. Our hunch is that the programme would certainly go some way in improving the economic viability of the small and medium cultivators by giving them remunerative subsidiary activities. But it is doubtful whether the programme would have much success in helping the labourers make the difficult transition towards becoming self-employed entrepreneurs. As can be seen from Table 6.5, column (2), the abandonment of IRDP schemes within the first two years of receiving the assistance was relatively the highest among the labourers.[6]

6 A SYNTHETIC SCENARIO

The effects of development programmes noted in the preceding sections have three features in common. First, they indicate the possibility of some diminution in the hold of the rural élite on the rural masses. With the cultivators gaining in viability, and the labourers turning to the state for economic support, it indeed seems unlikely that the rural élite could continue to wield the same power and authority as in the past.

Secondly, the development programmes have the effect of making the rural groups more outward-looking. Cultivators sell more of their output, use more of urban inputs and services, acquire interest in what the extension agencies have to offer, and become inquisitive about new supplementary activities bringing them in contact with new groups of suppliers and customers. Labourers find employment in new locations and move away more frequently than before from their traditional employers and types of work. They would also have more occasions to meet and mingle with labourers from a wider spatial spread. Interestingly, the group most prone to become outward-looking in the course of development is the group of rural élite. There are numerous findings indicating the growing participation of the rural élite in urban investments and activities. They also find it politically profitable to establish contacts at the higher echelons of political parties and government bureaucracy with a view to bringing more developmental funds and schemes into their villages.

Thirdly, state intervention for rural development enhances and sharpens the participation by rural groups in the political processes at the village and local levels. Puzzlingly, in a democratic polity, political activity appears to become self-perpetuating; economic growth as well as economic conflicts, successful development schemes as well as those which fail – all of these seem to provoke the actors on the political stage and their followers and observers into continual bouts of feverish activities.

While it is easy enough to enumerate the changes in rural community structure initiated by the state intervention, it is far from easy to predict the eventual shape assumed by the rural community as a result of these changes. A prime source of uncertainty is the impetus to the rural economy imparted by state intervention; it was seen in the preceding sections that there are constraints weakening the thrust of each one of the three interventions considered in this paper. With a weak thrust, the changes initiated by state intervention could be partial, short-lived, and reversible by other forces impinging on the rural economy. Also, a little reflection would show that the different changes described above are likely to occur at different speeds over time and space. To complicate the situation further, changes proceeding at different rates could give configurations with widely varying outcome for the rural community. For example, consider situations where politicisation of rural groups is accompanied by adequate economic thrust of development pro- grammes compared to the situations with serious imbalance between the two.

A desirable scenario from an economist's point of view is of a numerically large, viable and development-receptive middle strata in the rural community, which would keep in check the processes of polarisation. Aspiring young people from the strata take a lead in developing participatory and consultative systems in their local area. These systems, in their turn, make sufficiently adequate provision for the rural poor in the plans for area development, to prevent outbreaks of acute conflict and to provide upward mobility to the enterprising among the rural poor. The rural élite have little room or incentive for exploitative activities but find many new opportunities for retaining their leadership and status by promoting rural lobbies and taking up enterprises conducive to rural–urban integration. Village factions link up with political parties and enable the rural community to use competitive politics for development purposes. This, in a word, is a scenario of a successful integration of a rural community with the larger economy without losing its sense of identity and cohesion.[7]

Pessimism is so rampant among economists that it would be quite superfluous to mention the numerous ways in which the scenario could be one of rural stagnation, disintegration and immiserisation. It is precisely the uncertainty of the emerging scenario which makes it necessary for the theorist and policy-maker to monitor the rural changes in the wake of state intervention carefully, and in detail, without allowing preconceived notions to distort one's observations.[8] The intention of this paper is to stress this need, though we also believe that the Karnataka experiences would yield some positive lessons on how state intervention could help rural communities enter the main stream of growth and development.

Notes

1. In the period 1965–85, six years, roughly one out of every three years, witnessed severe drought in Karnataka. For details see Deshpande (1986).
2. For example, the perspective prepared for the Seventh Five Year Plan visualises the lifting up of all the rural poor above the poverty line by the turn of the century.
3. For an argument in favour of this proposition, see Rao and Deshpande (1986).
4. These findings come from the PhD dissertation in progress in ISEC by D. S. Gundu Rao on the theme of the economic impact of the technological changes in ragi in the southern part of Karnataka.
5. Such confrontations are particularly noticeable in rural pockets experiencing substantial increase in the demand for wage labour (see Thimmaiah and Rao, 1986).
6. ISEC's Concurrent Evaluation of IRDP covered two groups of beneficiaries – (a) current beneficiaries, that is, those who received assistance in a period of three months immediately preceding the date of interview, and (b) old beneficiaries, that is, those who received assistance in the corresponding period two years back.
7. This scenario relies in part on the insights provided by the two studies completed recently in ISEC – (i) M. V. Nadkarni's (1987) study on the farmers' movements in Karnataka, and (ii) V. S. Parthasarathy's (1986) intensive micro-level case study of rural élite.
8. Practicable procedure and indicators for such monitoring are suggested in V. M. Rao (1983c and d).

References

Deshpande, R. S. (1986) 'Drought: Some Issues and Problems', ISEC, July.
Nadkarni, M. V. (1987) *Farmer's Movements in India* (New Delhi: Allied Publishers).
Parthasarathy, V. S. (1986) Rural Elites and Development: A Case Study', monograph, ISEC.
Rao, V. M. (1983a) 'Barriers in Rural Development', *Economic and Political Weekly*, 2 July.
Rao, V. M. (1983b) 'Rural Diversification and the Strategy for Rural Employ-

ment', in Robinson E. A. G. *et al.* (eds) *Employment Policy in a Developing Country: A Case Study of India* (London: Macmillan).

Rao, V. M. (1983c) 'Information System for Rural Plan Implementation', ISEC.

Rao, V. M. (1983d) 'Indicators of Rural Change for Monitoring Rural Development', ISEC.

Rao, V. M. and Chandrakant, M. G. (1984) 'Resources at the Margin: A Note on the Karnataka Tank Irrigation Project', *Economic and Political Weekly (Review of Agriculture)*, June.

Rao, V. M. and Deshpande, R. S. (1986) 'Agricultural Growth in India: A Review of Experiences and Prospects', background paper prepared for the World Economic Congress, Delhi, December.

Thimmaiah, G. and Rao, V. M. (1986) 'Problems and Prospects for Sericulture Development in Karnataka: A Field View', in Hanumappa, H. G. (ed.) *Sericulture for Rural Development* (Bombay: Himalaya Publishing House).

Vivekananda, M. (1986) RLEGP in Karnataka – An Evaluation, ISEC, February.

7 What Can Agriculture Do for the Poorest Rural Groups?

Hans P. Binswanger*

WORLD BANK

and

Jaime B. Quizon*

CHASE ECONOMETRICS AND WORLD BANK

Africa
7180
1120
9140

1 INTRODUCTION

Most of the world's poorest people live in rural areas. They derive a large share of income from agriculture, as small farmers or as workers – or as both. Agricultural development is therefore often seen as the key to reducing poverty, especially rural poverty. In most of sub-Saharan Africa, for example, where the rural poor are mostly small farmers, it is clear that increasing the efficiency of these farmers *vis-à-vis* large farmers (or of the country as a whole *vis-à-vis* competing countries) improves the small farmers' condition. They can expand their sales and/or can produce their own subsistence with less effort or lower cash costs (for a full discussion see World Bank, 1986).

When the poorest rural groups are landless, as in South Asia, the issues are much more complicated. Small farmer-oriented strategies still help an important segment of the poor population to improve their competitive position. However, agricultural development measures do not affect the welfare of workers directly but only via the impact they have on the demand for labour and on the level of output prices. Agricultural development measures enhance efficiency of resource use. Therefore they normally reduce *labour input per unit of output*. How much they reduce it depends on the source of productivity gain. The reduction is larger for machines than for added irrigation, for example. *Labour demand* can only rise if the enhanced profitability of farming leads to an output increase which is sufficiently large enough to compensate for the initial reduction in labour requirements. The output expansion depends on the nature of the demand for agricultural output and on the elasticity of supply of agricultural output. The demand for agricultural output is price elastic for small open economies, but inelastic for closed or state trading economies. In closed economies the income effects of agricultural development and the income elasticities will condition the demand side along with the price elasticities. If output expansion is sharply limited from the demand side, agricultural growth will lead to reduced agricultural labour demand, but sharply lower food prices. The poorest rural group would lose as workers but gain as consumers. Which effect will be more important?

In this paper we use a general equlibrium model of India's agricultural sector to ask how much the poorest rural group can gain from agricultural development measures once output price and employment effects are accounted for. We first examine what happened to the income of different income groups during the last two decades of very successful agricultural growth. We then explore technical change as it applies to different crops under alternative trade assumptions, and consider the effects of expanding irrigation, declining fertiliser prices and removing trade restrictions on rice. The results suggest that consumer benefits are more important for the welfare of the largely landless than employment effects, and that they can benefit very substantially from agricultural growth only if food prices decline. This raises difficult policy dilemmas because declining prices erode the gains of the rural sector as a whole. We therefore explore food rations and direct income transfers as alternative means for the assistance of those in poverty.

2   A SUMMARY OF THE MODEL

The limited general equilibrium model used in our investigation determines quantities and prices in seven markets: three input markets (labour, draft power, and fertilisers); and four agricultural output markets (rice, wheat, coarse cereals, and other crops) (a mathematical exposition of the model can be found in Quizon and Binswanger, 1986). The model also determines residual farm profits. Given these prices and quantities, it then determines the real incomes of four rural and four urban income quartiles (R1, R2, R3, and R4 and U1, U2, U3, and U4, respectively).

The supply of the four agricultural commodities and the demand for the three factors of production are modelled as a jointly estimated system of output supply and factor demand equations. Output supply and factor demand shift in response to changes in exogenous endowment and technology variables: land (cultivable area), annual rainfall, irrigation, high-yielding varieties, roads, farm capital (animals and implements), regulated markets, and technological change.

The *supply of labour* is responsive to the real rural wage. Agricultural labour is supplied by rural groups and also by some urban emigration, which is responsive to the rural wage.

The *supply of draft power* is responsive to the real rental rate for draft animals and is supplied by each of the rural groups.

The *fertiliser supply* is treated as an aggregate of nutrient tons, which is responsive to the price of fertiliser relative to non-agricultural goods prices.

The *supply of land* is exogenously given as the cultivated area. This treatment still allows the cropped area to vary endogenously via changes in the extent of double and triple cropping. And, of course, the area allocated to different crops can vary. While the supply of land is exogenous, net returns to land (the residential farm profits after variable factors have been paid) are determined endogenously.

Consumer demand is responsive to the prices of commodities and the real income of each of the eight income groups. Poorer groups have higher income elasticities than richer groups. Each income group's demand must therefore be modelled separately. Demand was estimated econometrically; a flexible functional form was used, so that all (compensated) cross-price elasticities were directly estimated. Aggregate demand is the sum of the demands of all the income groups.

Nominal income is computed as each group's supply of agricultural production factors multiplied by the factor prices, plus an exogenously given component for non-agricultural income. *Real income* is calculated for each of the eight groups as their nominal income deflated by an endogenous consumer price index that is specific to that group's consumption patterns and reflects all endogenous changes in food prices.

Prices and quantities of commodities and factors of production are determined as those which equate aggregate supply and demand in each of the seven markets. The government can influence agricultural prices through the use of tariffs, food imports and exports, food grain storage, forced procurement at fixed prices, and sales in consumer ration shops at non-equilibrium prices. The model solves simultaneously for changes in endogenous prices and quantities and thus determines for each income group the change in its nominal income, price deflator, real income, labour supply, draft power supply, and level of consumption.

Non-agricultural prices are given exogenously and are used as the numeraire of the model. Because non-agricultural income is also given, non-agricultural production is exogenous and consumption of this output must adjust via trade.

The base year used in constructing the model is 1973–74. Initial values are computed largely from an extensive rural household survey conducted by the National Council for Applied Economic Research.[1] The entire model is written in logarithmically linear equation form.

There are several characteristics of the model which must be kept in mind while interpreting our findings. First, it is well known that the distributional outcomes from general equilibrium models depend crucially on labour market assumptions (Taylor, 1979). We model the real rural wage by equating supply and demand for labour; it is a full employment model. This treatment is consistent with empirical evidence that there is little year-round unemployment in rural areas and that most unemployment is seasonal (Krishna, 1976). Moreover, real wages are variable both within and across years; that is, no model of constant nominal or real wages is consistent with the data. Econometric studies of labour demand (Evenson and Binswanger, 1984) and supply (Bardhan, 1984; Rosenzweig, 1984) are also consistent with our equilibrium treatment of the rural labour market.

The model treats non-agricultural incomes (and implicitly urban wages and non-agricultural output) as exogenously determined. The purchasing power of the non-agricultural incomes, however, depends on agricultural prices. When agricultural prices rise, urban agricultural demand will fall because of both prices and income effects. But other feedback from agricultural activity to the non-agricultural sector is not allowed for in the model. One consequence of our treatment of the non-agricultural sector is that changes in food prices have no effect on the nominal urban wage; that is, reductions in food prices benefit urban wage earners and are not passed on to employers in the form of lower wages.

Although the model determines what happens to real farm profits and the incomes of the rural income groups, it does not treat endogenously what subsequently happens to private savings and private agricultural investment brought about by the changing fortunes of farmers. Thus our model is not a very long-run model. The reason for this treatment is that no econometric study exists which quantifies the link between farm profits and farm investment.

Finally, the model omits the effects of the market for foreign exchange on agricultural performance, and vice versa. India is modelled as a state-trading economy in which decisions to export or to import agricultural commodities rest with the government. These decisions are exogenous to the model.

Results from counter-factual analysis of the period 1960 to 1980 are reported in Quizon and Binswanger (1986). From our counter-factual analysis we note that our model is able to trace reasonably the major trends in Indian agriculture over the two decades 1960–61 to 1980–81.

3 WHAT HAPPENED TO RURAL INCOMES DURING THE GREEN REVOLUTION?

Longitudinal data on rural incomes, its components such as farm profits or its distribution, do not exist for the period 1960 to 1980. The model's equations can, however, be used in an *accounting model* to generate time series of rural incomes. We generate the income series for each of our eight income groups by using actual estimates of agricultural output, agricultural prices, wages and fertiliser consumption, as well as the exogenous variables that affect the income and factor market equations in the model. The numbers in Table 7.1 are indexes of the predicted levels and are calibrated so that the predicted level of each variable is equal to 100 for 1970–71, the end of the first phase of the Green Revolution.

We assumed that during the twenty-year period the across-quartile shares in ownership of factor inputs and within-quartile shares of non-agricultural and factor incomes in total income remained equal to their respective base-year (1973–74) values. We also assumed that the rates of growth in the population, in the agricultural capital stock, and in the non-agricultural income of each quartile were the same across the groups. Although the total endowments of the various groups change

Table 7.1 Simulated indexes of income distribution and their sources, India 1960–61 to 1980–81 (1970–71 = 100)

Endogenous variables	Agricultural year					
Real per capita income (actual)	1960–71	1965–66	1970–71	1973–74	1975–76	1980–81
National	92.0	95.0	100	95.1	95.4	105.9
Rural, by Quartile						
First	101.0	99.0	100	95.9	97.4	107.0
Second	96.9	95.8	100	94.6	94.8	99.9
Third	93.8	93.5	100	93.8	93.3	96.3
Fourth (Richest)	88.5	88.6	100	92.4	90.7	88.8
Aggregate[a]	92.9	92.4	100	93.6	92.9	94.9
Urban, by Quartile						
First (Poorest)	91.9	100.4	100	98.1	100.7	136.0
Second	90.9	102.8	100	99.3	102.6	141.9
Third	90.2	102.7	100	99.7	102.5	139.3
Fourth (Richest)	87.6	102.3	100	99.8	102.2	133.5
Aggregate[a]	89.4	102.3	100	99.4	102.2	136.7
Agricultural employment	98.2	100.1	100	112.3	118.8	118.5
Real agricultural wage bill	91.2	95.3	100	101.4	104.9	105.4
Real residual farm profits	64.2	67.9	100	86.0	85.1	76.4
Non-agricultural income	71.9	93.6	100	111.3	121.8	182.7
Real per capita disposable income	92.4	94.5	100	96.7	97.8	113.6
Total actual agricultural output	79.3	81.2	100	99.4	107.1	119.6
Actual prices = agricultural/non-agricultural goods	89.8	97.2	100	97.7	91.6	76.3

Note:
a. These estimates of per capita income are computed as in equation 1 = 17 of Appendix A (Quizon and Binswanger 1986), in which the subscript k now refers to either the rural quartiles (R1 to R4) or the urban quartiles (U1 to U4) only.

over time, the relative endowment position of each group was assumed to remain the same. But there may have been other causes of change in actual incomes that we were unable to account for, such as changes in taxation, in investment behaviour, in people's occupations, and in food subsidies. Table 7.1 shows what would have happened to real income as a result of changes in agricultural production and technology, agricultural output and input prices, non-agricultural incomes and prices, and population.

The last two rows of Table 7.1 show the actual growth of total agricultural output and the change in agricultural terms of trade. Agricultural production grew rapidly during the early Green Revolution period (1965–66 to 1970–71) and again from 1973–74 onward. Agricultural terms of trade rose prior to the Green Revolution, stayed fairly constant until 1973–74, and then dropped substantially by 1980–81.

These changes in quantity and price explain the changes in farm profits. Farm profits were depressed in 1960–61 and in 1965–66 but then moved dramatically upward by 1970–71. By 1973–74 they had declined to 86 per cent of their 1970–71 level, and by 1980–81 to 76 per cent of the 1970–71 level. In these years, declines in output prices outweighed rapid growth in agricultural output.

Employment in agriculture (estimated in our model) grew by about 20 per cent during the twenty-year period. Because real wages declined by about 5 per cent, the total real wage bill for the period rose by about 15 per cent. Non-agricultural real income more than doubled during the period, with the most rapid increases occurring just prior to the Green Revolution and between 1975–76 and 1980–81.

The trends in output and factor prices, and in agricultural and non-agricultural income, suggest that real aggregate per capita income among rural people grew by only about 8 per cent during the early stages of the Green Revolution, after which it declined and stagnated. Despite a drastic shift in the distribution of rural income from wages to profits in the early period, rural income distribution was remarkably stable for the period as a whole. The effect of adverse wage trends on the rural poor was partially alleviated because agricultural employment increased somewhat and because the poor participated to a small extent in the growth of farm profits. About 11 per cent of their income was derived from such profits. They also had substantial gains in non-agricultural incomes, and as consumers they benefited from the decline in agricultural prices during the last five years of the twenty-year period.

The first period of the Green Revolution was one of substantial gains in farm profits. But the rapid gains in production during the late 1970s did not translate into further advances in income because the prices of agricultural products fell. The production gains from the early Green

Revolution period were associated with rising prices because the government used the gains largely to replace imports. But once self-sufficiency in foodgrain production was more or less assured, the surplus grain production had to be absorbed domestically. This was a classic example of the process in which productivity gains in agriculture were transmitted to consumers (both rural and urban) by way of declining prices. In the late 1970s the combination of rapid non-agricultural growth and declining agricultural terms of trade greatly benefited the urban groups. The biggest beneficiaries were the urban poor, since they spend a larger share of their incomes on food.

4 HOW CAN SECTOR-SPECIFIC POLICIES AND PROGRAMMES HELP THE RURAL POOR?

The previous section offers only partial explanations as to why wages, farm profits, and income distribution evolved the way they did. An assessment of how each individual change in a policy or a trend affects the rural poor is required to separate the influences of different factors.

We do this by comparing the results of a simulated change in selected trends or policies with the 'base case'. Thus we simulate a change in a specific exogenous variable, such as technology, and trace the effect of the change in production, prices, employment, and farm profits. This then allows us to compare how real incomes would have been affected. Figure 7.1 illustrates this process. U_0U_2 is the path of the specific endogenous variable given actual policy trends and events, and 'a' is the value of U at U_1. The variable U could be one of those shown in the column headings of Tables 7.2 and 7.3. U_0U_2 is the simulation path of U if an exogenous change or intervention occurred, such as any of those shown in the left-hand column of Tables 7.2 and 7.3. The value b is the difference between U_2 and U_1, the induced change in U at T_1; and C is the percentage change in U, or b/a. T_0 to T_1 is perhaps three to five years, sufficient time for farmers to respond to changes in technology, policies, and prices by adjusting their production patterns.

For the technical change scenarios of Table 7.2, yields of rice or all crops are assumed to rise by 10 per cent, a change corresponding to a substantial varietal shift.[2] Because the share of rice in total crop output is 27 per cent, a 10 per cent yield gain has less powerful effects if it occurs in rice rather than in all crops. The two other development measurements considered are an expansion in irrigation by 10 per cent and the provision of a 20 per cent subsidy to fertiliser consumption.

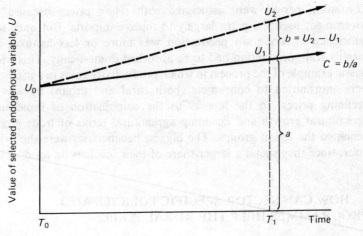

Note: *C* = percentage change in simulated value of *U* from its 'base' trend value,
         as the result of a simulated change in one or more exogenous variables.

Figure 7.1 Simulated changes in trends and policies: derivation of values

The technical changes are explored under two different trade regimes. In the first regimes (scenarios 1 and 2) the economy is considered closed and additional production is consumed in India. But in the second regimes (scenarios 3 and 4) a fraction of the extra yield is either exported or used to reduce imports of the commodity in question. The fraction of the extra yield which is exported is set so that the GNP deflator (not the individual commodity prices) is stabilised. Note that scenarios 3 and 4 correspond to an assumption of state trading; it is not an open economy model in many commodities.

When an increase of 10 per cent in rice yields has to be absorbed domestically, the result is a sharp decline in the price of rice (-15.4 per cent) and in the price of its closest substitute, wheat (-10.6 per cent). Rice production increases by about 10 per cent, while wheat production declines by about 3 per cent (for these details see Quizon and Binswanger, 1986). The GNP deflator (measured in terms of non-agricultural commodities) therefore declines by about 6 per cent, while total agricultural output increases by about 2.7 per cent. The price decline and the increase in agricultural output imply a real national income gain of about 2 per cent.

The increased agricultural output requires only moderately larger labour inputs, and the increased demand for labour results in modestly higher real agricultural wages. Therefore the real wage bill rises by a mere 1.3 per cent. The declines in agricultural prices, combined with the rise in wages, lead to a reduction in residual farm profits despite the increase in agricultural productivity. The price effects, the farm profit effects, and the wage largely explain the distributional outcome. Net buyers of food gain, the more so the larger their share of income spent on food. The urban poorest gain the most (6 per cent). The rural poor also benefit, since they also spend most of their income on food. Moreover, they benefit from the slight rise in wage levels. Since reduction in farm profits affects them only slightly, they end up with a net gain in real income of close to 4 per cent. However, since the rural rich derive much of their income from farm profits, their gain as consumers is not sufficient to offset their loss in profits. Their real income therefore falls by 0.7 per cent.

A decision to maintain the price level by exporting a portion of the expanded rice production (scenario 3) would sharply alter the distributional outcome. Farm profits rise by 8 per cent and therefore the rural rich are the main gainers. Their income expands by 3.7 per cent. The added demand for commodities with high income elasticities implies that relative prices must change in order to maintain overall price stability. The rice price then declines by 9 per cent, leaving the urban poor with a gain of only about 0.8 per cent. The rural poor gain only 2.1 per cent, less than with domestic absorption. Their consumption gain is eroded since additions to their wage income or farm profits are not sufficient to offset the consumer losses.

The sharp effects of trade on income distribution are also evident when technical change affects all crops, although magnitudes and other details differ significantly. The gains of the urban poor groups are larger than those of the rural poor when the extra output caused by technical change is absorbed domestically. In the all crops scenario trade policy is the major determinant of the distributional outcome of technical change. With domestic absorption the urban poor gain as much as 17.8 per cent. When trade is used to stabilise price levels their gains are eroded to a mere 2.3 per cent. For the rural rich the impact of trade is equally dramatic. With no exports their gains are only 1.8 per cent. With exports and stable prices they gain nearly 15 per cent.

The rural poorest gain nearly twice as much under domestic absorption than under price stability. When prices are stable they gain a little as consumers, a little as farm workers, and a little from higher farm profits in which they have a very small share. The only group who is hardly affected by trade policy changes is the small farmers whose consumer gains buffer producer losses and vice versa.

Table 7.2 The impact of technical changes, development measures and free trade in rice on real incomes (percentage change)

Scenarios/ endogenous variables	GMP deflator	Farm profits	Real wage bill	Real per capita income						Rice[a] exports	Domestic rice price	World rice price
				National average	Rural quartiles			Urban quartiles				
					Poorest	Second	Richest	Poorest	Richest			
Technical change												
A. Closed economy												
(1) 10% rice yield increase	−5.98	−3.77	1.34	2.05	3.76	2.53	−0.69	6.01	2.87	0.0	−15.43	0.0
(2) 10% increase in yield of all crops	−18.13	−4.31	0.50	7.20	9.95	7.26	1.84	17.78	9.83	0.0	−12.98	0.0
B. Exporting to maintain price stability												
(3) 10% rice yield increase[c]	0.0	8.03	2.48	2.47	2.09	2.80	3.70	0.84	0.02	2.69	−9.24	[e]
(4) 10% increase in yield of all crops[d]	0.0	31.35	1.49	8.55	5.49	8.58	14.78	2.25	0.66	2.28	0.39	[e]
C. Other development measures												
(5) 10% increase in irrigated area	−5.76	−4.79	1.14	1.71	2.92	1.71	−0.67	6.04	3.50	0.0	−6.93	0.0

(6) 20% decline in fertiliser price	−1.13	5.58	−2.67	1.30	−0.35	0.75	2.54	0.60	0.40	0.0	−1.76	0.0
D. *Free trade in rice*											
(7) Low international elasticities[b]	1.48	2.88	0.04	0.10	−0.42	0.06	1.07	−1.27	−0.70	0.59	2.69	−28.12
(8) High international elasticities[b]	7.11	13.85	0.20	0.46	−2.02	0.28	5.15	−6.08	−3.37	2.85	12.94	−20.94
(9) Exchanging rice for wheat (with high elasticities)	−0.42	−0.83	−0.05	0.07	0.08	0.04	−0.05	0.48	0.16	0.50	−0.20	−3.68

Notes:

[a] In metric tons.

[b] India's price at 70 per cent of world price, converted at official exchange rates. Elasticity of world import = $\alpha_w = -0.08$ for low elasticity and -0.87 for high elasticity scenarios. Elasticity of world exports = $\Sigma_w = 0.14$ for low elasticity and 0.55 for high elasticity scenarios.

[c] 54 per cent of the initial yield gain is exported, i.e. 5.4 per cent of base year rice production.

[d] 45.1 per cent of the initial yield gain in all four crops or crop groups is exported, i.e., 4.51 per cent of base year aggregate crop output.

[e] Level of world price decline depends on demand and supply elasticities in international markets (see note b).

Sources: Scenarios (1)–(7) from Quizon and Binswanger (1986).
Scenarios (8)–(9) from Quizon and Barbeiri (1985).

Finally, it is easy completely to erode the gains of the rural poor from technical change by more aggressive export-oriented policies which lead to increases in domestic prices (Quizon and Binswanger, 1986, Table 3). More aggressive export policies have a sharply regressive impact since they provide large benefits to the rural rich and hurt the urban poor.

4.1 Irrigation Investment

In row 5 of Table 7.2, the assumption is that investment in irrigation is accelerated enough to increase the percentage of area irrigated by 10 per cent. This leads to an increase in aggregate output of 2.7 per cent and a decrease in the aggregate price level of 5.8 per cent. Because irrigation requires labour, labour employment and real wages rise slightly. However, this labour demand effect on irrigation is not very large because inelastic final demand curtails the expansion of output. Residual farm profits, therefore, decline by 4.8 per cent as a consequence of slightly higher labour costs and lower output prices associated with domestic absorption. The income distributional outcomes follow from these changes in price and profit. The landless gain modestly (2.9 per cent), while large farmers lose (− 0.7 per cent). All urban households gain substantially, with the poorest showing the largest gain (6 per cent).

4.2 Fertiliser Price Decline

Declines in farm gate prices of fertilisers can occur in several ways. The government could eliminate the import tax now levied as part of its programme of subsidising and protecting domestic production of fertilisers. Or, for the given protection level of the domestic industry, it could reduce the farm gate price by increasing its financial subsidy to farmers. In the simulation reported in Table 7.2, we do not fully model the effects of the implied changes in government revenues, or the effects on the domestic industry.[3]

The poorest rural group loses with lower fertiliser prices because, with inelastic full final demand, fertiliser acts as a substitute for labour and the real wage bill declines by 2.7 per cent. For the poorest rural group the negative wage effect dominates the benefit from reduced output prices while the reverse is the case for the second quartile in which farm profits are a larger share of income. Farm profits rise sharply because of both lower fertiliser and lower wage costs. Therefore, declines in fertiliser prices benefit primarily the large farmers.

4.3 Liberalising the Rice Trade

The agricultural development alternatives so far can have a substantial benefit for the rural poor only if they result in price declines. This recognition lies behind India's consistent anti-trade bias in agriculture, and has resulted in domestic staple food prices being generally held at or below world market prices during the 1970s and early 1980s. The price differences have been particularly marked for rice.

We compared prices in two major producing states of India with world rice prices, i.e., the price of Thai 5 per cent broken (f.o.b. Bangkok), for the same period. In the period 1963 to 1972, Indian domestic rice prices averaged about the same level as world rice prices. But for the period after 1972, domestic prices have been significantly below world prices. This difference has been as large as 55 per cent and has remained high. In the simulations we will assume that the domestic rice price is 70 per cent of the world rice price prior to the opening of India to free trade in rice. Wheat prices were far less depressed compared to international levels (Quizon and Barbeiri, 1985, Tables 1 and 3).

An anti-trade policy in rice clearly hurts the rural sector as a whole. And because rice is a labour-intensive crop, it may even hurt the rural workers if expanding rice production had a large effect on the real wage bill. This issue is explored in Quizon and Barbeiri using a special version of the basic model; the results are shown in rows 8 and 9 of Table 7.2.

The world rice trade has always been small, particularly when compared to India's own rice production. Annual world gross exports of rice averaged only 11.24 million metric tons (m.m.t.) for the period 1978–80, whereas India's own rice production was 49.74 m.m.t. for the same period. Therefore, even if India exported only a small percentage of her rice production, say 5 per cent or 2.49 m.m.t., this alone could depress world prices, given that the world demand for and the world supply of rice exports are fairly inelastic. Evidently, the amount of rice India can trade is restricted by the size of the world rice market. In later simulations, we assume gross world exports of rice to be 9.60 m.m.t., the annual average for 1976–78.

Although the international rice market has been dominated by government-to-government contracts and long-term trade agreements, different empirical studies still suggest varying degrees of responsiveness of international rice supplies and demands to the world price. Whereas Falcon and Monke (1979–80), for example, conclude that the price mechanism is important in clearing the world rice market, Siamwalla and Haykin (1983) show that the role of prices, though positive, is extremely limited. Existing empirical evidence, however, supports the contention that the demand for, and supply of, rice exports are fairly inelastic, i.e., both α_W and ε_W are less than one. In later simulations we assume two extreme sets of elasticity values. The first set of elasticity estimates, i.e., $\alpha_W = -0.08$ and $\varepsilon_W = 0.14$, are a lower bound and correspond to Siamwalla and Haykin's (1983) estimates of the world demand and supply elasticities for rice for the year 1980. The second set of estimates, i.e., $\alpha_W = -0.87$ and $\varepsilon_W = 0.55$, are much higher. These correspond to the price elasticities of demand and of supply for rice in India which we estimated and used in our model.

The results show the large impact which India could have on the world rice price; even under the high elasticity assumption the prices would drop by about 21 per cent, while Indian rice exports would amount to a mere 2.85 per cent. India's rice prices would rise by about 13 per cent, curtailing domestic demand. Therefore domestic production would rise by only 2.6 per cent. Moreover, these increases would come at the expense of a reduction in coarse cereal production of 3.3 per cent and of other crops of 0.6 per cent. Aggregate agricultural output would rise only by about 0.3 per cent. With inelastic world supply and demand the aggregate domestic output effects decline to less than 0.1 per cent.

Because the impact on domestic output is so limited, there is very little impact on the labour demand and the real wage bill. Therefore the price effects dominate, and the welfare of the rural poorest declines, while the second quartile experiences virtually no change in its welfare level. The gainers are the rural well-to-do, who gain more, the higher the elasticity of world demand and supply of exports.

For the rural poor to gain from open rice trade, the additional income of the rural rich would have to have powerful effects on the non-farm economy via consumption linkage, which are not explicitly modelled here. In the absence of empirical estimates of consumption linkages, it is not possible to assess whether such trickle-down effects would be sufficient to offset losses of the poor.

Despite our conclusion that free trade in rice would hurt the rural poor, a simple simulation shows that if world elasticities are high, India has foregone significant arbitration opportunities in international markets during the 1970s and 1980s. With international rice prices exceeding wheat prices, India could have exported small quantities of rice in exchange for additional wheat imports. In scenario 9 we model the domestic impact of selling 0.5 million tons of rice and trading it in for 0.93 million tons of wheat, using 1978–81 international rice and wheat prices adjusted for the relevant transport costs. Because wheat and rice are substitutes in domestic consumption, the additional wheat depresses both domestic wheat and rice prices, although the rice price falls far less than the wheat price. National income rises by 0.07 per cent and the incomes of all groups, except the large farmers rise. While the rise for the rural poor is a very modest 0.08 per cent, it is significant relative to a loss of − 2.02 per cent which would occur under free trade in the high elasticity scenario.

5   FOOD AND REDISTRIBUTION POLICIES

Two points stand out from the previous discussions. First, it is not easy to find means of raising the incomes of the poorest rural group by using agricultural growth and trade measures. Secondly, changes in trade policy which would greatly benefit the rural sector as a whole, would tend to harm the poorest group. Indeed, in trade matters, this group tends to benefit from the same low food price policies which benefit the urban poor, although their benefits are somewhat smaller.

This leads to the following question: Can one find direct income distribution measures which would benefit the poorest groups without sharply reducing welfare levels of the rural sector as a whole? This question is explored in Table 7.3.

The first group of scenarios explores various excise tax financed food subsidy measures. The excise tax is levied on non-agricultural consumption. As its direct incidence is closely related to the share of income spent on non-agricultural commodities it falls most heavily on the richest urban group. The proceeds of the excise tax are spent on importing additional food and/or on subsidising food rations to various income groups. These rations are assumed to be inframarginal and can therefore be modelled straightforwardly as excise tax-financed income transfers. In scenario 1 the excise tax at the rate of 5.25 per cent is simply used to finance additional wheat imports at the level of US $560 million. The additional wheat is simply released into the open

Table 7.3 The impact of food subsidies and direct redistribution measures on real incomes

Scenarios/ endogenous variables	GNP deflator	Farm profits	Real national wage bill average	Real per capita incomes						Wheat output	Total output
				National average	Rural quartiles			Urban quartiles			
					Poorest	Second	Richest	Poorest	Richest		
Excise tax financed food subsidies											
(1) Foreign wheat supply released into opened market[a]	-9.30	-19.54	-0.80	-1.28	2.20	-0.80	-7.42	9.09	2.58	-9.75	-0.32
(2) Domestic procurement as rations to all urban groups[b]	6.62	8.68	-0.39	0.47	-1.82	-0.37	2.19	4.52	-2.40	0.79	0.19
(3) Foreign supply as rationed to rural and urban poor[c,d]	-5.73	-19.85	-2.04	-0.03	16.07	8.28	-9.07	18.16	-4.13	-14.68	-0.36

(4) Domestic procurement as rationed to rural and urban poor[d]	17.11	20.59	−0.89	0.50	10.07	8.70	4.82	−2.79	−14.51	2.20	0.65
(5) Importing to maintain price level[d, e]	−0.02	−9.76	−1.75	0.10	14.75	8.21	−5.60	12.92	−6.72	−10.46	−0.11
Direct distribution to rural poorest[d]											
(6) Land tax financed	1.84	−1.69	0.33	0.16	13.94	−1.13	−1.12	−1.81	−0.94	0.43	0.06
(7) Excise tax financed	6.49	8.35	−0.31	0.40	13.14	−0.41	2.18	−5.32	−5.12	0.99	0.20

Notes:

[a] This is 51 per cent of scenario (2), Table 1 in Binswanger and Quizon (1984). Excise tax is 5.25 per cent of non-agricultural consumption.

[b] The rations are scaled so as to increase the income of the urban poorest by 10 per cent initially. Excise tax at 5.25 per cent.

[c] Imports approximately US $1.7 billion.

[d] The transfers are scaled to increase the income of the rural poorest by 15 per cent initially. Excise tax 14.5 per cent.

[e] Combines scenario 3 and 4 in a ratio of 3 to 1, i.e., about 25 per cent of added demand is procured domestically.

Sources: Scenarios (1)–(4) are from Binswanger and Quizon (1984). Scenario 5 is computed as discussed in note e. Scenarios (6) and (7) are from Quizon and Binswanger (1986).

market. The same tax revenue is spent in scenario 2 to provide food rations to all urban income groups. The urban rations are not imported but domestically procured. The food rations are the same for each group and provide an initial transfer to the urban poor of 10 per cent of their income. The same ration provides an income transfer of 2.8 per cent of their income to the urban rich.

The simple importation of additional wheat benefits primarily the urban poor whose income rises by 9 per cent. The rural poor also benefit, but their gain is only about 2.2 per cent, smaller than the gain of the urban rich who bear the brunt of the taxation. The rural poor do not gain more because their wage income drops as does their (small) share of farm profits. The real incidence of the excise tax therefore falls on the rural rich who see an erosion of their incomes by 7.4 per cent.

Interestingly, an apparently equally urban-biased policy of providing food rations to all urban groups is made more favourable to the rural sector as a whole, if the supplies are domestically procured without adding to incomes. Consistent with Dantwala's (1867) hypothesis, the rural rich actually gain from such a policy because the price rises more than offset the direct incidence of the excise tax. (For discussions of Dantwala's hypothesis see Hayami *et al.*, 1982 and Schiff, 1986). On the other hand, the urban groups gain less than from a simple increase in imports, and the richest urban group ends up losing absolutely as the incidence of higher food prices and higher non-food prices exceeds the value of the food ration. The rural poor also lose but their loss is less than 2 per cent. Consistent with our earlier findings, neither of these policies is able to affect their real incomes sharply.

How about targeting food rations directly to all poor groups? In scenarios 3 and 4 the poorest and the second quartile of the rural and urban areas receive a fixed and equal food ration which is scaled such that the poorest rural group receives an initial boost of 15 per cent. The same ration translates into nominal income gains of 10 per cent for the second rural quartile, 11 per cent for the first urban quartile, and 9 per cent for the second urban quartile. Thus the programme provides nearly identical initial benefits to the urban poor as the previous programme of urban ration shops only. This targeted programme is much larger in magnitude than the urban fair-price shops, as half of the population now receives food aid. (The total urban population eligible in the previous scenarios is only 20 per cent of India's population.) To provide for the expanded programme by importing, 6 million tons of wheat and 2.1 million tons of rice would have to be imported. The excise tax rate would have to be at 14.75 per cent of household consumption of non-agricultural goods, a very high rate.

When the extra food for the programme is imported (scenario 3), the high income elasticity for food of the rural poor prevents the food prices from falling sharply because of the high level of taxation of the rich. But again, the combination of reduced prices and excise taxes implies that the heaviest burden of the programme falls on the rural rich. While wheat output declines substantially, aggregate agricultural output declines only by 0.36 per cent because the agricultural sector expands its non-wheat production because of changed relative commodity prices. The rural poor do lose some wage income but their gains on the price side more than offset this loss to give them a real income gain of 16 per cent, which exceeds the nominal transfer by 1 per cent.

By shifting from imports to domestic procurement the programme costs can be shifted entirely to the urban population. Prices now rise so sharply that the gain for the urban poor is completely eroded, while the urban rich face a loss of 14.5 per cent in their income. The rural rich, while taxed on their non-food consumption, experience such a sharp rise in farm profits that their real income rises by nearly 5 per cent. The rural poor who share to a very small extent in these profits, still gain about 10 per cent, down from the 15 per cent of the nominal transfer.

In order to achieve its poverty alleviation objectives and tax wealthy groups more evenly, the tax-cum food rations programme would have to be combined with a food import policy aimed not at stabilising food prices, but the price level of the economy. One such scenario is scenario 5 which combines scenarios 3 and 4 in a ratio of 3 to 1, i.e., about one-quarter of the food rations are domestically procured. Because the excise tax tends to increase prices, imports have to be sufficiently large to lead to a drop in agricultural prices and therefore a decline in farm profits. Under price stability, rich rural and urban groups are taxed about evenly. The initial gain of 15 per cent of the rural poor is only minimally eroded, while the initial gain of the urban poor of 10 per cent is increased by nearly 3 per cent because of the decline in food prices.

While scenario 5 appears evenhanded and quite efficient in distributing income, a coalition of the urban and the rural rich is likely to attempt to defeat it because of the high excise tax of almost 14 per cent on their non-food consumption. Can one help the rural poorest more directly with a modest programme aimed directly at them? Scenarios 6 and 7 aim at raising the income of the rural poorest initially by 15 per cent by providing a direct cash entitlement. Note that the transfer costs of these redistributive measures are ignored. The immediate cost of this redistribution is carried by the rural rich in the case of when a land tax is used to finance cash transfers. However, the land tax would also fall on smaller farmers. The excise tax has, of course, a much wider initial incidence, especially on the urban rich.

Redistribution to the poor adds to food demand because of their high income elasticity compared to the richer groups. This demand is not accommodated by imports so that food prices rise. The benefits to the poor rural group is therefore somewhat eroded, but not by much. The food price rises compete food away from the urban groups and the urban poor lose, especially when they also have to pay directly via excise taxes. The major difference from changing the financing from land or through land reform is that it shifts the costs entirely to the urban groups. The rural rich end up gaining because of the food price rises. Of course it is possible to combine these distributional scenarios with import policies which achieve price stability. When that is done the final incidence of the tax falls squarely on those who are taxed initially.

6 CONCLUSION

During the past two decades, Indian agricultural output has grown at an annual rate of 2.7 per cent, which is extremely high by international standards. The technical changes associated with the Green Revolution have been an important part of this increased output, and there is no question that, had they not occurred, India would be far worse off today than she is. During the early Green Revolution period (1965–66), the real per capita income of the rural population of India rose by about 8 per cent. However, these gains were rapidly eroded. The sobering point is that in 1980–81 real rural per capita income appears to have been only about 2 per cent higher than in 1960–61.

The early productivity gains of the Green Revolution were retained by the agricultural sector because Indian policy-makers used these gains to reduce imports of foods. Food prices therefore continued to rise slightly. But when near self-sufficiency was reached, all the extra output had to be absorbed domestically. Foodgrain prices declined, and terms of trade moved substantially against agriculture. The benefits of the productivity gains were thereby transferred to consumers, a classic case of the agricultural treadmill.

The early Green Revolution period was associated with a sharp rise in residual farm profits, while the real wage bill rose much more modestly. The real income gain of that period was distributed regressively; large farmers gained the most, while the rural poor gained very little. However, the subsequent rapid drop of about 25 per cent in residual farm profits reduced per capita incomes of the rural rich to their 1960–61 levels. By 1980–81 both the absolute level of real rural per capita income and its distribution appear to have returned to about what they were in 1960–61.

Real rural wages (as measured by actual data) appear to have risen somewhat during the early Green Revolution but then dropped back so that by 1980–81 they were barely above the 1960–61 level. Agricultural employment (as measured by the model) rose substantially, but at a rate slower than rural labour force growth. The rural poorest did not lose too much only because they shared somewhat in farm profit growth, in non-agricultural income growth, and in the consumer benefits from declining agricultural terms of trade.

The simulation suggests that it is extremely difficult to raise substantially agricultural labour incomes via agricultural development. When the expansion of agricultural output is confined from the domestic demand side, the initial reduction in labour requirements, arising from enhanced efficiency in agriculture, cannot be offset via output expansion. But even when export markets are used to prevent price declines, the real wage bills hardly rise. This conclusion could only be altered if higher farm profits were spent on labour-intensive home goods of the rural sector, a linkage not included in the model (but see, for example, Mellor, 1976 and Hazell and Roell, 1983). These consumer demand linkages, however, can operate only when farm profits are high, i.e., when food prices do not decline. But if prices do not decline, net food buyers, including poor rural workers, cannot benefit as consumers here. In a more complete model than the one presented here, a trade-off would therefore exist between benefiting the rural poor via price declines or via additional employment induced by consumer demand linkages.

What explains the remarkable stability of the agricultural wage bill in our basic model? The very small response in the wages is not caused by elastic labour supply. The total supply elasticity of rural labour, including the migration response, is less than 0.5. Demand for labour is also inelastic (-0.48) and thus cannot account for the limited wage response. Indeed, as shown elsewhere, when labour is withdrawn for rural areas because of reduced fertility, real rural wages increase sharply.

Instead the limited employment response arises from the inelastic supply of aggregate agricultural output. Even though individual crop supply elasticities are fairly large, when one crop expands it must compete with other crops for resources such as land, at least in the short run.[4] Thus the aggregate supply elasticity is what matters. Enhanced efficiency will result in increased farm profits/land rents rather than in expanded employment if aggregate supply is inelastic. Constraints on international demand for India's major crop rice and on the aggregate supply elasticity therefore suggests that trade liberalisation affecting only agriculture would not benefit the rural poor.

Agricultural development measures, on the other hand, assist small farmers, the other poor rural group, almost irrespective of the trade policy context. This is, of course, consistent with *a priori* expectations. The only caveat is that the measures actually do reach the small farmers.

Our food policy scenarios suggest that it is possible to increase the incomes of both the rural and the urban poor while taxing the rich groups in both sectors by using a combination of food rations targeted to all poor in rural and urban areas. But such a scheme can only be effective if the additional demand for food is accommodated by imports to stabilise the price level. The costs of such a programme can be shifted entirely to the rural rich by letting prices decline; or it can be shifted entirely to the urban sector by procuring the entire rations domestically. In the latter case the urban poor gain nothing from the elaborate tax-cum ration-shop scheme, while the gains of the rural poorest are substantially eroded. We also note that the taxation level required to implement a substantial redistributive scheme are very high. They can only be reduced by targeting the food rations or other cash transfers more narrowly to the poorest segments. As is well known, all these options are politically difficult. Sharper targeting erodes the political support for distributive measures, while less targeting leads to sharper opposition from the groups which have to be taxed explicitly.

Assisting the rural poor, who rely on labour income and are the net buyers of food whether the additional food is a result of agricultural development or direct transfers, is clearly not easy. Evenly spread efficiency improvements do help them, but not nearly as fast as one would hope. When then are the elements of a strategy for alleviating the plight of these groups? A strategy must focus on reducing labour supply in the long run via demographic change. We have explored such scenarios elsewhere, In addition, non-agricultural labour demand must start to grow more rapidly. This calls for accelerating non-agricultural growth (either on urban or rural land), and for reducing distortions which reduce the efficiency of capital and increase the capital labour ratios in all sectors of the economy. While these are old themes, this paper emphasises the crucial role of holding food prices down in economies where the poor are net buyers of food (see World Bank, 1966; or Mellor, 1976, and de Janvry and Sadoulet, in press). Agricultural development which increases self-sufficiency, but does not produce lower food prices, cannot help these groups very much. While the rural poorest are not as vulnerable to food price changes as poor urban groups, their income is not nearly as buffered with respect to food prices as that of the small farmers.

Notes

* The authors are staff members and consultants of the World Bank. However, the World Bank does not accept responsibility for the views expressed herein which are those of the authors and should not be attributed to the World Bank or to its affiliated organisations. The findings, interpretations and conclusions are the results of research supported in part by the Bank; they do not necessarily represent the official policy of the Bank. The designations employed and the presentation of material in this document are solely for the convenience of the reader and do not imply the expression of any opinion whatsoever on the part of the World Bank or its affiliates concerning the legal status of any country, territory, area or of its authorities, or concerning the delimitation of its boundaries or national affiliation.

1. For a fuller discussion of data sources and estimation of parameter values, see Pal and Quizon (1983).
2. For a detailed discussion of how technical change is introduced in the model, see Appendix III of Quizon and Binswanger (1984).
3. For a more complete analysis of fertiliser policy, see Quizon (1985).
4. For a detailed discussion of aggregate supply issues, see Binswanger *et al.* (1985).

References

Bardhan, P. (1984) 'Determinants of Supply and Demand for Labor in a Poor Agrarian Economy: An Analysis of Household Survey Data in Rural West Bengal', in Binswanger, H. and Rosenzweig, M. (eds) *Contractural Arrangements, Employment and Wages in Rural Labor Markets in Asia* (New Haven, Conn.: Yale University Press).

Binswanger, H. P. and Quizon, J. B. (1984) 'Distributional Consequences of Alternative Food Policies in India', Discussion paper 20, Research Unit, Agricultural and Rural Development Department, The World Bank.

Binswanger, H. P. and Quizon, J. B. (1986) 'Distributional Consequences of Alternative Food Policies in India', in Pinshrup-Anderson, P. (ed.),

Consumer-Oriented Food Subsidies: Costs, Benefits, and Policy Options for Developing Countries (Baltimore, Md.: Johns Hopkins University Press).

Binswanger, H., Mundlak, Y., Yang, M. C. and Bowers, A. (1985) *Estimation of Aggregate Agricultural Supply Response* (Washington, DC: World Bank, Agricultural and Rural Development) Report no. ARU-48, August.

Dantwala, M. L. (1967) 'Incentives and Disincentives in India Agriculture', *Indian Journal of Agricultural Economics*, vol. 22, pp. 1–25.

Evenson, R. E. and Binswanger, H. P. (1984) 'Estimating Labor Demand Function for Indian Agriculture', in Binswanger, H. and Rosenzweig, M., (eds), *Contractual Arrangements, Employment, and Wages in Labor Markets in Asia* (New Haven, Conn.: Yale University Press).

Falcon, W. P. and Monke, E. A. (1979–80) 'International Trade in Rice', *Food Research Institute Studies*, vol. XVII, pp. 279–306.

Hayami, Y., Subbarao, K. and Otsuka, K. (1982) 'Efficiency and Equity in the Producer Levy of India', *American Journal of Agricultural Economics*, vol. 64, Nov., pp. 655–63.

Hazell, P., and Roell, A. (1983) Rural Growth Linkages: Household Expenditure Patterns in Malaysia and Nigeria", International Food Policy Research Institute, Research Report no. 41, September.

Janvry, A. de and Sadoulet, E. (1987) 'Agricultural Price Policy in General Equilibrium Frameworks: Results and Comparisons', *American Journal of Agricultural Economics*, vol. 69, no. 2, pp. 230–46.

Krishna, R. (1976) *Rural Unemployment: A Survey of Concepts and Estimates for India* (Washington, DC: World Bank Staff Working Paper, no. 234).

Mellor, J. W. (1976) *The New Economics of Growth: A Strategy for India and the Developing World* (Ithaca, N.Y.: Cornell University Press).

Pal, R. and Quizon, J. (1983) *Factor Costs, Income and Supply Shares in Indian Agriculture* (Washington, DC: World Bank, Agriculture and Rural Development Department) Report no. ARU-6, December.

Quizon, J. B. (1985) 'Withdrawal of Fertilizer Subsidies: An Economic Appraisal', *Economic and Political Weekly*, vol. 29, 28 September pp. A.117–A.123.

Quizon, J. B. and Barbeiri, J. (1985) *The Economic Consequences of an Open Trade Policy for Rice in India* (Washington, DC: World Bank Agriculture and Rural Development Department) Report no. ARU-39, June.

Quizon, J. B. and Binswanger, H. P. (1984) Factor Gains and Losses in the Indian Semi-arid Tropics: A Didactic Approach. World Bank, Agriculture and Rural Development Department, Agricultural Research Unit Discussion Paper No. 9.

Quizon, J. B. and Binswanger, H. P. (1986) 'Modelling the Impact of Agricultural Growth and Government Policy on Income Distribution in India', *World Bank Economic Review*, vol. 1. September, pp. 103–48.

Rosenzweig, M. R. (1980) 'Neoclassical Theory and the Optimizing Peasant: An Econometric Analysis of Market Family Labor Supply in a Developing Country', *Quarterly Journal of Economics*, vol. 95, February, pp. 31–55.

Rosenzweig, M. R. (1984) 'Determinants of Wage Rates and Labor Supply Behavior in the Rural Sector of a Developing Country' in Binswanger, H. P. and Rosenzweig, M. R. (eds) *Contracted Arrangements Employment and Wages in Rural Labor Markets in Asia* (New Haven: Yale University Press).

Schiff, M. (1986) *India's Procurement Policy: Consequence for Producer and Consumer Prices* (Washington, DC: World Bank, Development Research Department) March.

Siamwalla, A. and Haykin, S. (1983) *The World Rice Market: Structure, Conduct and Performance* (International Food Policy Research Institute) Research Report 39, June.

Taylor, L. (1979) *Macro Models for Developing Countries* (New York: McGraw-Hill).

World Bank (1986) *Poverty and Hunger: Issues and Options for Food Security in Developing Countries* (Washington, DC: World Bank Policy Study).

Discussion on Part II

PAPER BY ALAIN DE JANVRY AND ELISABETH SADOULET

'Growth and Equity in Agriculture-led Growth'

Commenting on the paper, Professor Dasgupta noted that, instead of combining countries as they did, the authors could have classified the countries into different types of economies, i.e., those characterised by industrial-led growth into one group, those promoting both agricultural sector-led growth and industrial sector-led growth into another, and those with agricultural sector-led growth into another, and those with agricultural sector-led growth into a third. He asked if the authors had estimated an equity coefficient. He pointed out that the authors wrote about how equity helped produce agricultural growth, but did not write about how agricultural growth helped produce equity. Reductions in infant mortality and increases in levels of income were indicators of equitable growth. Their main conclusion that the greater the inequity of the income distribution the less the income-increasing effect will be was insufficient for policy purposes. Bruce has pointed out the importance of land reform in promoting growth and Mellor the importance of the demand for non-tradable commodities in increasing growth.

Professor de Janvry replied that time series would be required to provide an indicator of how equity in the income distribution increased over time. Infant mortality and income distribution were correlated. Agricultural sector-led growth led to growth in the informal non-traded commodity sector. Greater equity could result from a redistribution of land. Mellor and Johnston held that land reform led to peasant-based growth, and Mellor was right in holding agricultural sector-led growth led to more growth in the informal sector the more unequal the income distribution.

A discussant added that agricultural industry-led growth should be included. A country could capitalise on import substitution (wheat, for example, when the high-yield varieties replaced imported wheat in India), but then another agency of growth was needed – an industry.

de Janvry replied that the reason for this model stemmed from this exigency. It was necessary to capitalise on the engine of growth. Herein was the Indian economy's defect. The model basically portrayed a transitional strategy for capitalising on agricultural growth.

Another discussant commented, 'In several developing countries there are uneven growth rates in different regions. Is it possible to disaggregate this model by region? Agricultural policy has to be understood in the context of a general equilibrium model but, in doing this, one encounters large black boxes'. de Janvry replied that general equilibrium models do contain large black boxes. With a smaller, disaggregated model, we can pin down the income distribution effects of growth in an economy.

PAPER BY V. M. RAO

'Impact of Rural Development Programmes on the Economic Structure of Rural Communities'

Dr Gopalakrishna Kumar, the invited discussant, pointed out that the paper had two themes: the administrative and other dimensions of government intervention in rural development, and the socio-economic changes resulting from the process of agricultural development. Karnataka was a particularly interesting instance where both these themes could be developed together; the administrative system had become much more decentralised in recent years, and rapid socio-economic changes had also occurred, disrupting traditional class and caste hierarchies. While the analysis of the village communities in the paper contributed many valuable insights, a concluding section could have attempted to address the two themes referred to above more directly. In particular, the findings of the survey could have been assessed in the light of recent writings on the importance of market interlinkages in poor agrarian economies, and comments on the increasing economic role of caste alliances would have been interesting.

The author, Dr Rao, replied that his study was mainly impressionistic. It was meant to argue for state intervention to eradicate poverty. Creation of preconditions for development would then be positive. The object was to assess the impact of development programmes on income, asset formation, employment and shifts in internal household structure. It was also designed to gain an insight into how other rural dimensions were changing. Without entitlements, creation of assets and diversification of the internal structure of village economy, rural development was not viable. The salient finding was that in villages the landless were becoming more dependent on the government and less on the local élite.

Dr Binayak Rath (Indian Institute of Technology, Kanpur) then drew attention to the fact that the conclusion, on the basis of the Karnataka experience, was that state intervention could help rural communities to enter the mainstream of growth and development. On the basis of his own study (the evaluation of IRDP in Uttar Pradesh, including food-for-work programmes and other special component programmes, namely, low-cost housing and marketing complexes) this conclusion might not hold. Dr Rao had stated that cultivators gaining in viability and the labourers turning to the state for economic support were responsible for the diminution of the power of the rural élite. In fact, Dr Rath's study in Uttar Pradesh revealed, first, that the cultivators were not gaining any viability, and the labourers were not turning to the state for any economic support. On the contrary, the people felt these state interventions were responsible for their increased misery and heavier burdens. Second, Dr Rath and his colleagues had pointed out that these programmes were making the rural group more outward looking. But in the evaluation of some of the low-cost housing programmes it was found that the people were regressing and were not interested in participating in any of these schemes. Third, in the Uttar Pradesh study it was mentioned that rural groups were participating in the political processes of the village and on the local level. These rural groups were again the rural élitists. Findings from this study contradicted the observations in the paper that there was diminution of the hold of the rural élite.

The questions and comments that followed were concerned with whether it would have been better if small farmers with holdings below five hectares, and how they were benefited, would have been considered separately rather than combining them with landowners with holdings of five to ten hectares in the category of small- and medium-sized holdings. It was also asked which class group of what caste and income level was taking the lead and availing themselves of opportunity for alignment with political leaders.

It was noted that the conclusion that the programme would certainly go some way in improving the economic viability of the small and medium cultivators was too weak. The question was whether the programme would go the desired way and not some other way; and that the success of the programme as between labourers (people without land, resources, or skills) favoured the latter. What specific factors had made the difference in Karnataka between the small- and medium-sized farmers and the rural rich, or was this a supposition based on the small number of the rural rich? In regard to the wage, was it the market wage, the minimum wage, or any wage that the unemployed might accept in desperation?

Medium and small farmers were looking to other investments. The introduction of sericulture and eucalyptus oil extraction had made farmers move toward cash employment. It should have been questioned as to whether state intervention would really be useful since benefits did not percolate downward.

V. M. Rao replied, 'The paper had only described regional experience. The state could only implement schemes. The importance of voluntary organisations within a region had also to be considered'.

PAPER BY HANS P. BINSWANGER AND JAIME B. QUIZON

'What can Agriculture do for the Poorest Rural Groups?'

Dr Scandizzo, the invited discussant of the paper, commented that savings and fiscal flows were not accounted for in the model. This was a one-sector model. Trade-offs with other sectors were not taken into consideration. Conclusions, therefore, did not have a bearing on policy. For example, keeping agricultural prices low would benefit poorer groups, but what would the effects be on other groups? Trade liberalisation would also benefit poorer consumers.

Dr Binswanger replied that this was a three- to five-year model. Agricultural development helping the rural poor was not an assumption. The rural poor might suffer from higher agricultural prices because they were net buyers of food, spending as much as 70 to 80 per cent of their budgets on food. The employment multiplier of agricultural development might be less than one. The question was, what is more important to the rural poor, the employment benefits or the low food price benefits? Variables were omitted from the model, for example, agricultural investment and stock of non-farm goods. Agricultural investment in equipment reduced the demand for labour. If the rural poor increased their stock of non-farm goods, their non-agricultural activities would increase. But the conclusions of the model would be the same. A high price strategy for agricultural commodities would lead to more employment but food prices would increase.

Income redistribution effects of the high-yield varieties and concommitant price policies were of benefit to large farmers in the 1960s. The

1970s saw little efficiency growth. The rural rich lost, but the rural poor gained from the decline in wheat prices because the government decided not to export. The major conclusion was that gains from agricultural development are very much conditioned on governmental trade decisions.

Two questioners asked about differences between poor groups; intrahousehold differences; and which was more important for the economic welfare of the rural poor, trade reform or social institutional reform? Dr Binswanger replied that it was difficult to differentiate between income groups in so far as macroeconomic policy is concerned. It was also difficult to include intrahousehold differences in macroeconomic models. But India was certainly better off, because of the green revolution, than it would otherwise have been.

Part III

Agriculture and Industry under Capitalism

8 On the Nature and Implications of Intersectoral Resource Allocations: Argentina 1913–84*

Domingo Cavallo

INSTITUTO DE ESTUDIOS ECONOMICOS
SOBRE LA REALIDAD ARGENTINA Y
LATINO AMERICANO

Yair Mundlak

HEBREW UNIVERSITY OF JERUSALEM,
UNIVERSITY OF CHICAGO AND IFPRI

1 INTRODUCTION

Economic growth generates important changes in the sectoral composition of the economy. In the early stages of growth, the economy is largely rural, whereas in mature economies, agriculture constitutes only a small fraction of the economy. As a good part of the world's population still lives in rural areas, it is of great interest to understand the dynamics of this process. The subject of sectoral growth can be placed in a broader perspective, since the process of growth in mature economies generates other sectoral changes of great importance, such as a shift towards services. This process has many similarities to the process of industrialisation.

To review, the main determinants of sectoral growth operate along the following lines: Overall growth increases the consumption possibilities. The utility functions of consumers are not homothetic and the income elasticity for food is less than one, and in general, considerably less than one. Also, the price elasticity of demand for food is low. Thus,

143

an equiproportionate increase in output must cause an excess supply in the income inelastic sector. As a consequence, its relative price declines, and the lower the price elasticity the larger is the decline in price caused by a given amount of excess supply. As a result, the value output to be distributed to factors of production in agriculture declines, their rates of return decline relative to those obtained in non-agriculture and resources move away from agriculture to non-agriculture.

This is a simplified statement of the process and as such it abstracts many pertinent details which do not change the overall picture. Yet the above description applies to a closed economy and therefore, on the face of it, the behaviour of open economies, such as Argentina, should be different. However, the world is a closed economy, and since the process is common to all countries, a global excess supply is generated by the aforementioned process, causing world agricultural prices to decline, and thereby exporting countries are affected. In a recent study it was reported that the trend components of prices of the main agricultural products, deflated by US wholesale prices, declined over the period 1900–84 at a rate of 0.5, or more, per cent per annum (Binswanger *et al.*, 1985). Thus, the adjustment called for in factor allocation does not skip over exporting countries.

The basic determinant of the process is the income elasticity which is an empirical quantity. Many of the studies report income elasticities of food. As income increases, food is purchased with an increasing component of non-agricultural inputs and, therefore, the income elasticity for the agricultural product is smaller than that reported for food (see Mundlak, 1985b).

The description of the process is conditional on the existence of economic growth. While the subject of the determinants of growth is beyond the scope of this paper, and therefore growth is in general taken to be exogenous, yet, some aspects of this are pertinent for our discussion. Growth is generated by an accumulaton of physical and human capital and technical change which itself depends on the pace of capital accumulation. This is true, both for the rate of technical change and for its factor bias. The bare fact is that increases in the capital–labour ratio generate incentives for innovations of labour-saving techniques (Mundlak, 1985a). Thus, even though the process of sectoral growth calls for a movement of resources out of agriculture, it is applied differentially to labour and to capital.

With these qualifications we can introduce the main subject of this paper, the intersectoral resource allocation. It is well known that there are wide intersectoral gaps in wage rates. Thus it cannot be assumed that the resource allocation at any time is in equilibrium in the comparative statics sense. This has repercussions on almost any empirical question, specifically the evaluation of the determinants of resource allocation and the changes that can be expected to take place over time. The implication of this in studying the sectoral growth path of the economy is demonstrated in our study of the growth of the Argentinian economy over the period 1947–72 (Cavallo and Mundlak, 1982). The particular formulation used for sectoral growth made it possible to evaluate the consequences of important economic policies implemented in Argentina, which were largely taxing agriculture, either directly through export tax, or indirectly by protection of non-agriculture, maintaining a large and highly inefficient public sector and, not independently, a highly appreciated peso. This policy, our study has shown, caused agricultural growth to lag behind that observed in other countries growing grain and livestock, such as the USA.

In view of the importance of the findings, we have made an effort to enlarge the data base and a time series of the main variables has been constructed for the period 1913–84.[1] In what follows we bring some preliminary results based on the extended data.

2 LABOUR ALLOCATION[2]

The intersectoral labour allocation can be analysed within the framework of occupational choice. However, in the case of agriculture, a choice of non-agricultural occupation often implies a geographical mobility and as such entails a cost of migration. The cost depends on the distance from the non-agricultural labour markets. In mature economies, such as Western Europe, Japan, and important parts of the USA, this distance has shrunk due to motorisation, elaborate transportation systems, and the urbanisation of rural areas. It has been reduced to the extent that it is now possible to choose a convex combination of two occupations rather than be faced with a discrete choice. As a consequence, large parts of agriculture have become part-time farming, with the family labour divided between agriculture and non-agriculture.

In formulating the problem of occupational choice a distinction is made between landless labour and farm owners. Many of the issues can be introduced in the framework of landless labour, with which we begin. The choice can be studied within the framework of time allocation. Let $U(y,t_L)$ be the utility function expressed in terms of income y, and time spent on leisure, t_L. The function is weakly separable with respect to the composition of consumption and therefore y is a sufficient statistic for the non-leisure consumption. The allocation of time between leisure and work (t_w) is determined so as to maximise the Langrangian equation

$$L = U(y,t_L) - \lambda_1(y - wt_w) - \lambda_2(t - t_L - t_w) \qquad (1)$$

where w is the wage rate, t is the time availability and assuming no other source of income. Solving the problem and introducing the optimal quantities, $t_L(w)$ and $t_w(w)$ into the utility function results in the indirect utility function:

$$v(w) = \max \{U(y,t_L); y = wt_w, t = t_L + t_w\} \qquad (2)$$

$$v'(w) > 0$$

The problem can be formulated as a lifetime choice. In this simple formulation the decision in one period does not affect the decision in another period. Thus, the disconnected stream of utility evaluated for an individual of age g is

$$V(w,g) = \int_g^T e^{-r\tau} v(w(\tau)d\tau) \qquad (3)$$

The indirect utility is derived for each of the possible occupations and the choice is for the occupation with the highest level of utility taking into account the cost of changing occupation, which is referred to here as the cost of migration.

The cost of migration can be introduced into the indirect utility function. Thus, $V(w_n, C(\cdot))$ is the level of utility achievable at wage rate w_n in non-agriculture, and cost of migration $C(\cdot)$, $\partial V/\partial C < 0$. Let the path of wage rate in agriculture be w_a. Then a landless labourer will migrate from agriculture if

$$V(w_n,g,C(\cdot)) > V(w_a,g) \qquad (4)$$

The off-farm labour migration is a universal phenomenon which continues over a long period of time. The question is why it takes so long before it comes to an end. If non-agriculture is more attractive, then all the labour should leave at once. Thus, in order to allow for a gradual adjustment, other considerations have to be brought in. First is age (g). Other things being equal, the younger the person is, the larger the integral in (3) and at the same time, by assumption, the smaller the cost of migration. Thus, we write $C(g)$.

Another variable which affects the cost of migration is the distance, d, from the non-agricultural labour market. The larger is the distance, the larger is the cost, thus the cost is written as $C(g,d)$.

Migration takes place in spite of existing unemployment in non-agriculture. This phenomenon was explained by Toddaro (1969) by suggesting that the decision takes place according to expected wage rate rather than actual wage rate, where the expected wage is the product of the wage rate and the probability of getting a job, q_n. This implicitly assumes risk neutrality. When the wage differential is high, it pays to migrate even when the probability of getting a job is less than one. The same consideration also applies to agriculture. Thus, we can rewrite (4) as:

$$V(w_n q_n, \ g, C(g, \ d)) > V(w_a \ q_a, g) \qquad (5)$$
$$+ + \quad - -(+,+) \qquad + \ + \ -$$

where the signs indicate the sign of the partial derivatives. Other variables may influence the decision. Education may contribute in various ways. It is likely to reduce the cost of migration and increase the probability of getting a job.

The choice faced by a farm operator is between operating the farm or working in non-agriculture. Whenever the distance to the non-agricultural labour market allows it, a convex combination of the two is also possible. The employment opportunities on the farm can be summarised by deriving a constrained profit function. Let x be the output, p its price, v a vector of variable inputs including hired labour, but not own labour, and k a vector of constraints, including quasi-fixed inputs. The production function is $F(x,v,k,t_a) = 0$, where t_a is the farmer's time worked on the farm. Then, the restricted profit function is:

$$\pi(t_a, \ p, \ w, \ k) = \max \{px - wv; \ F(x,v,k,t_a) = 0\} \qquad (6)$$
$$+ \ \ + \ \ - \ \ + \quad v,x$$

In what follows, we write $z = (p,w,k)$. The evaluation of the present value of the stream of the restricted profit is discussed briefly in the next section. Let the maximum of the present value, obtained by choosing an optimal path of inputs over time, be $\Pi(t_a,z)$ (see Epstein, 1981). The prices and k are now the present expectations of the future values. The time allocation of the farm owner is determined by replacing $\Pi(t_a,z)$ for wt_w in (1). Substitute the solution $t_a(z)$ in $\Pi(t_a,z)$ to obtain $\Pi(z)$. Then, the indirect utility function for the farm owner is $V(z,g)$, and the farmer will remain in agriculture as long as

$$V(z,g) > V(w_n q_n, g, C(g,d)) \tag{7}$$

The analysis can be generalised to accommodate part-time farming by rewriting the constraints in (1) to allow for off-farm work and income. This is not essential for our purpose.

The main difference in the decision between the farm owner and the landless labourer is that the determinants of agricultural profitability enter explicitly into the decision criterion of the farm owner. Thus, other things being equal, the larger the profitability of agriculture, the smaller should be the off-farm migration.

In order to derive a migration function we introduce an index function h which takes values 0,1 to be determined by:

$$
\begin{aligned}
[V_j(n) - V_j(a)]h_j &\geqslant 0 \tag{8}\\
+ \quad & 1\\
-,0 \quad & 0
\end{aligned}
$$

where $V_j(n)$ and $V_j(a)$ are the indirect utility functions for an individual j evaluated for the conditions in non-agriculture and agriculture respectively. The arguments of $V_j(a)$ are those appearing in (7) and (5) for farm operator and landless labourer respectively. The argument of $V_j(n)$ is the same in (7) and (5). Thus, $h(a,n)$ is a function of the arguments of $V_j(n)$ and of $V_j(a)$. Summing h_j over the agricultural labour force gives the number of migrants:

$$M(a,n) = \sum_{j=1}^{L_a} h_j(a,n) \tag{9}$$

Before continuing, it should be mentioned that the analysis could be made symmetric and applied to non-agricultural labour, in which case the cost of migration will appear in $V(a)$. In that case, the summation will be over the individuals in non-agriculture. Let this be denoted by an expression similar to (9) with the sectoral order in the argument reversed:

$$M(n,a) = \sum_{j=1}^{L_n} h_j(n,a) \tag{10}$$

and the net off-farm migration will be:

$$M = M(a,n) + M(n,a) \tag{11}$$

Of course, M is a function of (a,n).

To suppress the scale, we deal with the migration rate, $m = M/L_a$, the migration as a proportion of the agricultural labour force.

The empirical formulation of the migration equation is explained in Mundlak (1979). The basic form is:

$$1n(m + c_0) = \beta_0 + \beta_1 1n(\delta - c_1) + \beta_2 1n(RL) + \beta_3 z + e$$

$$e \sim N(0,\sigma_e^2)$$

where δ is a measure of intersectoral wage or income differential, $RL = L_n/L_a$ is the ratio of the labour force in the two sectors, and z stands for other variables that might enter the equation. The βs are coefficients to be estimated, c_0 is a non-negative constant. When there is negative migration, c_0 is set to be positive. In this study it was taken to be 0.04. The second constant, c_1, determines the value of δ at which migration becomes zero. In this study it was set to zero for computational convenience and the analysis will later on be extended to search for other values of c_1. In Cavallo and Mundlak (1982) we used $c_1 = 1.25$.[3]

In the present study we use the intersectoral wage ratio for δ, $\delta = w_a/w_n$, RL as defined above. Unemployment in non-agriculture, U, is computed from $([\bar{Y}_n(t)]/[Y_n(t)] - 1 + 0.05) = u$, where Y_n is non-agricultural GDP, $\bar{Y}_n(t)$ is the $\max_{0 < i < t} Y_n(t - i)$. It turns out that the best results were obtained with unemployment lagged three years. Finally, we use the price of land, PA, as a summary variable for agricultural profitability. It is a price index divided by the *GDP* deflator. The best empirical result was obtained with a 2-year lag for PA.

The data are discussed in *Estudios* no. 39 (IEERAL, 1986). The major task was to construct a consistent labour series based on the

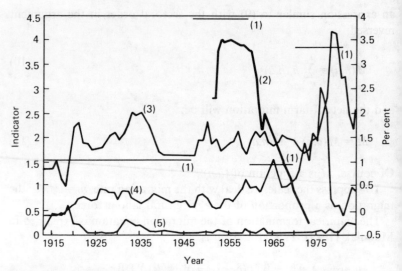

Figure 8.1 Labour migrations compared with wages, land prices and un-employment (Argentina 1913–84)

(1) Intercensus average migration rate (right scale)
(2) Annual migration rate (right scale)

Agricultural migrants as percentage of agricultural labour (see text)

(3) Wage ratio (agricultural/non-agricultural)$^{-1}$ (left scale)
(4) Price of land (left scale)
(5) Unemployment (left scale) in non-agriculture related to GDP (actual) (see text)

census data and other existing time series for part of the period. The variables used in the analysis are plotted in Figure 8.1.

The estimated equation for 1914–80 is:

$$ln(m + 0.04) = -4.393 - 1.476\, ln(wR) + 0.074\, ln(LR)(t - 2)$$
$$(11.4) \quad (3.31) \qquad\qquad (0.64)$$

$$- 0.256\, lnU(t - 3) - 0.871\, lnPA(t - 2)$$
$$(1.71) \qquad\qquad (4.15)$$

$$R^2 = 0.993, \text{ D.W.} = 2.282$$

where: m is the (net) proportion of the labour force that migrated from agriculture during year t. Numbers in parentheses are t-statistics. The elasticities with respect to the wage ratio and land price are:

$$E(m,wR) = -4.32 \quad E(m,PA) = -2.55.$$

All the variables have the correct sign and the two price variables are significantly different from zero. The composition of the labour force, as measured here by LR, is not significant. That implies that the size of the labour force in non-agriculture did not affect the migration rate. This can be explained in part by the importance of the unemployment variable. It appears that unemployment was the dominant force. The elasticities of migration with respect to prices are sizeable indeed. In Cavallo and Mundlak (1982) estimates of the migration equation were presented for the period 1940–73, with a somewhat differently constructed labour data, and all the variables were 3-year moving averages, a procedure which introduced serial correlation. To eliminate it, the equation included a lagged dependent variable. The equation was obtained with a value of $c_1 = 1.25$, and $c_0 = 0.06$. The equation did not include the price of land. The elasticity of migration with respect to wage ratio was -4.4. The similarity of this value to the one obtained here is surprisingly close. Furthermore, it was quite robust to some modifications in the specification.

3   CAPITAL ALLOCATION – EMPIRICAL RESULTS

The intersectoral allocation of capital is done primarily through the allocation of gross investment. Recent analysis of investment behaviour is centred on the cost of adjustment, an idea initiated by Eisner and Strotz (1963) and developed by Gould (1968), Lucas (1967), and Tradeway (1969). The idea was developed to account for the fact that whenever there is a gap between the existing and optimal stocks of capital, firms do not close it in one jump. The adjustment requires time to complete. It was therefore postulated that investment requires diversion of resources away from production. This view implies a transformation curve representing a trade-off between output of final product and the build-up of the capital stock of the firm. The empirical work that has evolved from this approach is not quite conclusive.

The internal cost of adjustment seems to be primarily important in analysing the behaviour of the individual firm. However, when dealing with the industry as a whole, there is another important force that dictates a gradual adjustment of the capital stock. This is related to the availability of resources as reflected in the supply of capital goods. Thus, there are limitations which are external to the firm which are referred to as external cost of adjustment. External cost of adjustment was recognised in the original work of Eisner and Strotz and was applied by Mussa (1977). In some sense, the limitation of the factor supply function is similar to the limitation that the demand for the final product imposes on a competitive industry, a subject incorporated by Lucas and Prescott (1971) in their study of investment.

It is difficult at this point to assess the quantitative importance of the internal cost of adjustment. Be it what it may, it is postulated that the main force that drives the intersectoral allocation of investment is related to the competition of a particular sector with other sectors for existing resources. The limitation of resources reflects saving behaviour in the household and public sectors, as well as international mobility of capital. These are not very responsive to sectoral investment decisions, and can therefore be considered to be exogenous in the present analysis. As a consequence, just as in the analysis of intersectoral allocation of

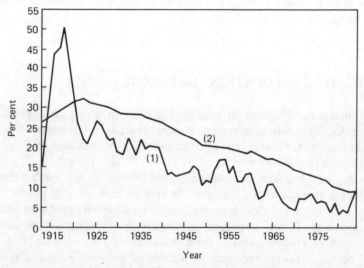

Figure 8.2 Shares of investment and capital stock in agriculture (Argentina 1913–84)

(1) Share of agricultural investment in total investment
(2) Share of agricultural capital stock in total capital stock

labour, the allocation of investment will depend on the intersectoral differential rates of returns. Since empirical studies often do not show dependence of investment on the rates of returns, we begin the discussion by first presenting the empirical results.

The shares of agriculture in total investment and in the capital stock are plotted in Figure 8.2 It is seen that the share of agriculture in the capital stock reached its peak in the early 1920s where it amounted to over 30 per cent, and it has declined since then to a level of 10 per cent. This followed a decline in the share of investment, which was subject to some volatility. The differential returns to capital are plotted in Figure 8.3 together with the price of land. The sectoral rate of return was computed as non-wage income divided by the capital stock, where in agriculture capital stock includes land. The inclusion of land accounts for part of the differential rate of return and therefore the figure should be viewed more as an index number series.

The empirical analysis consisted of regressing the natural logarithm of the share of agriculture in total investment (I_a/I) on the share of agriculture in the capital stock (K_a/K), the differential rate of return,

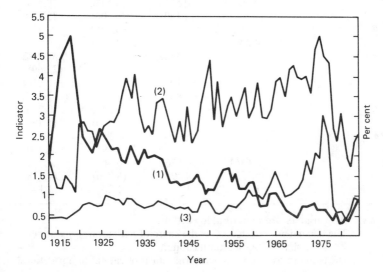

Figure 8.3   Allocation of agricultural investment in relation to land price and differential returns on capital (Argentina 1913–84)

(1) Share of agricultural investment in total investment (scale on the right) (as in Figure 8.2)
(2) Differential returns on capital (non-agriculture/agriculture) (see text)
(3) Price of land as in Figure 8.1, graph 4

which is decomposed into an anticipated component (DR^e) obtained from an $AR(4)$ process, and an unanticipated component (DR^u) which constitutes the difference between the actual (DR) and the anticipated ratio. Also included are the price of land (PA) current and lagged one year, and the dependent variable lagged one year. All variables were taken as natural logarithms. The results are reported in Table 8.1.

The most important result is the strong effect of the differential rate of return on the allocation of investment. When decomposed to its

Table 8.1 Intersectoral allocation of investment (Argentina 1913–84)

Variable/equation:	1	2	3	4
Period	1914–84	1917–84	1914–84	1917–84
R^2	0.904	0.903	0.909	0.905
D.W.	1.794	1.888	1.891	1.901
Constant	0.3411	0.4048	0.3991	0.4836
	(2.620)	(2.335)	(2.081)	(1.901)
Z^k	0.5001	0.5326	0.5330	0.5579
	(3.167)	(3.180)	(3.308)	(3.120)
DR	−0.3523	—	−0.3964	—
	(−4.344)		(−3.533)	
DR^e	—	−0.4602	—	−0.4982
		(−3.268)		(2.569)
DR^u	—	−0.1056	—	−0.2166
		(−0.859)		(−1.557)
PA	—	—	0.2486	0.2067
			(2.200)	(1.803)
PA_{t-1}	—	—	−0.2080	−0.1287
			(−1.195)	(−1.050)
Z_{t-1}	0.5861	0.5367	0.5627	0.5327
	(5.922)	(4.796)	(5.726)	(4.578)
$E(Z,Z^k)$	1.20	1.15	1.28	1.19

Notes: All variables are in natural logarithms.
   The dependent variable, Z, is the share of agricultural investment.
   Z^k is the share of agricultural capital.
   DR is the ratio of non-agricultural return of capital to agricultural return on capital.
   DR^e is the expected values from an $AR(4)$ process for DR.
   DR^u are the residuals from this autoregression.
   PA is an index of the price of land divided by the GDP deflator.
   Subscripts indicate lags in the variable and t-statistics are in parenthesis.
   $E(Z,Z^k)$ is the elasticity of Z with respect to Z^k.

components, it is the anticipated component that has done most of the explanation. The unexpected component becomes marginally important when the price of land is introduced. The price of land constitutes another measure of anticipated profitability. In many ways it appears to be an ideal measure, but this is not quite the case. The price of land includes other components, such as tax shelters, which are not directly related to the present discussion. Still it is informative as a predictor of the profitability of agriculture. In any case, the two measures, price of land and differential rates of returns, seem to be important in explaining investment. The share of agriculture in the capital stock is introduced here to scale the investment. As argued in Cavallo and Mundlak (1982), in the absence of price signals the elasticity of I_a/I with respect to K_a/K should be unity. The actual result appears at the last line of the table. The numbers are somewhat larger than 1. Thus, the reason that the I_a/I is declining is attributed to the differential probability of agriculture.

4 INTERSECTORAL ALLOCATION OF INVESTMENT – THE CONCEPTUAL FRAMEWORK

The underlying optimisation problem is to choose a time path of inputs, where the investment in a given year affects profits in subsequent years. The first part of the discussion is general and, therefore, sectoral designation is omitted. Assume that agriculture produces a single output x with capital, K, labour L, and raw materials v, using a production function $x = f(K,L,v,t)$. The function has constant returns to scale, is concave, and twice differential. To simplify, assume that the supply of labour and raw materials is perfectly elastic with prices w_L and w_v respectively.[4]

The supply price of capital is q. At the industry level q is assumed to depend on the level of investment, $q = q(I,t)$. All the variables are functions of time. The net cash flow of a competitive firm at time t is:

$$R(t) = P(t)F(K(t)), L(t), v(t),t) - w_L(t)L(t) - w_v(t)v(t)$$
$$- q(t)(\dot{K}(t) + \delta(K(t)) - c(\dot{K}) \tag{12}$$

where $c(\dot{K})$ represents the internal cost of adjustment. The non-stochastic problem calls for selecting a time path of inputs that will maximise the present value of the stream of $R(t)$:

$$\max R = \int_0^\infty e^{-rt} R(t) dt \tag{13}$$

subject to

$K(0) = K_0$, where K_0 is given, and
$I(t) = K(t) + \delta K(t)$,

where δ is the rate of depreciation.

$$\lim_{t \to \infty} e^{-rt} R(t) = 0$$

The first-order conditions call for

$$\frac{\partial R(t)}{\partial L} = 0 \to \frac{\partial F}{\partial L} = w_L/p \tag{14}$$

$$\frac{\partial R(t)}{\partial v} = 0 \to \frac{\partial F}{\partial v} = w_v/p \tag{15}$$

and the Euler equation

$$\frac{\partial R(t)}{\partial K} - \frac{d}{dt} \left(\frac{\partial R(t)}{\partial \dot{K}} \right) = 0 \tag{16}$$

The first two conditions imply that along the optimal path, the employment at time t of the inputs which have no effect on revenue in subsequent periods is determined by equating the marginal productivities to their real prices in each period. Consequently, the problem can be solved in steps. First, determine at each period the optimal levels $L(t)$ and $v(t)$ as functions of prices and $K(t)$, $L(K, \cdot)$, $v(K, \cdot)$ respectively, substitute the result in $R(t)$ and obtain a restricted profit function:

$$\Pi(K, \cdot) = PF(K, \cdot_L) - w_v v(K, \cdot) - w_L L(K, \cdot) - q(\dot{K} + \delta K - c\dot{K})$$

where $(K, \cdot) = (K, w_L, w_v, P, t)$

Suppressing the dependence on prices, the problem is to maximise

$$R = \int_0^\infty e^{-rt} \Pi(K(t), \dot{K}(t)) dt \tag{17}$$

subject to the same constraints as (13).

Differentiating, suppressing the time index, the Euler equation is:

$$P\frac{\partial F}{\partial K} - q(\delta + r - \hat{q}) + C'(\dot{K})(\hat{q} - r)q + qC''(K)\ddot{K} = 0 \tag{18}$$

In the absence of internal cost of adjustment, i.e. $C(\dot{K}) = 0$, the optimal time path of $K(t)$, say $K^*(t)$, is obtained by solving (19):

$$\frac{P\partial F(K^*)}{\partial K} - q(\delta + r - \hat{q}) = 0, \tag{19}$$

stating that at the optimal level, the value of marginal productivity is equal to the user cost of capital, allowing for price appreciation. Since K^* is a function of the prices that enter the restricted profit function, a change in prices requires an adjustment in $K^*(t)$, which in the present formulation should be performed in one step. As it is believed that this is not the mode of behaviour of firms, a cost of adjustment was introduced to determine the pace of adjustment from any arbitrary $K(t)$ to the optimal level $K^*(t)$. Let the cost of adjustment be $C(\dot{K}) = \frac{1}{2}\gamma\dot{K}^2$, substitute its derivatives in (18), and solve to obtain a non-explosive solution for the differential equation $(d\dot{K}/dt)$ (Sargent, 1979, chapter 6).

$$\dot{K} = [pF_k - q(\delta + r - \hat{q})]/\gamma q(r - \hat{q}), \ \gamma > 0 \tag{20}$$
$$r > \hat{q}$$

A difference between the marginal productivity of capital and the user cost is closed by adjusting the capital stock. The smaller is the cost of adjustment, as represented by γ, the larger is the adjustment made in any one period, as $\partial\dot{K}/\partial\gamma < 0$.

For reasons stated above, we prefer to examine the behaviour under external cost of adjustment. To simplify things, this is done without internal cost, although the latter can be added when it is pertinent. To begin, suppose that at time t, $K^*(t)$ which solves (19) is different from the available capital, $K(t)$. Thus, a demand for investment is generated at the firm (i) level: $I_i^d(q,t) = K_i^*(q,t) - K_i(t)$. Summing over all firms in the industry, we obtain the industry demand $I^d(q,t) = \Sigma_i I_i^d(q,t)$. And by (19) $\partial I^d(q,t)/\partial q < 0$. Let the supply of capital goods be $q(I^s,t)$, $dq^s/dI > 0$. Write the inverse function, $I^s = I(q,t)$. Then q is determined by equating

$$I^d(q,t) = I^s(q,t). \tag{21}$$

This analysis shifts the gradual response of investment to scarcity of investment goods. This scarcity simply reflects the fact that, at any time, resources are finite, and if more of them are demanded in one industry they have to be bidden away from another industry, a process which requires adjustment in price to equate supply with demand. When properly measured, each firm will fulfil (19). But the price will be so determined as to allocate the investment goods among all producers.

The above result can be obtained as an optimal solution by maximising the social welfare to be determined here as the difference between the consumer surplus and the cost of the capital goods to the industry. The essence of this analysis is that there is a difference between the price of the investment good observed by the firm and the supply price to the industry. This is analogous to the difference that exists in a competitive industry facing externalities between the horizontal summation of the marginal costs of the firms and the industry supply curve.

Applying the analysis to the two-sector economy, the supply of investment good to agriculture $I_a^s(q,t)$ is equal to the investment less the demand by non-agriculture. The latter depends on the profitability in non-agriculture. This outlines the foundation of the empirical analysis.

5 IMPLICATIONS

The two equations discussed above determine the dynamics of the economy as follows. The labour force in agriculture grows at the natural rate less migration. In this we abstract from changes in the participation rates. The labour force in non-agriculture grows at the natural rate plus the off-farm migration. The capital accumulation in the two sectors is determined by the investment allocation equation and the overall investment rate. That outputs change over time according to the resource change and the change in their productivity is a subject not discussed here. The change in outputs and the demand function determines the product prices, which in turn determines factor returns. This process has been formulated in a form which allows a numerical solution. Exogenous changes, which may come from the world markets or from government policies, affect sectoral returns and thereby affect the growth path of the economy. This has been demonstrated in Cavallo and Mundlak (1982) for the period 1950–72 and is now extended to the period 1914–84.

To illustrate the analytic importance of this formulation, we can refer to the numerical evaluation of the aggregate agriculture supply.

Empirical analyses generally conclude that the elasticity of such a function is nearly zero. Such studies relate output to some form of price expectations but, in so doing, the dynamics of the system are ignored. Alternatively, the supply response can be evaluated by computing the response of resource allocation and productivity to a change in the time path of prices.[5] When this is done, substantially different results are obtained.

Notes

*   This chapter reports on a part of a research project on agriculture and economic growth in Argentina conducted jointly by IEERAL and IFPRI. We thank Roberto Domenech for the empirical analysis and José A. Scheinkman for comments.

1.   The data are reported in *Estudios* (IEERAL, 1986). A main change from the previous study is that the analysis is now carried out with annual data rather than 3-year moving averages.

2.   This discussion is based on Mundlak, Lecture Notes: Agriculture and Economic Growth: Theory and Measurement.

3.   The choice of c_1 affects the estimates of the βs. However, the elasticities of m with respect to δ are fairly robust to variations in c_1.

4.   The assumption on the supply price of labour may seem to be inconsistent with the determinants of the agricultural labour force above. It is introduced here in order to simplify the discussion. The integration of the present discussion with the formulation of labour migration does not affect the results in a qualitative way (see Mundlak, *Agricultural and Economic Growth*).

5.   For review and analysis of this subject, see Mundlak (1985c).

References

Binswanger, H., Mundlak, Y., Yang, M. C., and Bowers, A. (1985) 'Estimation of Aggregate Agricultural Supply Response' (Washington, DC: The World Bank, ARU48).

Cavallo, D. and Mundlak, Y. (1982) *Agricultural and Economic Growth in an Open Economy: The Case of Argentina* (Washington, DC: IFPRI).

Eisner, R. and Strotz, R. H. (1963) 'Determinants of Business Investment', in *Commission on Money and Credit, Impact of Monetary Policy* (Englewood Cliff, NJ: Prentice Hall).

Epstein, L. G. (1981) 'Duality Theory and Functional Forms for Dynamic Factor Demands', *Review of Economic Studies*, vol. 48, pp. 81–95.

Gould, J. P. (1968) 'Adjustment Costs in the Theory of Investment of the Firm', *Review of Economic Studies*, vol. 35, pp. 47–55.

IEERAL: *Estudios* (1986) Instituto de Estudios Economicos sobre la Realidad Argentina y Latino Americano, no. 39 (Cordoba, Argentina).

Lucas, R. E. (1967) 'Optimal Investment Policy and the Flexible Accelerator', *International Economic Review*, vol. 8, pp. 78–85.

Lucas, R. E. and Prescott, E. C. (1971) 'Investment Under Uncertainty', *Econometrica*, vol. 39, no. 5.

Mundlak, Y. *Agricultural and Economic Growth: Theory and Measurement*, Lecture Notes (The University of Chicago).

Mundlak, Y. (1979) *Intersectoral Factor Mobility and Agricultural Growth* (Washington, DC: International Food Policy Research Institute).

Mundlak, Y. (1985a) 'Capital Accumulation, the Choice of Techniques and Agricultural Output' (The Center for Agricultural Economic Research), Working Paper no. 8504, and in Mellor, J. W. and Ahmed, R. (eds), *Agricultural Price Policy for Developing Countries* (Johns Hopkins University Press (forthcoming).

Mundlak, Y. (1985b) 'Agricultural Growth and the Price of Food' (Rehovot: The Center for Agricultural Economic Research), Working Paper no. 8505 (1985), and in Maunder, A. and Renborg, U. (eds), *Agriculture in a Turbulent World Economy* (Oxford: Gower, 1986).

Mundlak, Y. (1985c) 'The Aggregate Agriculture Supply' (Rehovot: The Center for Agricultural Economic Research), Working Paper no. 8511.

Mussa, U. (1977) 'External and Internal Adjustment Costs and the Theory of Aggregate and Firm Investment', *Economica*, vol. 44, pp. 163–78.

Sargent, T. J. (1979) *Macroeconomic Theory* (Academic Press).

Toddaro, M. P. (1969) 'A Model of Labor Migration and Urban Unemployment in Less Developed Countries', *American Economic Review*, vol. 59, pp. 135–40.

Tradeway, A. B. (1969) 'On Rational Entrepreneurial Behavior and the Demand for Investment', *Review of Economic Studies*, vol. 36, pp. 227–39.

9 The Choice of Tenancy Contract

Clive Bell*
VANDERBELT UNIVERSITY

As the textbooks tell us, when there is a complete set of perfectly competitive markets, including those for contingent commodities, it does not matter whether capital hires labour or labour hires capital. This indeterminacy denies any significance to the question of who actually organises production. Moreover, there is no room for diversity of contracts. For prices convey all relevant information and individuals can buy or sell as much of each contingent commodity as they please, taking prices as parametrically given.

When peasant agriculture in Asia is examined in the light of these propositions, three general features stand out. First, a large proportion – usually a majority – of households do not participate in the market for tenancies. Secondly, tenancy takes diverse forms: share-cropping, fixed rents payable in kind in arrears, and cash payable in advance are all found. In some areas one form of lease is dominant, while, in others, two or (rarely) all three forms coexist in fair numbers, even at the level of the individual village. Thirdly, virtually all farmers, owner-cultivators and tenants alike, employ hired hands.

This paper is an attempt to assess whether these general features can be plausibly explained by specific and empirically relevant departures from the so-called complete markets model,[1] and what these departures imply for the allocation of resources. While the choice among alternative forms of tenancy will be our main concern, the choice between tenancy and self-cultivation with hired labour will also be discussed. Section 1 deals with the case in which insurance and certain other markets are absent, but contractual enforcement is costless; so that the main emphasis is on risk-sharing rather than incentives. In Section 2, the discussion is extended to cover costly enforcement, including the effort of hired labourers. The effects of imperfections in credit markets are taken up in Section 3; and a general synthesis is offered in Section 4. Section 5 examines the extent to which the incidence of particular forms of tenancy in several regions of Asia is consistent with that synthesis. Finally, there are some tentative remarks on some possible consequences of certain public policies.

1   INCOMPLETE MARKETS: COSTLESS ENFORCEMENT

One set of markets that is conspicuously absent in the risky environment of peasant agriculture is that for insurance, owing to moral hazard and adverse selection. The markets for supervisory and husbandry skills also do not exist in many areas, and are very thin where they do. The same is true of the services of draft animals in many parts of India (Bliss and Stern, 1982) – though animals are readily traded as assets. Equally importantly, households belonging to certain social groups will not hire out female and child labour. There is, therefore, an extensive category of non-tradable inputs. In analysing these particular departures from the complete markets model, it will be helpful to start with the assumption that agents incur no transaction costs in their dealings in the markets that do exist.

1.1.   Missing Insurance Markets

As a first step, suppose that only insurance markets are absent. Then if output is produced under constant returns to scale, a competitive equilibrium will exist and be (constrained) efficient (Newbery, 1977). This result imparts some pattern to the choice of activity from individuals' endowments and tastes. At one extreme, a very risk-averse individual can avoid risk altogether by hiring out his labour, land, and other tradable endowments at the (certain) prevailing rates. At the other, those prepared to run considerable risks may rent in land beyond what they own, and cultivate the whole with the help of hired hands in addition to their own labour. Thus, the pattern of tenancy and labour hiring will be generated by individuals' willingness to bear risk, which will depend, in part, on their endowments.

The special case in which there is multiplicative risk and (at least) one risk-neutral individual yields a definite pattern of trade and a first-best allocation of resources. Since this individual requires no premium to bear risk and there are constant returns to scale, no risk-averse individual will be able to compete with him in cultivation. Hence, as he is the sole risk-neutral individual, he will cultivate all land and hire all labour in the system, thereby acting, in effect, as an insurer for everyone else.

That a perfectly competitive equilibrium exists in the absence of insurance markets does not, of course, shed much light on why most households operate exactly the land they own, since it is unlikely that it would be efficient to spread risks by trading in labour alone. Moreover, the fact that the equilibrium is constrained efficient appears to rule out sharecropping, despite the supposed risk-sharing advantages of that form of tenancy. Newbery proves that share contracts are at best equivalent to a suitable combination of wage and fixed rent contracts, even when share contracts contain explicit and costlessly enforceable stipulations about the technique of production to be employed.[2] As sharecropping involves more severe problems of enforcement than fixed rental arrangements, the former will be strictly inferior to mixtures of fixed rent and wage contracts. Solving the puzzle of why sharecropping exists at all will, therefore, require some changes in assumptions.

1.2. Risky Wages (Rentals)

Newbery's solution to the puzzle appeals to risk in factor markets. Suppose wage (rental) rates depend on the state of nature, but are revealed only after inputs of labour (land) are committed. Newbery proves that if there is multiplicative risk and wages are not perfectly correlated with output, then production will be efficient in a competitive equilibrium in which share contracts are also available. In the case of non-multiplicative risk, sharecropping still affords additional advantages, even though production will not, in general, be efficient. Thus, sufficient conditions have been found for sharecropping contracts to make an appearance. Indeed, under the above assumptions, virtually all individuals who choose to cultivate some land, whether owned or rented, will also choose to have both fixed and share contracts; for only by chance will the first-order conditions hold as strict equalities with contractual specialisation. Unfortunately, this conclusion is at odds with the empirical evidence that households rarely mix different tenancy contracts.

The above formulation of risk in factor markets is also rather strained. While cultivators often do not know what the ruling spot wage rates for subsequent operations will be, they certainly know the spot wage they must pay for current operations. For example, when a farmer wants to engage ploughmen, he knows the wage rate he must offer them, although he does not know what the wage rate will be at harvest time. Naturally, if harvest wages depend on the state of nature, the associated risks will usually affect his choice of how many ploughmen to engage; but this is not at all the consideration that opens the door to sharecropping in the above framework. What is needed, therefore, is a demonstration that share contracts offer advantages over mixtures of wage and fixed rental contracts when there are dated inputs of labour in production and, at each stage, future wages are not known.

1.3. Non-tradable Inputs

The absence of insurance markets alone will not do: something else must be amiss. The next step is further to reduce the set of functioning markets by introducing the non-tradables referred to above. As the mixing of factor (wage and rental) contracts at certain and parametric prices played a central role in sub-section 1.1, the lack of such trading opportunities will affect not only the pattern of activities, but also efficiency and the choice of contract.

If some inputs are not tradable, households can attempt to adjust by trading in the markets that do exist. Thus, households which have abundant (scarce) supplies of draft power, husbandry and managerial skills relative to their landholdings will tend to lease in (out) land to complement them. In a risky world, however, those with relatively abundant endowments of non-tradables must also be willing to take on the additional risks of cultivating tenancies. If there is a competitive wage-fixed rent equilibrium, it turns out that landlords can devise profitable sharecropping contracts that will induce such households to assume these risks. The intuition for this result is that when any household possessing a non-tradable does not undertake cultivation, the economy's aggregate endowment of non-tradables is not fully used.[3] On this interpretation, therefore, sharecropping arises as a device to induce very risk-averse individuals to supply non-tradables by undertaking cultivating in a risky environment.

Consider the case in which there are constant returns to scale in land (H), labour (L), and a non-tradable (M); risk is multiplicative (represented by the random variable θ, with $E\theta = 1$; and there are perfectly competitive wage and fixed rental markets with parametric prices (w,R) in terms of output. Let household i have endowments of land, labour, and non-tradables of $(\bar{H}_i, \bar{L}_i, \bar{M}_i)$, respectively, all of which are supplied inelastically. Suppose further that the household maximises the expected utility of income, where income is given by

$$Y_i = \theta F(H_i, L_i; \bar{M}_i) + w(\bar{L}_i - L_i) + R(\bar{H}_i - H_i). \tag{1}$$

If the household chooses to cultivate some land $(H_i > 0)$, the usual assumptions on the production function, $F(\cdot)$, imply that $L_i > 0$. For an inferior solution, therefore, the first-order conditions (*FOC*) are

$$EU_i' \cdot \theta F_1 = EU_i' \cdot R \tag{2}$$

$$EU_i' \cdot \theta F_2 = EU_i' \cdot w. \tag{3}$$

Hence,

$$\frac{F_1}{F_2} = \frac{R}{w}, \tag{4}$$

that is, the expected marginal rate of substitution between the tradables land and labour is equal to the rental–wage ratio. If there are constant returns to scale in land and labour alone, so that the non-tradable is not productive, (4) implies the existence of a unique labour–land ratio which is independent of the household's characteristics. Thus, technique will be identical on all farms. If $U_i(\cdot)$ is concave, then $(EU_i'\theta/EU_i') \leqslant 1$, with strict equality if the household is risk-neutral. The quantity $p_i = 1 - (EU_i'\theta/EU_i')$ may be thought of as the price of risk for household i. Clearly, if the technique of production is identical on all farms, all cultivating households will face the same price of risk.

If the non-tradable is productive, however, it is most unlikely that all households will cultivate with the same technique. Consider, for example, two otherwise identical households, one risk-neutral and the other (slightly) risk-averse. The former will choose (H,L) such that $F_1(H,L,\bar{M}) = R$ and $F_2(H,L,\bar{M}) = w$. The fixed factor $\bar{M}$ ensures that H and L are unique and finite, so that there is room for risk-averse households to compete in cultivation. The risk-averse household will choose somewhat smaller values of land and labour, since its price of risk is positive. Hence, its technique of production will be more intensive in the non-tradable relative to land and labour than the technique selected by the risk-neutral household. In contract to the case of risky wages considered in sub-section 1.2, production is not efficient because there is a non-tradable coupled with the absence of markets for insurance.

At the household's optimum, the shadow price of its non-tradable endowment is $EU'_i \cdot \theta F_3$, which will vary across households. If the non-tradable were actually tradable in a perfect market, the quantity $(1 - p_i)F_3$ is the market price that would induce household i to use exactly $\bar{M}_i$ on its operational holding. This price will vary across households.

Starting with a competitive fixed rent–wage equilibrium, the next step is to ask whether a landlord and a tenant can both improve their positions by entering into a share contract. The terms thereof may be derived as the outcome of a bargaining game (Bell and Zusman, 1976), or they may set unilaterally by one party (usually the landlord) in a principal–agent relationship (Stiglitz, 1974). In the absence of a share contract, the landlord (i) and tenant (j) have access to parametric trading opportunities at (w,R) and self-cultivation. Let their expected utilities at their respective optima be V_i^* and V_j^*, and let these be their respective disagreement pay-offs in the game. For simplicity, suppose the landlord does not possess the non-tradable, and so does not cultivate. Let (H_i,L_i,M_i) denote the bundle of inputs applied to the share tenancy leased by i and cultivated by j. With costless enforcement, they will negotiate over the variables that both can observe: the area to be sharecropped, the labour and non-tradables to be applied to it, and the share (α) of the resulting output going to the tenant. Their incomes are, respectively,

$$Y_i = (1 - \alpha)\theta F(H_i,L_i,M_i) + R(\bar{H}_i - H_i) \qquad (5)$$

and

$$Y_j = \alpha\theta F(H_i,L_i,M_i) - RH_j + \theta F(H_j,L_j,\bar{M}_j - M_i) + w(\bar{L}_j - L_i - L_j). \qquad (6)$$

Note that although the landlord has no interest in the amount of land (H_j) and labour (L_j) the tenant employs under fixed rent contracts with other landlords, these inputs nevertheless depend on (H_i,L_i,M_i,α).

To establish that a share contract may be mutually attractive, suppose the landlord is risk-neutral, and let the terms be such that $(1 - \alpha)F(H_i,L_i,M_i) = RH_i$, so that the landlord will be indifferent between leasing out H_i under those terms and fixed rent at the going rate. Furthermore, let the share contract call for the technique employed on fixed rent tenancies. With identical technique on all plots, the income of the tenant with the sharecropping lease is

$$Y_j = Y_j^* - H_i[(1 - \alpha)\theta x - R], \tag{7}$$

where $x = F(H,L,M)/H$, the common expected yield per hectare on all plots. For H_i sufficiently small,

$$\tag{8}$$
$$EU(Y_j^* - H_i[(1 - \alpha)\theta x - R]) \simeq EU(Y_j^*) - EU_j'[(1 - \alpha)\theta x - R]H_i.$$

Hence,

$$EU(Y_j) \simeq EU(Y_j^*) - EU_j'(\theta - 1) \cdot RH_i. \tag{9}$$

If the tenant is risk-averse, $EU_j'\theta < EU_j'$ under the alternative of fixed rent leasing alone. Hence, $EU(Y_j) > V_j^*$, i.e., the tenant is better off with the share contract. By continuity, there will exist a share contract under which both parties gain over their alternatives at parametric (R,w).

This example illustrates the important point that each landlord–tenant pair must be complementarily matched in both their tastes for risk-bearing and their endowments of tradables relative to non-tradables. It has already been shown that a risk-neutral tenant will not choose a share contract and that a very risk-averse tenant will not cultivate without one. Thus, the absence of markets for certain factors as well as insurance yields conclusions about both the direction of trades in the market for leases and the choice of contract which are more consistent, in certain respects, with the evidence than the case of risky factor markets. What both fail to explain is the mass of households which do not lease at all, to which we now turn.

2 COSTLY ENFORCEMENT

In the face of transaction costs, some of which are indivisible, households whose endowments match their desired use of factors in production sufficiently closely will choose not to trade in those markets. Thus, the transaction costs associated with tenancy contracts can be invoked as an explanation for the fact that many households do not lease. It is not an especially satisfying one, however, because the notion of a 'sufficiently close match' is not well defined. Something more precise is needed, particularly as the transaction costs associated with share contracts are appreciably higher than those with fixed rent ones. Moreover, as most farms hire labour, it also begs the question of how labour effort is enforced. For if the sharecropper has an incentive to undersupply inputs, the hired field-worker, who is paid a flat daily rate, will not exert himself, except under the goad of supervision, threat of dismissal, or moral scruple. For the owner of land, this bears on the choice between own cultivation with the help of hired hands and leasing out land to tenants.

If shirking were the only consideration, the efficient pattern of leasing would be one in which each family's *operational* holding was proportional to its endowment of labour. As we have seen, however, such an allocation will generally result in an unsatisfactory pattern of risk-spreading and risk-sharing, as well as a poor matching of non-tradables to land. The fact that the overwhelming majority of owner-cultivators and tenants make some use of hired hands suggests that these considerations are certainly powerful enough to overcome the presumptive costs of moral hazard in the labour market, even though the latter may be significant.

The principal mechanism of enforcement is supervision. As supervisory labour is not tradable, there will be an incentive for the owner-cultivator to lease out some of his land when the scale of his operations becomes sufficiently large. Such a move will displace some of the burdens of moral hazard in the labour market on to his tenants, since most tenants hire labour. There are, however, gains from this shift because supervision is jointly produced with management as the cultivator attends to his fields. Thus, while tenancy can be viewed as a response to the non-tradability of certain skills and inputs, it also indirectly mitigates moral hazard in the labour market as a whole by inducing a greater supply of supervisory effort.

A simple way of incorporating the joint production of labour, supervision, and management into the model of sub-section 1.3 is to introduce the time (L_0) the cultivator spends working in his fields, either alone or alongside hired hands. L_0 is also a measure of the cultivator's supervisory effort when he hires labour. Let the amount of real effort put out by N hired hands, measured in units of the cultivator's own labour, be given by

$$L_1 = \lambda(N, L_0). \tag{10}$$

For simplicity, let $\lambda(\cdot)$ be strictly concave in N for given L_0, with (λ/N) approaching unity as N becomes very small for all values of L_0.

Suppose only fixed rent contracts are available. The household's income is

$$Y = \theta F(H, L_0 + L_1, L_0) + w(\bar{L} - L_0 - N) + R(\bar{H} - H). \tag{11}$$

Its decision problem is to

$$\underset{(H, L_0, N)}{\text{maximise}} \ EU(Y) \tag{12}$$

subject to (10), (11), $L_0 \leqslant \bar{L}$ and the non-negativity of its choice variables. The usual assumptions on $F(\cdot)$ will ensure that $L_0 > 0$ if cultivation is undertaken, so that there will also be some supervisory effort and inputs of family labour. Assuming that $\lambda(\cdot)$ is continuously differentiable, the *FOC* are

$$EU' \cdot \theta F_1 - EU' \cdot R \leqslant 0 \tag{13}$$
$$H \geqslant 0 \quad \text{complementarily}$$

$$EU' \cdot \theta[F_2(1 + \lambda_2) + F_3] - EU' \cdot w \geqslant 0 \tag{14}$$
$$L_0 \leqslant \bar{L} \quad \text{complementarily}$$

$$EU' \cdot \theta F_2 \cdot \lambda_1 - EU' \cdot w \leqslant 0 \tag{15}$$
$$N \geqslant 0 \quad \text{complementarily}$$

Hence,

$$\frac{w}{(1 + \lambda_2)F_2 + F_3} \leqslant \frac{EU' \cdot \theta}{EU'} = \frac{R}{F_1} \leqslant \frac{w}{F_2 \cdot \lambda_1}. \tag{16}$$

If some labour is hired, (14) and (16) imply that all family labour will be employed on the farm, as intuition suggests, and that

$$R/w = F_1/F_2 \cdot \lambda_1. \tag{17}$$

A comparison of (17) and (4) shows clearly how the need to supervise labour affects the scale of cultivation. As in sub-section 1.3, production will not, in general, be efficient.

If the family is not too risk-averse to undertake cultivation, there will be an endowment $(\bar{H},\bar{L})$ such that its optimal policy is autarky with respect to inputs, that is, $L_0 = \bar{L}$, $H = \bar{H}$, and $N = 0$. In this case, $\lambda_2 = 0$ and $\lambda_1 = 1$. Hence, from (16),

$$\frac{w}{F_2 + F_3} \leqslant \frac{R}{F_1} \leqslant \frac{w}{F_2}, \tag{18}$$

where the derivatives are evaluated at autarky for inputs and at most one of the relations holds as an equality. By continuity, there exists a neighbourhood including $(\bar{H},\bar{L})$ in the space of endowments such that autarky is the best policy. By virtue of constant returns to scale, if $(\bar{H},\bar{L})$ is an autarkic endowment, then so is any scalar multiple thereof, provided that the household's price of risk also stays within the limits set by (18), a requirement that does not seem to put strong restrictions on preferences. Hence, the set of endowments that induces autarky will be roughly cone-shaped, with its apex at the origin.

While logically sound, however, this will not do; for in Asia at least, peasant households which own, but do not lease, land almost invariably hire labour. As long as they do so, continuous changes in their endowments can induce continuous changes in the amount of land leased without violating (17). Thus, one must appeal to the costs of negotiating and enforcing tenancy contracts to explain why a large proportion of landowning households do not lease.

When the rent is payable in advance, the landlord's costs of enforcement will be zero. For his part, the tenant must have the assurance that once he has paid the rent, he will obtain (or retain) the tenancy. As other potential tenants live in the same village, the landlord will damage his reputation by reneging, so that this assurance should be virtually complete. That leaves the usual 'frictional' costs of search and negotiation to drive a wedge between the respective net returns to leasing in and out a particular plot.

A share tenant has an incentive to undersupply inputs – even non-tradables, if he also cultivates land of his own and/or a fixed rent tenancy. Hence, if monitoring is costly, a landlord with share tenancies will incur enforcement costs. At the very least, he (or his agent) must keep an eye on the crop as harvest approaches, since there is an obvious temptation for the tenant to conceal output. Certain inputs may be prohibitively costly to monitor and their levels will, therefore, be chosen by the tenant. Unlike a fixed rent payable in advance, the landlord's (expected) pay-off from a share tenancy will then depend on the characteristics of the tenant, as can be seen from a glance at (5) and

(6). Moral hazard therefore widens the 'frictional' wedge discussed above. The same argument applies in the case of a fixed rent payable in kind in arrears if all the landlord can claim is the entire crop when this is not large enough to meet the rent. For then the landlord's *expected* return will depend on the tenant's characteristics. Thus, not only do transaction costs generate a measurable set of endowments such that the households possessing them would not wish to lease, but the size of that set also depends on the tenancy contract in question.

What are the compensating advantages of share tenancies that induce landlords to offer them? As argued above, share contracts may be attractive to farmers who are unwilling to assume the risk of a fixed rent contract. Conversely, landlords who are risk-averse will prefer fixed to share rent tenancies, *ceteris paribus*. Hence, if reasonable standards of cultivation can be induced and/or enforced on share tenancies, the expected value of the share rent yielded by a piece of land will normally be greater than the fixed rent that piece can command. This is corroborated by the evidence.

3 IMPERFECT CREDIT MARKETS

When credit markets are imperfect, sharecropping will have an additional advantage over fixed rents payable in advance.[4] As production takes time, the tenant must have access to working capital, from his own savings, the landlord, or third parties. If he is rationed in the credit market, then he will be less willing to pay a fixed rent in advance, for this will be a drain on the working capital available for cultivation and the subsistence of his family and animals. A sharecropping contract, however, makes no claims on the tenant's working capital. As the landlord forgoes payment in advance, the share of the crop he receives as rent is a reward for waiting, as well as a payment for the services of his land and risk-sharing. Moreover, if the landlord's shadow price of funds is lower than the tenant's, sharecropping will have the additional advantage of providing some implicit financial intermediation. On this account, therefore, the choice of contract is determined by the sizes of the landlord's and tenant's funds of working capital. In general, production will not be efficient, even with costless enforcement.

As the advantage stemming from payment in arrears is also shared by a fixed rent (in kind or cash) payable in arrears, the issue is not fully settled. The latter contract must provide for the contingency that the output of the tenancy is less than the rent payable. If the landlord can claim only what the tenant produces, then as noted above, moral hazard intrudes. Even if the landlord converts the unpaid portion of the rent into a loan to the tenant, his chances of recovering the loan (and any interest thereon) will still depend on the tenant's future performance. Moreover, if the tenant cannot borrow from third parties, the landlord will have to keep the tenant on and finance much or all of the tenancy's requirements for capital. With a run of bad luck, incompetence, or onerous terms, the tenant could slide into debt-peonage. The clear advantage of sharecropping to the tenant is that it reduces the chances of such an unpleasant fate.

In some areas of India, contracts specifying a fixed rent in kind often contain a provision whereby the payment is commuted to sharecropping if the landlord is persuaded that a poor crop is nature's doing rather than the tenant's negligence. It is hard to make sense of such a provision unless the costs of collecting the stipulated rent in full through deferred payments are prohibitively high.

4 A SYNTHESIS

We have examined, in turn, four influences that shape the extent and nature of tenancy: (i) the absence of insurance markets; (ii) the non-tradability of certain productive inputs; (iii) asymmetries in information and costly monitoring, which lead to moral hazard; and (iv) imperfect credit markets. When they are drawn together, they imply the following qualitative pattern of leasing behaviour.

First, households which have abundant endowments of non-tradables relative to land will tend to lease in. Conversely, households which have abundant endowments of land relative to non-tradables will tend to lease out. Secondly, households which lease in on a fixed rent basis will tend to be less risk-averse and to have better-than-average access to working capital, *ceteris paribus*, than those which lease in on a share basis. The converse will hold for those leasing out. Thirdly, among households leasing out, other factors making share tenancies more attractive, *ceteris paribus*, are (a) big endowments of labour for supervision, and (b) residence in the same locality (village) as the tenant.

Finally, there remains the mass of households that do not lease at all, and how it relates to those that do. Consider a household which is not particularly risk-averse and is leasing in on a fixed rent basis. Let its endowment of land ($\bar{H}$) increase steadily, so that the amount of land it wishes to lease in will fall.[5] In the presence of negotiation costs, the household will leave the market for tenancies before $\bar{H}$ has reached a value such that $EU' \cdot \theta F_1 = EU' \cdot R$. At that point, let $\bar{H}$ increase slightly. Negotiation costs will deter the household from leasing out a small parcel on fixed rent, even if $EU' \cdot \theta F_1 < EU' \cdot R$ at the larger endowment of land. As the household is not particularly risk-averse, it may consider leasing out on a share basis. Now, while offering a higher expected rental income, a share tenancy will entail the diversion of valuable time from supervising the plots that remain under the household's own cultivation. In the fact of such fixed costs, which are not incurred with a fixed rent lease, $\bar{H}$ will have to be somewhat larger before leasing out on a share basis becomes worth while. When $\bar{H}$ is large enough, the choice will fall on sharecropping if enforcement costs are not too high. In that case, the range of $\bar{H}$ over which the household will choose not to lease will be quite large.

Now consider a rather risk-averse household owning little land. If it leases in, its choice probably will be sharecropping. As before, let its endowment of land increase. Depending on how closely its landlord monitors the tenancy and its own capacity to supervise and manage, there will come a point at which it no longer desires to lease in. As before, frictional costs will generate a range of $\bar{H}$ over which it does not desire to lease at all. Once $\bar{H}$ has become large enough for leasing out to be desirable, the household will choose a fixed rent lease if it is sufficiently risk-averse. As there are no enforcement costs, the said range of $\bar{H}$ may be quite narrow, in contrast to the above sequence for a not very risk-averse household.

When the credit market is imperfect, households may consider leases fixed rent payable in kind in arrears. With that option, the range of $\bar{H}$ over which a household will choose to not lease will be larger still.

Thus far, the household's endowments have been taken as fixed. Given enough time, the household's size and composition can be altered, to some extent, by fertility, and its holdings of land and other assets by purchases or sales. Leaving aside endogenous fertility, the opportunity to buy or sell land or draft animals provides an alternative to leasing land when there is no market for the *services* of draft animals. It is not, however, a complete alternative, for two reasons. First, the spatial specificity of land imposes a lower bound on the size of plots that will attract buyers. Draft animals, which usually work in pairs, are also significantly and inherently indivisible. Secondly, imperfections in the credit market exacerbate the problem of lumpiness. As Binswanger and Rosenzweig (1986) persuasively argue, draft animals are poor collateral for loans, and the value of land will usually exceed the (expected) present value of its returns when the credit market is imperfect because of its acceptability as collateral. Hence, financing purchases of either asset may be difficult or unattractive. In fact, while animals are fairly actively traded as assets, the market for land as an asset is thin. As noted above, the converse is true of their services, which partly reflects the limited adjustments that can be accomplished through sales and purchases alone.

5   A READING OF SOME EVIDENCE

The qualitative features of tenancy contracts in certain regions of India and peninsular Malaysia will now be examined in the light of the above. Such a selective examination will not, of course, constitute a test of the theory in any formal sense; but the evidence should be consistent with the theory, and theory should enlighten interpretation.

Both the Kemubu and Muda areas of Malaysia are coastal plains devoted to rice cultivation. Rainfall is high and not very variable. Before irrigation from public canals made double-cropping feasible in the early 1970s, the dominant forms of lease were, respectively, sharecropping and fixed rent payable in kind in arrears. Average incomes and landholdings were appreciably lower, and the concentration of land ownership somewhat greater, in Kemubu than in Muda. Also, whereas Kemubu was and remains rather isolated, Muda is fairly close to the industry and commerce of Penang, and has had a more diversified economic base. Thus, the opportunities for reasonably remunerative and secure off-farm employment were also much more superior in Muda. The introduction of an irrigated second crop greatly improved farmers' incomes and cash flow. At the same time the government made determined efforts to ensure that adequate credit was available through the banking system, and encouraged cultivators to establish deposit accounts. These efforts enjoyed fair success in Muda, but indifferent results in Kemubu. By the mid-1960s, cash rents in advance were quite common in Muda; by the mid-1970s, share tenancy had virtually vanished, while cash rent tenancies had become dominant. In Kemubu, however, fixed rent arrangements appeared to be making only modest inroads at the expense of sharecropping.

Three regions of India will be compared: the Godavari delta; the Gangetic plain of Bihar; and the Punjab. The Godavari delta is ecologically quite similar to Muda. Rice is the principal crop, sugarcane being a minor alternative on irrigated land and tobacco on unirrigated upland. The canal irrigation system is of long standing, parts of it dating back to the nineteenth century. Land ownership is much more concentrated than in Muda, and the credit market, while functioning fairly well by the standards of rural India, is noticeably more fragmented. The dominant form of lease in rice and tobacco cultivation, respectively, is fixed rent in kind and cash.

The Gangetic plain of Bihar is subtropical. Although it receives about 50 inches of rainfall annually, most of the rain falls in July, August, and September. When there is adequate residual moisture, a second crop can be taken in the winter season on unirrigated land. Rice is the principal monsoon crop; wheat and pulses are grown in winter; and jute, maize, and rice in the summer. There are several very large canal systems, and there has been private investment in tubewells in some tracts, but much of the land is still dependent on the rains. Despite this diversity, sharecropping is virtually the only form of lease. The explanation for this lies in appreciable natural risks coupled with grinding poverty and great inequalities in the ownership of land and other wealth. Tenants are usually much poorer than landlords, and employment and wages are uncertain, even in the irrigated tracts. Moreover, the credit market is highly fragmented, with most co-operatives effectively defunct and the few branches of the (nationalised) commercial banks reluctant to add to an already heavy burden of bad loans. Under these conditions, sharecropping is an understandable response to wholesale failures of, or imperfections in, other markets.

The Punjab plain is ecologically quite homogeneous and virtually all land is irrigated. It is also exceptional, in that share and cash rent tenancies are found in roughly equal proportions. Indeed, both forms are often found in the same village, and very occasionally in the same household. Thus, a more discriminating appeal to the theory is needed. Such an attempt has been made by Bell and Sussangkarn (1985), using data on a sample of landowning households (almost a half of which were leasing in or out) drawn from ten villages in Ferozepur and Jullunder districts. They construct a bivariate probit model based on the synthesis of Section 4, using indicator functions for endowments of non-tradables relative to own land and capacity to bear risk. With the introduction of endogenous ranges of 'friction' to represent transactions costs, the structure is able, in principle, to generate all five qualitative choices: fixed renting in, sharecropping in, fixed renting out, sharecropping out, and not leasing at all. The estimation is fairly successful, and the results are consistent with the above theory.

6 CONCLUDING REMARKS: PUBLIC POLICY

It has been argued that the observed patterns of (i) share and fixed rent leases and (ii) self-cultivation, tenancy, and wage employment stem from the absence of, or imperfections in, insurance and other markets and the structure of enforcement costs. This is not particularly startling, but it makes drawing firm conclusions about public policy hazardous. For if there is not a complete set of markets, it is well known that 'local' improvements in structure that fall short of completeness may yield outcomes that are Pareto-inferior to the status quo. Hence, the following remarks about the possible consequences of certain policies are tentative.

The provision of irrigation by public canals has absorbed a substantial share of public expenditures on agriculture, and private investment in tubewells has been facilitated by rural electrification and subsidised credit. While irrigation should reduce risk and, by increasing incomes, make households more willing to bear risk, the associated techniques of production may involve greater risk, in that irrigated agriculture demands a lot of working capital. The examples of Kemubu, Bihar, and even the Punjab suggest that extending the area under irrigation will not consign sharecropping to the annals of economic history. Indeed, the contractual innovation of cost-sharing in respect of key inputs like fertiliser has demonstrated sharecropping's adaptability and tenacity. The introduction of cost-sharing and the other examples do suggest, however, that share tenancy's fate may be determined, ultimately, by whether the credit market begins to function fairly well. In any event, the latter seems to be necessary if the full potential of irrigated agriculture is to be realised. Unlike dams, of course, markets cannot be constructed by fiat; and much intervention in credit markets has attracted criticism (see, for example, von Pischke *et al.*, 1983).

Another intervention to reduce risk is to set up large schemes of employment in rural public works, thereby assuring a safe income to those households which depend mostly on employment for subsistence. From sub-section 1.1, it appears that such schemes might reduce the demand for share tenancies somewhat; but in view of the other forces favouring share arrangements, and the fact that most tenants are net hirers of workers, rural employment schemes appear unlikely to affect the extent and pattern of leasing very much.

Finally, there is the question of mechanisation. As noted above, the services of draft animals are non-tradable, to which tenancy is a partial response. When tractors are introduced, an active market in tractor ploughing services soon springs up, so that a non-tradable input becomes tradable. Although families with relatively large endowments of labour will have a cost advantage in rearing and maintaining animals, they will have no such advantage in owning and operating tractors – if anything the reverse will be true when credit markets are imperfect. Thus, although tractors are land-saving compared to animals, their introduction is more likely than not to reduce the area under tenancy. In that case, there will be greater demands on landowners' time to supervise the additional field labourers they will need to carry out cultivation on the land that was formerly under tenancy. It is also probable that, on balance, they will have less time to manage share tenancies. In that case, fixed rent tenancies would gain in relative importance. Be that as it may, the tenants who now profit from the non-tradability of animal draftpower services appear to be almost certain losers.

Notes

*   I am indebted to Irma Adelman for valuable editorial comments but I retain full responsibility for any errors that remain.
1.   Binswanger and Rosenzweig (1986) adopt a similar starting point for their inquiry into the diversity of organisational arrangements in agriculture. An excellent survey of the sharecropping literature, which emphasises asymmetries in information, is provided by Singh (1987).
2.   This proposition was proved earlier by Stiglitz (1974) and Reid (1976) under the restrictive assumption of multiplicative risk.
3.   The formal proof, which is omitted here for want of space, follows that of Newbery's Proposition 1, which itself draws on a theorem in Arrow and Hahn (1971).
4.   This proposition has a central place in the classical economists' discussion of tenancy, as Jaynes (1984) emphasises.
5.   If the household's price of risk falls, too, the amount it desires to lease in may not be monotone; but the assertion in the text will be true in the large, since the price of risk can be no lower than zero.

References

Arrow, K. J. and Hahn, F. H. (1971) *General Competitive Analysis* (San Francisco: Holden-Day).

Bell, C. and Sussangkarn, C. (1985) 'The Choice of Tenancy Contract', World Bank, processed.

Bell, C. and Zusman, P. (1976) 'A Bargaining-Theoretic Approach to Crop-sharing Contracts, *American Economic Review*, vol. 66, pp. 578–88.

Binswanger, H. and Rosenzweig, M. (1986) 'Behavioral and Material Determinants of Production Relations in Agriculture', *Journal of Development Studies*, vol. 22, pp. 503–39.

Bliss, C. J. and Stern, N. H. (1982) *Palanpur: The Economy of an Indian Village* (Clarendon Press: Oxford).

Jaynes, G. D. (1984) 'Economic Theory and Land Tenure', in Binswanger, H. and Rosenzweig, M. (eds), *Contractual Arrangements, Employment and Wages in Rural Labor Markets in Asia* (New Haven: Yale University Press).

Newbery, D. M. G. (1977) 'Risk-sharing, Sharecropping and Uncertain Labour Markets', *Review of Economic Studies*, vol. 44, pp. 585–94.

Pischke, J. D. von *et al.* (1983) *Rural Financial Markets in Developing Countries* (Baltimore: Johns Hopkins University Press).

Reid, J. D. (1976) 'Sharecropping and Agricultural Uncertainty', *Economic Development and Cultural Change*, vol. 24, pp. 549–76.

Singh, N. (1987) 'Theories of Sharecropping', WP 155 University of California, Santa Cruz (forthcoming in Bardhan, P. K. (ed.), *The Economic Theory of Agrarian Institutions* (Oxford University Press)).

Stiglitz, J. E. (1974) 'Incentives and Risk-sharing in Agriculture', *Review of Economic Studies*, vol. 41, pp. 219–55.

Discussion on Part III

PAPER BY DOMINGO CAVALLO AND YAIR MUNDLAK

'On the Nature and Implications of Intersectoral Resource Allocations: Argentina 1913–84'

The invited discussant of the paper, Professor Fernando de Holanda Barbosa, averred that the rate of off-farm migration was not a function of wage differentials alone. Other variables such as educational facilities, housing, etc., played an important role in the landless labourer's decision to migrate to urban areas. The government's role in investment allocation should have been represented in the relevant equation. The analysis ought to have been in terms of amounts, net of tax, as there were large differences in the tax treatment of the agricultural and non-agricultural sectors. The risk variable needed to be included in the immigration equation. The analysis should also have included both the price of land and the ratio between the price of land and the lagged price of land as explanatory variables. The estimation should have taken into account both expected and unexpected components and problems of bias, and inconsistency should have been considered. For long period studies like the present one, unstable coefficients were to be expected as coefficients changed over time.

In the general discussion following this paper, it was noted that the paper needed to take into account the question of agrarian class relations and changes in these relations as it dealt with a long period of time. A single equation for the whole period involving a large number of exogenous and structural shifts might not be appropriate. The stability of the entire system required testing.

One commentator stated that in countries like India migration took place among the poorer classes for reasons not mentioned in the paper which related only to a very specific situation. The push-and-pull factors leading to migration had relevance in this case for mere survival and not simply to account for wage differentials.

Further comments were that the trend in the increase of landlessness and the impact of migration on urban unemployment and wage levels ought to have been taken into account. Dynamic equations were more useful for modelling the real structural dualities built into the system. Land profitability related to factors like ownership and investment.

179

Tenancy might be banned in the eyes of the law but might continue to proliferate in different concealed forms leading to distortions of the investment market. And since income from agriculture was more stable than land prices, it, rather than land value, should have been used as a proxy for profitability.

It was suggested that the paper would have been more useful if the changing distribution pattern for land, which led to varying degrees of land concentration and migration, were included as an additional explanatory variable and it was pointed out that expected values could not explain phenomena which were also influenced by unexpected variables.

The author, Professor Mundlak, agreed that some of the determinants that were mentioned in the discussion were pertinent, and in fact have been used in some of his other studies. However, it was important to emphasise that the wage differential was a key variable in that it had a dominant effect on the dynamics of the economy. It was for this reason that all other variables were viewed as auxiliary in obtaining, when relevant, a more accurate effect of the wage differential.

PAPER BY CLIVE BELL

'The Choice of Tenancy Contract'

In the comments, following the presentation of Professor Bell's paper by the invited discussant, Professor Alain de Janvry noted that both landlords and tenants had non-tradable inputs, and input combinations have a large number of variations. Of these, one particular set of input combinations had been examined and given policy importance. Further, the form of the combination of management and supervision embodied in household labour and the form of the transaction functions had not been specified. Simply scrutinising the relative efficiency of alternative contracts had neglected welfare considerations and other variables such as collective action or the role of the state affecting the choice of tenancy contracts.

The instance of bullocks and bullock carts in Janpur (India) was cited in the general discussion to illustrate that, even if inputs were non-tradable, their services might be tradable. Studies in the Philippines, it was then said, showed that rent controls did not result in an appropriate sharing of risk, nor did they induce land improvement or increased production. An alternative was the wage contract. There was no proof that tenancy contracts were more efficient than other arrangements. Historically, since share contracts predated wage contracts, the continued existence of share-tenancy had to be explained and its policy implications explored. And it was also said that, since sharecropping led to incentive and moral hazard problems, more complex contracts providing appropriate incentives were indicated.

An important question was raised relating rural unrest referring to sharecropping in Bihar (India). The issues were whether tenancy increased productivity and production and whether it was conducive to the reduction of inequalities in the distribution of income and productive assets or wealth, both vital for the success of poverty programmes.

One commentator noted that in tenancy there was also a partnership aspect that gave the sharecropper the illusion of being a partner which served an ideological function. Another added that the paper did not deal with why sharecropping had come into existence, e.g., absentee landlords, the outflow of the élite from rural areas, and others. Having accepted the relative inefficiency of the system, measures necessary to change it and advocacy for a better alternative were indicated. Rural industrialisation was important in this context as tractors led to a decrease in tenancy contracts and an increase in landlord supervision.

The Chair observed that the paper made a major contribution to our knowledge concerning sharecropping but how the contract was managed had not been brought out. The author was interested in the relative efficiency of alternative contracts but neglected the welfare aspects. The demand for land as an asset did not allow landowners to dispose of it and, hence, the system continued. Abilities were not completely tradable. The theory advocated requires testing using both time series and cross-section data.

Part IV

Agriculture and Industry in Socialist Experience

10 Economic and Social Development of Czechoslovak Agriculture

V. Jeniček

ECONOMIC RESEARCH INSTITUTE FOR
AGRICULTURE AND FOOD, PRAGUE

Economic and social changes in the Czechoslovak countryside have been marked since 1945. There have been changes in the mode of production, in the social structure, in the structure of the residential network, in the functional use and spatial arrangements in rural residential areas, and, particularly, in the quality of living of the rural population.

1 CHARACTERISTICS OF THE CZECHOSLOVAK COUNTRYSIDE[1]

Czechoslovakia has a large proportion of its population living in rural communities and a relatively small proportion in large cities. The largest group of rural communities comprises villages with 200–500 inhabitants (30.1 per cent of the total population) and villages with 500–1000 inhabitants (28.4 per cent of the population). The proportion of the smallest communities, that is, those with fewer than 200 inhabitants, has been steadily decreasing. In 1950, 4.5 per cent of the Czechoslovak population lived in these communities; in 1960 it was 2.3 per cent, in 1970 1.7 per cent, and in 1980 only 0.7 per cent. The smaller the village the greater the rate of decrease. There has been a steady decrease in the size of the population in villages with fewer than 600 inhabitants, a slow decrease in villages with 500–1000 inhabitants, and little or no decrease in the majority of villages with more than 1000 inhabitants. Overall, in 1950 villages with 5000 or fewer inhabitants had a population of 7.7 million; in 1970, 7.4 million, and in 1980, 6.1 million.

The countryside is characterised by a dense network of compact villages. About 90 per cent of the rural population lives in these villages. This high degree of concentration of rural settlement has a number of advantages. It simplifies the provision of services to the population, reduces the costs of construction of public amenities, and makes for a better social climate: contacts between people are easier, neighbours' help is more readily available, and so on.

Agriculture remains a permanent and important component of the socioeconomic base of the rural communities. It is collectivised, and modern large-scale farming makes it easier to keep farm operations outside villages and to co-ordinate the interests of agricultural production with the overall interests of society.

Natural and geographic conditions are generally favourable in the rural areas. This is due to the climate in Central Europe, the microclimatic conditions for the majority of rural settlements, the varied landscape, the appropriate ratio between arable land and grassland (meadows and pastures), the high proportion of forests, and an adequate area of water courses and reservoirs.

Railways, roads, and other communication facilities provide for ready access to rural communities and for easy social interchange between rural and urban communities.

2   CHANGES IN THE STRUCTURE OF THE RURAL POPULATION

As a result of the industrialisation of the Czechoslovak economy, particularly in the 1950s and 1960s, today's villages are far from being purely farming communities. Their populations engage in both agricultural and industrial activity and frequently migrate.

A greater proportion of the population of towns is employed, compared with that in the villages. The proportion of adults is larger in the towns; the proportion of the young (adolescents) and the old lower. Villages have a higher percentage of pensioners and other persons who are not wage-earners (17.0 per cent in the villages, 15.4 per cent in towns) and more persons supported by wage-earners, that is, children and other dependants (36.1 per cent in the villages, 33.8 per cent in towns and cities).

There are also large differences in the type of economic activity between towns and villages. Some 42.5 per cent of the urban and more urbanised population is employed in industry, as opposed to 35.2 per cent of the rural population. Some 10.5 per cent of the urban working population is employed in the transport and distribution sectors, as opposed to 6.6 per cent of the rural population. The tertiary or service sector is larger in the towns (26 per cent of total employment, as opposed to 10.9 per cent in the rural areas). There is almost no difference in the proportions employed in construction. The proportion employed in the agricultural and forestry sector is higher among the rural population (32.1 per cent in the rural areas, 4.9 per cent in the towns).

One of the main trends in the rural areas is the steady decrease in the proportion of the population engaged in farming. Persons permanently engaged in agriculture now constitute about half of the working population in the rural areas.

The decrease in the size of the farming population accompanying the increase in size and the higher degree of urbanisation of the towns is not directly the result of the increase in the proportion of the population working in industry. The growth of the relative proportion employed in industry characterises only communities of 10,000 or less. In more populous communities the tertiary sector is the fastest growing. In the large cities and towns (those with populations of 50,000–100,000) industrial workers are about a third of the working population; in cities of over 100,000 the proportion is even lower.

Currently, in only 41 per cent of rural area households (all of whose working members would probably have been employed in agriculture in the past) are there both men and women employed in agriculture. This is because of local area industrialisation, farm and non-farm job opportunities in the village, available transport, and so on.

The increase in the similarity in living conditions in towns and villages is related to the proper allocation of labour between urban and rural areas, and between industry and agriculture. The traditional concentration of industry and other economic activity in towns and cities, and the accompanying higher levels of technical, cultural and information dissemination activity, is closely related to rural mobility.

3 SOME FEATURES OF THE PROCESS OF BRINGING TOWN AND VILLAGE CLOSER TO EACH OTHER

Factors that are bringing the urban and rural areas closer together include:

  (i)   the short average distance between villages, and between villages and towns and cities;

  (ii) the heterogeneity of the rural enclaves;

 (iii) the non-existence of a boundary between the farming population and the other professional groups living in the rural areas;

 (iv) the removal, to varying extents, of the socioeconomic differences between the more advanced and the industrially backward, mainly agricultural, regions. This applies particularly to southern Bohemia, the Bohemian–Moravian uplands, and the generally less-industrialised Slovakia. The greatest advance has occurred in small and medium-sized towns (20,000–50,000 inhabitants) and the cities did not grow in population at the expense of rural regions;

  (v) the increasingly mixed occupational structure of rural households. The number of household members engaged in agricultural production has decreased and the number working in industry, transport and the service sector has increased.

 (vi) the fact that the standard of living and living and working conditions of those engaged in agriculture and the other economic sectors are now very similar. Like workers in the industrial and service sectors, a large proportion of agricultural workers have a five-day week and work in shifts. The social security benefits and health care available to farmers' families do not differ from those available to other workers. Agricultural workers have the same recreational resorts available to them as other workers. The average wage of agricultural workers is about the same as that of industrial workers. And the durable equipment in farm family households is about the same as that in the households of non-farm families.

4 INDUSTRIALISATION OF AGRICULTURE AND THE PROCESS OF BRINGING CLOSER TOGETHER THE WORKING CONDITIONS IN AGRICULTURE AND INDUSTRY

The industrialisation of agriculture and its recognition as a basic sector of production has, together with other factors, influenced the incomes

Table 10.1   Household fixed assets in Czechoslovakia (number per 100 households)

| Assets | Households of: | | |
	workers	employees	farmers
Refrigerator	99.4	101.6	98.5
Freezer	2.7	3.6	10.3
Washing machine: automatic	36.9	45.0	39.0
without centrifuge	30.2	26.4	29.6
with centrifuge	38.9	34.2	47.2
communal house	15.5	17.8	4.0
Colour TV sets	8.8	9.2	12.0
Black-and-white TV sets	98.6	100.6	95.0
Radio receiver: table	50.2	49.5	53.6
battery	82.1	86.9	78.8
cable	13.4	13.5	4.3
Radio-phonograph	30.8	37.4	29.7
Stereo-listening equipment	8.6	11.9	4.2
Tape recorder, record player	51.3	56.7	41.6
Piano	4.8	11.6	5.2
Other musical instruments	12.7	21.8	12.6
Cooker: gas	69.0	70.8	30.7
electric	22.7	23.1	40.4
Bicycle	88.5	84.9	120.9
Motor bike	5.4	5.0	9.9
Motor cycle, scooter	16.5	10.2	27.0
Car	58.5	59.4	70.4
Caravan	0.9	0.9	1.1
Houseboat	0.3	0.7	0.6
Garage	35.3	36.9	53.2
Weekend chalet	7.1	10.2	2.4
Recreation cottage	3.0	6.9	1.1
Telephone	29.1	44.4	15.1

Source: Statitická ročenka ČSSR 1985.

of agricultural workers, their standard of living, and their mode of living. This has led to a significant closing of the gap between the social and economic status of workers in agriculture and those in comparable sectors of the national economy (see Table 10.1). Wages in agriculture have been brought to the same level as those in comparable sectors of the economy (see Tables 10.2 and 10.3). Under the social security system, health care benefits first, then old-age and other pensions, were made uniformly available to farmers and all other workers. Under the Agricultural Co-operative Act, the legal status of farmers is the same as that of all other workers, and this applies to provisions regarding working house, leave, working relations, and so on.

Scientifically-based advanced technology applied to agriculture has led to larger production units (see Table 10.4) and a greater division of labour. The pre-1945 private farmer did everything for himself. His work was varied but his productivity was low. The worker in the modern large-scale agricultural production unit is a specialist who can no longer perform all the farming operations. Some types of agricul-

Table 10.2   Relationship between monthly wages in the national economy and in agriculture (Index monthly national average wages = 100)

	1955	1970	1980	1983
Average monthly wage of workers in state sector of agriculture Index	74.8	93.2	97.3	100.3
Average monthly wage of co-operative farmers Index	69.6	83.8	100.1	100.4

Source: As Table 10.1.

Table 10.3   Movement of wages in the national economy and in agriculture (1955 = 100)

	1970	1980	1983
Average monthly wage of a worker in the national economy	161.4	219.8	232.5
Average monthly wage of a worker in the state sector of agriculture	201.1	285.9	311.6
Average monthly wage of co-operative farmers	194.4	316.2	349.0

Source: As Table 10.1.

Table 10.4   Number and size of farms in Czechoslovakia

Parameter	1955	1970	1980	1983
Number of co-op. farms	6795	6200	1722	1697
Average size of co-op. farmland (hectares)	270	638	2486	2526
Number of state farms	179	331	200	225
Average size of state farmland (hectares)	4517	4329	8604	8676

Source: As Table 10.1.

tural employment are disappearing and others appearing in response to advances in technology. Successful development of society, the enterprise and the individual will increasingly depend on the individual's ability to adapt to new conditions and the further integration of agriculture and industry. The change in the position of agriculture in the national economy is shown in Table 10.5.

Table 10.5   Position of Czechoslovak agriculture in the national economy

Parameter	1965	1970	1975	1980	1985
Contribution of agriculture to social product of national economy (%)	11.9	12.1	10.8	9.5	9.8
Contribution of agriculture to national income of national economy (%)	11.9	10.1	8.3	7.2	7.5
Share of agriculture in total capital investment in production sectors of national economy (%)	10.1	14.4	18.4	14.7	17.1
Share of agriculture in value of fixed assets of national economy (%)	14.1	14.6	14.8	15.2	15.2
Proportion of persons employed in agriculture out of total number of working people in whole production sphere of national economy (%)	24.4	21.5	17.9	17.0	16.8

Source: As Table 10.1.

5   AGRICULTURE, INDUSTRY, AND THE AGRO-INDUSTRIAL COMPLEX

The increased level of interdependence and the strengthening of the linkages between agriculture, industry, and the other sectors of the economy have resulted in an integrated agro-industrial complex (AIC) with one objective – to produce consumer goods and exports requiring agricultural raw materials. Figures in Table 10.6 indicate that almost 20 per cent of the nation's fixed assets and a quarter of its labour power are employed in this effort. Within the complex, 65 per cent of the fixed assets and 70 per cent of the labour are devoted to agricultural production. Input industries employ 10 per cent of the fixed assets and 9.3 per cent of AIC labour. Only 3.2 per cent of input industries' products are destined for the agricultural sector. The chemical industry is an exception; more than 8 per cent of its output is destined for agriculture.

The growth of farm output and food production was made possible by the high rate at which labour was provided with technological inputs. This rate increased 2.8 times over the period from 1970 to 1984.

Table 10.6 Distribution of fixed assets and labour by industry

Industry	Fixed assets (%)	Labour (%)
Agriculture	12.9	16.8
Food industry	4.3	4.7
Input industries	2.7	2.5
Agro-industrial complex	19.9	24.0
Production sectors of the economy, total	100.0	100.0

Source: As Table 10.1.

Table 10.7 Fixed assets in Czechoslovak agriculture
(year 1948 = 100)

Year	Total	Out of the total:	
		buildings	machines, equipment
1960	162.5	152.9	209.8
1970	272.3	250.2	380.1
1980	504.4	331.8	810.1
1983	597.8	517.9	987.8

Source: As Table 10.1.

A number of factors underlie the importance and irreplaceability of agriculture both in the past and in the future. First, agriculture is, and will remain in the foreseeable future, almost the only source of an increasing output of food and other organic products stemming from renewable resources. Secondly, agriculture provides the means of production for the firms in the agro-industrial complex. Agriculture and its requirements also dictate the extent, orientation, and to some extent the distribution of suppliers' facilities. Thirdly, the structure, volume, and distribution of the production of farm commodities directly influence allocations to the firms that process farm products. They also underlie directions of development and levels of production in the food industry. Fourthly, the value of equipment, chemicals, and other agricultural inputs depends upon their value in agriculture itself. Fifthly, the higher the labour productivity in agriculture, the lower the cost of food, the lower the proportion of food expenditure in total expenditure and the higher the national income.

6 FUTURE TRENDS

Since 1950 Czechoslovakia has had a relatively high rate of growth in farm output (see Table 10.8). A relatively high rate of labour productivity and the increasing availability of fixed assets have contributed to a substantial improvement in self-sufficiency in food production, stability in the domestic market, and regularity in the food supply. Food security has two aspects – meeting society's requirements and doing so

Table 10.8 Indices of gross farm output in Czechoslovakia (the year 1948 = 100)

Year	Total	Per worker	Per hectare of farm land
1960	134	205	137
1970	163	310	172
1980	200	469	218
1983	212	509	233

Source: As Table 10.1.

at the least cost. Development of the food system in the future will require the utilisation of the fruits of scientific and technical research.

The objectives of food policy are to provide the population with a nutritionally adequate high-quality diet, to have a sufficient domestic food supply responsive to requirements, and to attain complete self-sufficiency in the production of foods whose components can be grown in the nation's climatic zone.

Increased food production will depend on the use and quality of animal feed, vitamin or feed supplements, organic and commercial fertilisers, pesticides, farm equipment, preservatives and other technological inputs.

Food consumption should be in accord with scientific findings concerning nutrition. The consumption level of nutrients for individuals should correspond to, and be planned to accord with, recommended dietary allowances. The trend is towards further improvement in food consumption habits (see Tables 10.9 and 10.10) and greater reliance upon household resources leading towards more self-sufficiency in food production.

Specific product category expectations include an increase in the consumption of milk and dairy products of 0.8 per cent annually and of meat by about 0.4 per cent annually. The consumption of fruits and vegetables, prime sources of vitamin C, of which there are seasonal deficiencies, and of other irreplaceable nutrients, will increase by about 15–20 per cent annually as diets and life-styles change. Domestic agriculture will provide more products with higher nutrient content. Increased consumption of Southern hemisphere fruits is also expected.

Although the planned consumption of food accords with nutritional requirements, it also reflects the fact that some of the eating habits of the population cannot be changed within a short period of time. In the future, the balance between the consumption of animal and vegetable protein is expected to improve, and the requirements for vitamins and minerals will be fully met. The consumption of energy will be partially reduced, particularly the consumption of saccharides. Vitamin consumption is expected to increase substantially.

Higher levels of consumption of different groups of foodstuffs will be attained through systematic, purposeful, and economically effective efforts influencing the whole process of primary production, processing, and distribution of food, as well as conditions for its ultimate use in households and public catering. It will also depend on shopping behaviour and meal preparation techniques. Behaviour will be influenced by providing nutrition education to women and children,

Table 10.9 Consumption of basic foods in Czechoslovakia (kg per capita per annum)

	1960	1970	1975	1983	$\frac{1983}{1960}$ index	Expected 1990	Expected 1995
Meat, total	45.7	71.9	81.1	83.3	182.3	88	91
Fish	4.7	5.2	5.8	5.0	106.4		
Milk and milk products in the value of milk without butter	172.8	196.2	210.4	241.8	139.9	250	255
of this, cheese	2.3	3.9	4.6	6.0	260.1	260	265
Eggs, no.	142	277	297	328	230.1	325	325
Fats, oils, total (in the value of 100% fat)	13.7	19.9	19.9	22.2	162.0	22	21.5
Sugar	22.4	37.7	38.0	37.8	168.7	38	37
Cereals (in the value of flour, including rice)	105.8	111.1	108.1	107.8	101.9	101	96
Potatoes	75.8	103.4	95.8	78.7	103.8	88	92
Vegetables, total (in the value of fresh vegetables)	89.1	76.3	73.7	71.2	88.9	82.5	92
Fruits, total (in the value of fresh fruits)	50.9	46.6	47.7	62.7	123.2	62	66

Source: As Table 10.1.

Table 10.10 Recommended and expected food allowance per capita per diem

		Food allowance	Expected for: 1990	1995	Index: 1955 Food allowance
Energy	kJ	11,640.0	12,511.0	12,417.0	106.7
Protein, total	g	101.0	101.4	101.9	100.9
of this, animal	g	60.0	58.6	59.8	99.7
Fats	g	95.0	121.9	121.8	128.2
Saccharides	g	380.0	370.0	364.8	96.0
Calcium	mg	930.0	943.0	965.0	103.8
Iron	mg	13.6	16.6	17.0	125.0
Vitamin B_1	mg	1.43	1.80	1.82	127.3
Vitamin B_2	mg	1.88	1.87	1.91	101.6
Vitamin C	mg	112.0	88.4	96.0	85.7

Source: - As Table 10.1.

and launching publicity campaigns aimed at disseminating information on nutritional requirements. Mass communication media and active co-operation of social organisations will help to promote this programme.

Note

1. Statistics in this and the following section are taken from Statistická ročenka ČSSR 1985.

References

Sociálně-ekonomický rozvoj československého zemědělství (Socioeconomic development of Czechoslovak Agriculture) (1983) (Prague: State Agriculture Press).
Statistická ročenka ČSSR 1985 (Czechoslovak Statistical Yearbook) (Prague).

11 Socialist Technically Oriented Production Systems: the Case of Hungarian Agriculture

Aladár Sipos

INSTITUTE OF ECONOMICS, BUDAPEST

Hungary

7/00
7 110
0520

1 INTRODUCTION[1]

Between the two world wars Hungary was one of the most backward countries in Europe, both in regard to its economic development and to its social structure. Per capita national income in 1937 was a mere 60 per cent of the European average. Even in 1945 Hungarian agriculture had many feudal traits. Inequalities in land tenure were the rule. At the end of the 1930s 68.7 per cent of farms had an area of less than three hectares and they accounted for only 9 per cent of all the arable land. At the same time, 0.1 per cent of farms were large holdings with more than 600 hectares each and accounted for 26 per cent of the arable land.

The war was not yet over when, in December 1944, in the liberated part of the country, the Provisional National Government was formed, and its first programme, which included land reform, was publicly decreed in March 1945.

During the land reform 35 per cent of the country's arable land (3.2 million hectares) changed hands. 650,000 families were entitled to three hectares each on average: 49 per cent of former agricultural workers, 53 per cent of farm hands and 20 per cent of small-holders received land. Every third Hungarian peasant was, partly or totally, a new landholder as a result of this reform.

When the distribution of land was completed the dominant form of land tenure became the small holding, because land was given to peasants as private property.

197

Some years later, when the nationalisation of manufacturing, transport and wholsesale trade was completed, the development of the retail trade on a co-operative basis and the establishment of craftsmen and peasant co-operatives became the norm. Under such circumstances the question naturally arose; how could small-holders be won over to the cause of the co-operative movement?

2   THE INITIAL MODEL

The original idea was that profitability considerations by themselves would induce small-holders to form co-operatives as the inadequacy of small-scale production was evident from past experience. During the great crisis of 1929–32, the Hungarian economy, and especially agriculture, were severely affected as products could be sold neither domestically nor on the world market. Bur during the 1940s circumstances changed radically. Industrialisation enhanced the purchasing power of the indigenous urban population and world market demand stabilised. Under such conditions the pressure to combine was weakened.

At this time two schools of thought concerning the socialist reorganisation of agriculture crystallised in political circles. The first held that under the then circumstances socialist reorganisation of agriculture was not an urgent task. Tolerance and working out a new concept were favoured. The other, which later became dominant, sought to replace market pressure with executive force. This included the compulsory delivery of agricultural produce, compulsory sowing coupled with low purchase prices, progressive taxation and direct pressure on well-to-do peasants.

This resulted in the loosening of the worker-peasant alliance, in stagnating agricultural production and in constant shortages. Even the newly-formed co-operatives had no way to establish themselves firmly. The area of untilled land grew rapidly.

The new leadership in 1956 faced grave problems. The former regime had pursued a voluntaristic economic policy, did not take into account the endowment and traditions of the country, and looked on agriculture merely as a source of material for rapid industrialisation. Its ill-found economic goals were supplemented by forced establishment of co-operatives. These methods were so alien to the mentality of the Hungarian peasantry that the original goal could not be reached. The leadership of the pre-1956 era could not work out and implement an agrarian policy which would accomplish the double task of effecting the development and socialist reorganisation of agriculture. In the middle of 1956 the co-operative sector accounted for slightly more than 20 per cent of the country's arable land, and even this was 11.3 per cent by the middle of 1957. The reasons for this decline were the forced collectivisation and the confusion caused by the counter-revolution.

3 THE NEW MODEL

Following the defeat of the counter-revolution a new agrarian policy was formulated as early as the end of 1956. Its central idea was to improve living conditions in the countryside and to eliminate peasant backwardness step by step. The government took measures which gained the confidence of the peasantry. It openly condemned the failures of the pre-1956 era, notably the forced collectivisation, and tried to remedy previous wrongs. Another important task of agrarian policy was to strengthen the role of material incentives with the aim of boosting agricultural production under the new socioeconomic conditions. This aim was pursued by increasing agricultural prices and reducing taxes. The government strongly backed state and co-operative farms in their efforts to consolidate their standing and gave aid to individual peasants in order to increase their production and wellbeing. Policy was based on the principle that higher living standards and not administrative force should convince the peasantry of the advantages of socialism and co-operation.

From among agrarian policy measures taken at that time the most important one was the abolition of compulsory delivery and its substitution by a standard buy-up system. As a result, the previous hierarchical system was replaced by horizontal commodity relationships based on contractual arrangements. This decisive step was not only the main factor behind the political and economic successes of the period, but also a contribution towards Marxist economic theory and management practice of the transitory stage of development from capitalism to socialism.

Previously, all farms were subject to directive state planning. However, with the abolition of compulsory delivery in the two most important sectors of agriculture – co-operative and private farms – direct management was abandoned and replaced by indirect regulation. New price, tax, credit and transfer policies had to be worked out in a way that would take into account all the effects that these policy measures would trigger off in agriculture and the contiguous sectors of manufacturing and trade, and even in the whole of the economy. These far-reaching steps were considered the first in the series of measures which resulted in the reform of the entire system of macroeconomic management, the so-called new economic mechanism.

The new agrarian policy proved to be correct. As a result of its implementation there was growth in agricultural production and preconditions for a new and more successful attempt at collectivisation were created. This drive began at the beginning of 1959 and was completed by the spring of 1961. At that time co-operatives held 74 per cent of the arable land and produced 70 per cent of agricultural output.

The Hungarian leadership based its collectivisation efforts first on political factors. Collectivisation was coupled with technical progress and growth of production. This policy objective, termed at that time the 'double task', was attained. It is a remarkable achievement of Hungarian agriculture that even in the years of collectivisation both its net and gross output increased. Livestock numbers grew, and so did the number of hectares of irrigated land.

The establishment of agricultural co-operatives was made much easier because the principle of voluntariness was adhered to, with few exceptions. Another important principle was gradualness, which still applies. In the main, large, integrated, producer co-operatives were established, but simpler types of co-operatives also survived, providing vegetables, fruit and wine, or if located where the soil was poor, engaged in raising animals or bees.

Gradualness applied to producer co-operatives implied differentiated land rent; household organisation units (for example, employing family labour) and remuneration (for example, share cropping) in accord with local circumstances, type of activity and level of technology.

An important part of the reorganisation strategy was alliance with middle-income peasantry. Middle-income peasants entering the new co-operatives had a favourable impact on small peasants and contributed to the economic base in land, implements and knowledge.

The handling of the kulak problem was a political success. The Hungarian political leadership gave the membership of the co-operatives a free hand in deciding whether to admit a wealthy peasant or not. The majority of the applications were accepted. Many of the former kulaks were voted into management and some of them became chairmen. Democracy was the prime principle applied in dealing with the affairs of the co-operative. Members chose managers of their own liking. Outside interference was prompted only by serious infighting which endangered the survival of the co-operative, or by extremely poor showings in production.

Another favourable political factor was the application of social policy, namely providing pensions, old age benefits and health insurance for members of co-operatives.

State and co-operative farms became the dominant forms of agricultural enterprise but not the only forms. Co-operative and state farms are large, highly concentrated firms with an average area of 4158 hectares for co-operatives and 7630 hectares for state farms. Large farms began with plant cultivation but gradually diversified into animal husbandry and horticulture. A phenomenon right from the beginning was vertical integration which, from the 1960s onwards, included several industrial activities such as mixed fodder production, food processing, construction work, maintenance and repair of own machinery, the production of engineering, chemical and light engineering products, and so on.

At present, more than two-thirds of large farms are engaged in some kind of industrial activity. Half is food processing, which largely contributes to the domestic supply. The industrial activity of agricultural enterprises makes up to a large extent for the lack of small- and medium-scale service industries, thus lessening the outflow of the rural population. It increases farm income by better utilisation of local resources – buildings, equipment and labour.

Experience thus far has demonstrated that industrial activity on the part of agricultural units is efficient, and it has developed rapidly. In 1960 only 3 per cent of the gross output of agricultural units came from industrial activity. At present the figure is 30 per cent.

Although large-scale farming is overwhelmingly the case in Hungary, the role of small farms is not negligible. For years they have accounted for one-third of agricultural output. Nowadays some 1.5 million families are engaged in farming; 674,000 are members of co-operatives who received their household plots under statutory provisions. Another form of small-scale farming is the so-called auxiliary plot. These number 800,000 at present. Their proprietors are not peasants but people working in manufacturing, private and public services. The average area of auxiliary plots is rather small; in most cases they are simply gardens.

1.5 million small agricultural producer households mean, with family members included, 4.5 million people. Only 17.5 per cent are actively engaged in agricultural production and consider it their occupation; 25.2 per cent of them are working in manufacturing or other sectors of the economy. Dependent family members account for 4.3 per cent of the small producers and 14.3 per cent of the population are pensioners.

Household and auxiliary farms produce for their own consumption. Recently, however, specialisation and commodity production for sale have gained ground. Specialised small farmers generally co-operate with co-operatives and other large farms. A universal form of such co-operation is the putting-out system whereby the household receives the necessary livestock, fodder, machinery and other services from the large farm, which also sells the produce which the household has contracted to produce. What remains from the proceeds after the cost of inputs is deducted is the income of the small producer. In most co-operatives, household production is organised by a separate division under the leadership of trained specialists.

Some large farms have specialised groups engaged in the production of one particular product. The group includes everybody, not only employees, who are engaged in the activity. The most popular animal husbandry groups raise rabbits, poultry, pigeons and beef cattle. There are also groups that raise fruits and vegetables, make wine, garden or grow grain. Apart from raising hogs, these are the categories in which household and auxiliary farm production has a considerable share. They are all characterised by the major importance of manual labour. In the production of grain and rough and bulk feed, the growing of sugar-beet or sunflowers, or the procesing of canned vegetables, the role of the household and auxiliary farms is negligible. Production of the last-named commodities is relatively easy to merchandise and large farms have an insurmountable advantage in doing so. Large farms also have the lion's share in the raising of poultry and beef cattle.

The foregoing discussion suggests only that close integration between large and household and auxiliary farms enables the latter to produce one-third of the extra agricultural output on a relatively tiny area.

The long-term objective of Hungarian agrarian policy is to favour small-scale production. Contractual arrangements provide for security of income. Efforts to improve the supply of implements, materials and equipment were made in the past and will probably be intensified in the future.

4 INDUSTRIALISATION OF HUNGARIAN AGRICULTURE

Hungarian agriculture underwent more change during the two decades of its collectivisation than during previous centuries. Before collectivisation, output fluctuations from one year to another were large; the overall rate of growth was low. After the introduction of large-scale farming and the establishment of modern large-scale agricultural units, the rate of growth accelerated and fluctuations were dampened.

At present Hungarian agriculture produces 100 per cent more on a 10 per cent greater land area with a 50 per cent smaller work force than it did 25 years ago. Per capita food consumption rose twofold during the last 25 years. At the same time, agricultural exports increased. Agricultural expansion was particularly rapid during the last 15 years.

The growth of Hungarian agriculture appears outstanding even by international standards. Between the two world wars and in the 1950s and 1960s Hungarian agriculture ranked between 14th and 18th among European counties, and for a long time could not improve its position. In the 1970s and 1980s, however, quite a few parameters ranked between. Per capita grain production was 1.4 tons in 1983, second only to Denmark in Europe. Hungary is among the foremost in Europe in per capita apple, pork, poultry and egg production.

This showing is largely explained by the qualitative change in production technology, namely, the industrialisation of agricultural production. This means a total reshuffle of agriculture's technical basis. In several sectors mechanisation is in an advanced state if not completed, with the employment of complex machine systems. Animal traction and manual work are being performed more and more by machines. Whereas in 1950 only 14.4 per cent of total traction power used by agriculture was mechanical, the remainder being animal traction (mainly horse), in 1960 this figure stood at 50.2 per cent, and today it has nearly reached the limit.

The strategy for the industrialisation of Hungarian agriculture was first devised by scientists at the end of the 1950s. By the second half of the 1960s the programme was endorsed by the political and economic leadership. The industrialisation of Hungarian agriculture comprises:

1. Large-scale implementation of modern technologies based on progress in chemistry and biology, coupled with continuous general and professional education of those working in agriculture. As a result of this process, agricultural work, from a technical point of view, becomes similar to industrial work.
2. As in industry, large-scale production becomes the rule in agriculture, In accordance with the needs of concentrated mass production, modern organisational methods gradually gain ground.
3. In industrialised agriculture the importance of co-operation and

integration is much more important. On a microeconomic level it means vertical expansion of the individual firm's profile and more co-operation between firms. On a macroeconomic level, as a result of the above-mentioned process, an integrated food economy and agro-industrial complex arises.

The industrialisation of Hungarian agriculture was started right after collectivisation, in the early 1960s, and was speeded up after the 1968 reform. The rapid development of production resulted in a total change in the technical basis of agriculture. As previously noted, animal traction and manual work were and are being replaced more and more by machines.

4.1 Mechanisation

Beside the substitution of machine power for animal and human power, mechanisation had the effect of increasing yield and diminishing costs. Cost reduction as a result of mechanisation prevails only if yields surpass a certain minimum.

The level of mechanisation in Hungarian agriculture is at present about average. The mechanisation of soil cultivation, sowing, care of plants and grain harvesting is sufficient, although it cannot meet recent requirements, but that of transport is only at 60–65 per cent of requirements, and that of loading at 10–15 per cent. Mechanical traction capacity is not yet sufficient for the optimal completion of every task in the autumn peak period. The mechanisation of harvesting of root crops (corn, sugar-beet, potatoes) and rough fodder is at an advanced level.

Mechanisation in horticulture is at a low level. That of animal husbandry is also below the level of crop cultivation (the only exception being poultry), mainly because of lack of money, but sometimes also of suitable technology. After socialist reorganisation, demand for large structures increased, but it could not be satisfied all at once.

4.2 Specialised Inputs

Industrialisation of agriculture resulted not only in larger investment but also in the use of more materials, tools, energy and in circulating capital. This fact explains why, in the early 1980s, the quantity of material purchased from industry was more than the quantity of agricultural origin. Chemicals and industrially-produced fodder had an especially large role but energy and fuel consumption were not negligible. In the plant cultivation sector, fertilisers and pesticides were 48 per cent of total costs.

The use of fertilisers has risen dramatically. On every hectare of ploughed land, orchard or vineyard, two kilogrammes of fertiliser were used in 1938, 6 kg in 1950, 29 kg in 1960, 150 kg in 1970 and 309 kg in 1984 – all well rewarded by better yields.

Modern agriculture is characterised by the optimal composition and rationing of fertilisers used. Microelement enriched solid fertilisers, fluid ammonia and other fluid fertilisers have been introduced in Hungary.

Pesticide use has increased too, reducing somewhat the heavy loss of plants. Nevertheless, losses amounting in some years to 10 per cent of gross crop output occur.

Modernisation of agriculture increased energy consumption considerably. From 1978 onwards, total energy consumption in Hungarian agriculture diminished, the increase of output not withstanding. Before that date there was an almost 10 per cent increase yearly. This and other facts has indicated that in recent years a greater stress has been laid on capital efficiency. One can observe a shift towards cheaper solutions, both in investment and operation (reconstruction as opposed to new investment, better utilisation of by-products and waste).

4.3 Production Systems

As industrialisation of agriculture unfolds, an ever-growing importance must be accorded to the optimal combination of production factors, that is, to the systems approach. In a technically operated system, every factor of production is equally important. If one of them is not applied at the agreed level, the efficiency of the total production is jeopardised. The proportions between different factors of production are strictly prescribed by technology. The slightest deviation can have serious consequences in terms of efficiency of the overall system. This means that the professional knowledge of workers must be raised.

Technically operated production systems offer a suitable organisational framework for the optimal combination of production factors. In some sectors, for example, in field crop production, they are the main forces behind production yields.

The possibilities of creating technically-operated production systems are not the same in every agricultural firm, not even in different subdivisions of the same firm. But the point is that not every firm has to go through all phases of research and development. They can simply adopt or buy a tried technology. In Hungary the most frequently used method of diffusing proven large-scale agricultural technology is the establishment of a technically-operated production system.

The technically-operated production system as an economic institution is a specifically Hungarian phenomenon. It has no counterpart in the agrarian sector of other countries, save a few such systems in other socialist countries, all of which are of Hungarian origin. Its conception and development are due largely to self-reliance and initiative at the level of the firm.

The production system is a partnership formed with the aim of producing a particular product using a well-defined technology. The conditions of its functioning are fixed through free bargaining by potential members. The leader is that particular farm which worked out the technology of producing the product using industrial methods, that is, the system centre. In principle, every large farm has the right to work out such a technology but a production system (partnership) based on that technology cannot be formed without previous state licensing. No farm has a monopoly on formulating a production system, so that production using industrial methods of one and the same product may be organised concurrently by several large farms. Experience shows that competition among organising farms has – and will most probably have in the future – an important role in the rapid spread and improved outcomes of production systems. Every firm which wants to enter such a system can now compare different offers with different conditions before making a final decision. In this way, every large farm can enjoy voluntarily the advantages of suitable concentrations, specialisation of modern technology and organisation without impairing its self-reliance. The system centre takes an active part in the organisation of member farm production; it works out, improves on and adapts industrial production methods to special needs, provides a variety of services and controls technology at member farms.

Production systems first appeared in Hungarian agriculture in the early 1960s in poultry farming and egg production, because these were the areas where outside factors (notably weather conditions) had the least impact. They were initiated by some outstanding state farms. Later on, pork, beef and milk production systems became universal.

Based on experience gained from animal husbandry and on scientific and technical progress, the organisation of crop production systems was begun in the 1970s. The first were corn-producing systems, their lack having been acutely felt by animal farms which needed more certain fodder provision. In subsequent years, through crop association, the technically-operated production of other crops began. Production systems for vegetables, fruit and wine also evolved.

The number of technically-operated production systems increased rapidly from 1972–73. There were five systems in the country in 1972, 74 in 1982. Cultivated area in the scope of these systems grew from 6000 hectares in 1970 to 2.5 million hectares in 1983. Besides one-profile systems, multi-profile systems spread quickly, having originated either by the merger of former one-profile systems, or by profile enlargement of previous corn-producing systems. Organised crop associations helped in better use of machinery, mainly in cases where the types of machine in use for different cultures was essentially the same. The equipment for wheat and corn production is identical (apart from some special implements). Therefore they are plausible candidates for association. Apart from wheat, many other plants (sugar-beet, sunflower, soy bean, potato) could be successfully associated with corn.

An important characteristic of technically-operated production systems is a considerable increase in yields both compared to the firm's own previous results and to the country average. Our experience attests to the fact that complex production systems are based on modern technology, genetics and organisational principles are an efficient method of industrialising both crop cultivation and animal husbandry.

There are, however, big differences in production yields among members of the same system. Some farms entering the system thought of it as a vehicle for free distribution of machinery and fertiliser. Although scientifically based production methods and technologies were readily available, they failed to adapt them to their specific needs. System centres also have to bear blame because they accepted so many applications that in the end they were unable to supply all members with personnel and material.

Last but not least, we have to stress that system-based production methods are not only knowledge-intensive, but also require many more assets than traditional systems. Not only are production yields greater, but so are raw material costs and depreciation. For efficiency and net income to improve, farms have to have all the factors necessary for their types of production to make the transition to the new production methods; complex technology, suitable breeds, etc.

The changes of the 1970s, among them an increase in the prices of the means of production surpassing by a large margin the increase on state purchase prices, strengthened the role of efficiency considerations. Yield increase had to be subordinated to profit maximisation. An important condition for the further success of production systems is to establish an identity of interest between members and the system centre. Moreover, future viability of production systems increasingly depends on their ability to provide a great variety of services differentiated according to the needs of the customers. The renewal of production systems would be made easier if purchase of factors of production was less complicated.

In appreciating the performance of production systems, it has to be acknowledged that up-to-date, efficient production can also be maintained outside of production systems. Production systems might reach a stage when they have nothing more to offer – their members being raised to the highest conceivable level. It does not detract from the value of technically-operated production if such systems dissolve.

4.4 Partnerships

After the collectivisation of Hungarian agriculture, partnerships spread rapidly – most of them among co-operatives. This movement was reinforced by the modest size and financial means of co-operatives at that time. With the unfolding of the reform of macroeconomic management, the number of partnerships formed by agricultural firms – first of all co-operatives – grew rapidly.

At present the majority of partnerships in the Hungarian economy is in agriculture. From among 1000 or so partnerships, 892 were created by agricultural, food industrial or sylvi-cultural firms, most of them co-operatives. Some 80–85 per cent of partnerships are engaged in agriculture or in some contiguous activity (construction, food processing, sales etc.). In 1981 every Hungarian agricultural firm was a member of six such partnerships on average. This was the area first liberated from central regulation, hence the area of greatest liberty in contracting, or entrepreneurship, etc. The best results were achieved by production systems.

Partnerships deserve particular attention because they can further efficient, well-organised production and sale without endangering the independence of members. Thus partnerships are an alternative to mergers. Partnerships are a mobile element of the institutional structure because their birth and death are an issue of firm level decisions without adminstrative interference from the state.

Concerning the future of partnerships, we have to stress the importance of their being based on interests at the level of the firm. Any campaign to organise such partnerships would only detract attention from the much more serious problems of efficiency and the mobilisation of reserves. Unfortunately the distribution of partnerships among fields of activity is uneven. There are very few food-processing firms in the partnerships. From the middle 1970s to 1980 their number decreased from 59 to 15. This problem cannot be solved without raising the level of incentives. In the future, the role of co-ordinative partnerships (where capital is not pooled) will be enhanced. They can further interfirm relations without draining investment resources.

Efficient development of agriculture involves the inclusion of farmer interests into the system of macroeconomic management, first of all the system of regulators. The development of the management of agriculture is an integral part of the reform process started in the mid-1960s. The essence of the reform is to further the self-reliance of individual firms and to assure financial reproduction on an increasing scale. These aims were pursued by repeated and significant price increases, by government subsidies intended both for investment and for operation costs, by the credit system, by financial regulators influencing both the occurrence and the spending of firm incomes, and by the regulation of trade with input producers.

Another important feature of Hungarian agrarian policy was to integrate agriculture more firmly into the national economy.

5 THE PROBLEMS OF THE PRESENT

The guarantee of food on a satisfactory level for the whole population is an historic achievement of Hungarian agrarian policy. This result was achieved by increasing the quantities produced. Incentives served this objective. If we have problems today, they arise not from shortage but from overproduction. The problem is the more acutely felt as the Hungarian food sector is export-orientated and the industry is hard hit, both by increasing costs and by a more exacting world market. Hungarian agriculture has no other alternative but to accommodate.

In shaping future agrarian policy we have to stress the importance of quality and efficiency instead of quantity. This is a new policy objective.

Note

1. Statistics in this chapter are taken from Hungarian Central Statistical
   Office 1985 and 1987.

References

Hungarian Central Statistical Office (1985) *Statistical Yearbook* (Budapest:
Hungarian Central Statistical Office).
Hungarian Central Statistical Office (1987) *Mezőgazdasági statisztikai évkönyv*
(Yearbook of Agriculture Statistics) (Budapest: Hungarian Central Statisti-
cal Office).

12 China's Economic Structural Reform and Agricultural Development

Luo Yuanzheng

ECONOMICS INSTITUTE OF THE CHINESE
ACADEMY OF SOCIAL SCIENCES, BEIJING

Population is a basic factor in determining economic and social development. Changes in and development of the population structure are an important indicator of the growth of social productivity and the level of social development.

The development of human social productivity, and particularly the development of commodity production and commodity exchange, give rise to the emergence of cities inhabited by non-agricultural populations. The further growth of the social division of labour and the commodity economy and the rise of labour productivity accelerate the process of population urbanisation. The growth of cities, in turn, spurs the development of the social economy as a whole. On the other hand, along with the improvement in the social and economic life in many countries, an increasingly large number of the surplus rural labour force and the rural population flows into cities, causing the dramatic growth of the urban population. This has caused numerous problems in cities in the provision of employment, medical services, housing, food, transportation and the maintenance of public order, and has led to a widening gap between cities and the rural area.

Prior to the founding of the People's Republic of China, China's rural areas remained in a permanent state of poverty and backwardness. When famines struck, large numbers of peasants were forced to flee to cities to seek survival; hence the emergence of large slums in cities.

Following the founding of the new China, the Chinese government adopted the policy of mutual assistance and exchange between urban and rural areas. However, the percentage of rural population in the whole population remained more or less unchanged. The discrepancy between cities and the countryside, and between workers and peasants, was not eliminated. The self-supporting economy still prevailed in China's rural areas. Owing to the rapid growth in population after the new China was founded, and in particular the loss of control over the rural population, China's current rural population still accounts for about 80 per cent of the national total. Such a large rural population has aggravated the long-standing problem of food security. Efforts over several decades failed to modernise China's agriculture and to control effectively the massive influx of the rural population into cities. Numerous administrative means were adopted in an attempt to check this influx. For example, peasants were denied a stable food supply and residential permits, and their children were denied access to schooling in cities. However, these measures succeeded only to a limited extent in reducing urban population growth. They failed to bring about a rational balance between the rural and non-rural population and to provide employment for the surplus rural labour force. This remains an acute problem in China's socialist economic development.

After the Central Committee of the Communist Party of China held the Third Plenary Session of the 11th Central Committee in 1979, China adopted a series of new strategies for social and economic development. The new strategies have resulted in major achievements during China's Sixth Five-Year Plan Period for National Economic and Social Development. During this period, the effective reform policies and guidelines, suited to China's rural conditions, pursued by the Chinese government, have brought about profound changes in China's rural areas.

China is a developing country with its economy still backward and its productivity low. According to the criterion in a 1979 FAO report, an average monthly income above 700 dollars is a high income; that between 300 and 700 dollars is a medium income; an average monthly income below 300 dollars is a low income; that between 50 and 70 dollars means poverty and that below 50 dollars destitution. The average income of China's rural labour force in 1985 was 993 yuan (the standard unit of Chinese currency), which came to 30 dollars a month according to the exchange rate of the time. Although the value of China's industrial output amounts to 73 per cent of the total value of its industrial and agricultural output, it is still not developed. China's rural labour income is 74 per cent of the national total and the rural population amounts to 77 per cent of its total population. Agriculture, the main source of the people's livelihood, as well as the foundation of the national economy, has a vital bearing on China's overall growth. Hence agricultural development has top priority in China's social and economic development plans.

China started the reform of its economic structure in the rural areas and remarkable progress has been made. The introduction of a more flexible rural economic policy has invigorated the rural economy. It not only promotes the growth of rural productive forces but also causes a rational change in China's population structure, distribution and movement. On the one hand, the economic reform seeded peasant initiative and raised agricultural productivity. A large number of the agricultural labour force was freed from agricultural production and could thus seek employment in non-agricultural sectors. On the other hand, the development of the rural economy, and in particular the mushroom growth of township industry and service trades in the rural areas, now provide abundant and stable employment opportunities for seven million rural young people aged between 17 and 18 who join the labour force every year. The development of township industry not only absorbs large numbers of the rural population, but also makes the townships in China's vast rural areas more prosperous. It advances the progress of urbanisation of China's rural areas and points to the direction of future development of China's urban areas.

According to statistics, at the end of 1985 the total value of output of China's rural township industry, including collective peasant factories and individual peasant factories, reached 248 billion yuan. (It reached 49.3 billion yuan in 1978. Since 1979 the annual increase in the value of the total output of China's township industry has averaged 26 per cent). This figure represents 15.3 per cent of the value of total national output and 40 per cent of the rural output, and equals the value of national output in 1964. Its industrial output reached 180 billion yuan, which amounted to 20 per cent of the total value of national industrial output for the year, and equalled that of 1969. There are 64 million workers in China's township industry, the same number as in industries owned by the people as a whole. Thus, employment is created for a large number of the surplus rural labour force without driving them into cities. The advantages are obvious. Ample employment opportunities are provided, thus avoiding severe social problems. A lower amount of state investment in fixed assets is needed to provide employment for the surplus labour force. It could reach 1340 billion yuan, as 21,000 yuan is needed to create a job. Excessive urban population growth and concomitant investment in urban infrastructure is avoided. It enables those remaining in the agricultural sector to earn more because of the absence of many competitors. More wealth is created. For example, each farm labourer creates only about 900 yuan annually, while that created by a worker in a township workshop is 4000 yuan. What is more, it helps to rationalise the rural economic structure.

In addition to the above-mentioned advantages, China's rural township industry has other unique advantages. First, the potential contributions of both the labour force and the means of production are fully realised, with maximum absorption of various types of labour, including the auxiliary labour force, and maximum utilisation of makeshift workshops and equipment. Secondly, it accommodates the present level of labour skill and management expertise, re-employs the surplus rural labour force, and gives ample scope to the initiative and wisdom of the Chinese peasants. Thirdly, it saves capital, reduces consumption of energy, and helps to protect the environment and maintain the ecological balance. In short, township industry is small in scale, requires less capital and yields quick returns. It is a good tool for developing commodity production and the rural economy.

The employment structure of China's rural labour force, which remained relatively unchanged for 30 years, has begun to go through remarkable changes in the past five years. By the end of 1985 China had a total rural labour force of over 370 million. Among them, 307 million were engaged in primary industry, and that number showed an increase of 6.9 per cent over that of 1980. The number in the labour forces employed in secondary industry grew to 39 million, an increase of 73.7 per cent over that of 1980. Some 28 million work in the tertiary industry sector, representing an increase of 135 per cent. The percentage of secondary industry labour force in the total rural labour force rose from 7 per cent in 1980 to 10.4 per cent in 1985, and the percentage in the tertiary industry sector rose from 3.8 per cent in 1980 to 7.7 per cent in 1985. During the same period, China's grain output increased by 100 million tons. This shows that China's rural economy has moved away from the traditional rural economy in which all labour activity was confined by the limited farmland. The lopsided single grain economy that long prevailed in the past has been replaced by an economy characterised by integrated growth of agriculture, industry and commerce. This is of crucial importance in effecting a fundamental change in the work pattern of 800 million peasants engaged in farming and in raising agricultural productivity.

The growth of township industry, peasant households engaged in specialised undertakings, and the development and improvement of various production contract systems, are all playing an important role in ensuring the rational development of the rural population structure. The transformation of China's self-supporting rural economy into one characterised by large-scale commodity production, and the transformation of its traditional agriculture into modernised agriculture, offer brighter prospects and richer forms of reorganising China's population structure.

China is going through a unique process of transferring agricultural labour into non-agricultural sectors. During this process numerous township enterprises and family workshops absorb labour and create job opportunities. It thus alleviates pressure on large cities and at the same time increases non-agricultural output value in the rural areas, and raises rural consumption and asset accumulation.

A historical study of the path of economic growth which the developed countries have taken shows that the growth of non-agricultural undertakings in the rural areas is a universal economic trend. Admittedly, countries vary as to social systems, their level of economic development, natural endowments and resources, and in their approaches toward creating employment for the rural labour force. They have, however, pursued more or less the same policy in promoting the integrated and comprehensive development of their rural economies, and in rationalising their economic and employment structures.

With the development of society and the economy, rural labour migration is inevitable. What is important is to find an appropriate way to handle it. I believe that economic structural reform in China's rural areas opens up wide prospects for the rational development of China's population structure. It is imperative to take into consideration the specific conditions in China – a vast country with a population of one billion and varying degrees of development in different regions – in rationalising the population structure. Strategies and policies should be formulated which are suited to China's national conditions and which take into account the fact that 80 per cent of China's population is rural. As China has just started to rationalise its population structure, we still lack experience. However, we have reason to believe that as economic reform deepens, better and more comprehensive ways will be found to deal with the problems related to China's population structure, distribution and movement.

13 Intensification of Land Utilisation

Tigran Khachaturov

ASSOCIATION OF SOVIET ECONOMIC SCIENTIFIC
INSTITUTIONS, MOSCOW

U.S.S.R.
7172
0520

1 THE LAND RESOURCES OF THE USSR

Under socialism, which entails the people's ownership of land as well as other natural resources, there is the possibility of having a planned, efficient approach to land use. The entire land area of the USSR constitutes an integral state land fund. It is the people's property.

Population distribution and production in the USSR is highly concentrated. Two-thirds of the population (180 million people) live in towns, which comprise a total settled area of less than 100,000 square kilometres, or 0.4 per cent of the vast territory of the USSR (22.3 million square km). Industrial enterprises situated outside towns occupy 70,000 square km, or 0.3 per cent of USSR territory. All modes of transportation account for 40,000 square km, or less than 0.2 per cent. About 420,000 square km of land are provided for health resorts, national parks and other such entities. The major part of the USSR population, its industry and transport are, therefore, concentrated in an area slightly over 210,000 square km, or less than 1 per cent of the USSR territory. Taking into account the land occupied for other uses, the figures would be slightly over 600,000 square km and 2.7 per cent.

Agricultural land (6.1 million square km) and forest land (8.1 square km) covers a little less than two-thirds of the USSR territory. The remaining one-third of the country's territory is almost uninhabited arctic tundra, glaciers, deserts and mountains.

The development of agriculture in the USSR has fallen behind that of industry, although agriculture's share in the national income (including turnover tax) was 27.5 per cent in 1984. At the 27th Congress of the CPSU Mr Gorbachev said that 'the lag in agriculture is being overcome slowly. A decisive turn is needed in the agrarian sector'. According to the 'Guidelines for the Economic and Social Development of the

USSR for 1986–90 and for the period ending in 2000' adopted at the 27th Congress, the following objectives are envisaged: steady growth of agricultural production; and the promulgation of the necessary measures so that the management, planning and financing of the agro-industrial complex would function as a unified system. Scientifically-grounded systems of agriculture, use of soil-protective methods of farming, anti-erosion measures, increasing soil fertility, and the intro-duction of intensive technologies, are all to contribute to the accele-ration of agricultural development.

In comparison with other countries of the world, the USSR has the largest territory. It also has the largest agricultural area, a greater area than that of the USA, Australia, China or India. Its area in crops also exceeds that of any other country. Concomitantly the USSR's agricul-tural output is less than that of the USA. The major reason for this is the worse climatic conditions. Agricultural lands are mostly situated in the so-called 'risky agricultural zone' with relatively low temperatures, prolonged periods of frost and low humidity. The USSR agricultural areas of overriding importance, the Ukraine, North Caucasus, the Middle and Lower Volga areas, Southern Urals, Northern Kazakhstan and Western Siberia lie at 45–55°N; large areas extend farther north. The entire US territory lies south of 48°, whereas two-thirds of the USSR territory is to the north of this latitude. The difference in temperatures and humidity is significant. 60 per cent of arable land is in the areas with a mean annual temperature of about + 5°C in the USSR. Only 10 per cent of arable land is in areas with such temperatures in the USA. About 1.1 per cent of arable land in the USSR is located in areas with annual precipitation of 700 mm or more, as opposed to 60 per cent in the USA. In areas with annual precipitation below 400 mm the corresponding figures would be 40 and 11 per cent respectively.

Judging by the mean annual temperatures, agricultural areas of the USSR, especially in its Asian region, have more in common with Canada, with its vast uninhabited northern expanses, than with the USA. The level of grain yield in the USSR is also nearer to that of Canada than that of the USA.

During the years of Soviet power, and especially in the post-war period, measures to expand arable land, specifically crop areas, have been undertaken. In 1913 there were 118 million hectares of crop area in the country; in 1940 there were 115 million hectares and in 1950 the figure was 146 million hectares. The reduction resulted from allotting some crop areas to the non-agricultural sector. In the 1950s crop areas expanded dramatically, due to an enormous development of virgin and long-fallow lands, primarily in Kazakhstan, adding more than 42 million hectares.

In 1960 cropped areas of the USSR comprised 203 million hectares; in 1983 there were 213 million hectares (with 227 million hectares of arable land). Possibilities for further expansion of arable land and pasture are very limited. There is little long-fallow land left – a total of 700,000 hectares as a whole in the country. There might be some expansion of agricultural land provided saline areas and bushlands are re-established and made stone-free.

Hand in hand with extensive development of crop lands, efforts have been made to increase the crop yield on existing agricultural land. For instance, the average grain output had more than doubled by the end of the 1970s as compared with the beginning of the 1950s.

The basic method of upgrading agricultural productivity is seen as being a changeover to the most productive modern systems of agricultural management rather than in the extensive expansion of arable and other agricultural land. These systems vary according to regional differences among zones in, for example, soil, climate, organisation and management.

1.1 Agricultural Zones

Viewing the country's agricultural zones from the point of view of their importance in agricultural production, the bulk of production comes from the vast plains of the European part of the USSR, Siberia and Kazakhstan, the forest-steppe and steppe zones of the USSR. Here nearly two-thirds of the country's arable is to be found, predominantly black fertile soils in both zones. Feed and fodder grain crops, soy beans, vegetables, sugar-beet, potatoes and sunflower are grown there. Livestock breeding for both milk and meat production and pig breeding are well developed. The climatic conditions differ in specific parts of both zones. Mean temperatures are higher in the south and diminish northwardly; eastwardly the aridity increases dramatically. The probability of arid years is 20–45 per cent. North of the forest-steppe zone is the taiga zone with its south-western part accounting for 15 per cent of all the arable land. The mean temperatures here are lower than in the wooded steppe zone but humidity is sufficient and in some places too much (Western Siberia). The soils are mainly soddy podzolic, boggy here and there. Among grain crops, rye and barley are cultivated. Vegetables, potatoes and flax are also grown. Dairy cattle breeding is well developed. To the south of the steppe zone is the arid steppe with higher temperatures and extremely low humidity, especially in the areas off the left bank of the Volga and in Kazakhstan. The soils are chestnut and dark chestnut, here and there sandy loam and sandy solonetzic. The western part of the zone is largely ploughed. In the Volga and Kazakhstan areas pastures account for a large part of agricultural land.

Other zones – the arctic deserts and tundra in the north and deserts and semi-deserts in the south – are unfavourable for agriculture because of their climatic and soil conditions, that is, low temperatures in the north and extreme aridity in the south. A considerable part of the agricultural lands in the desert and semi-desert zones is pasture. To plough land in these dry zones requires irrigation.

The analysis of land resources by zones highlights possible ways for their essential improvement. We are unable to increase the warmth required by agricultural zones, although we can transform the land, upgrading fertility and yield capacity of soils, eliminating soil acidity, salinity, bog, swamp and rockiness, and reduce losses caused by drought.

2 INTENSIFICATION OF LAND USE

Intensification of agricultural land use calls for intensive cultivation, land management, erosion control, lime and gypsum application and application of fertiliser. Such measures are provided for by the general scheme of land resource utilisation and should be vigorously put into practice.

The productive capacity of soils is of the utmost importance. It is not only a natural property of land itself, as well as climatic conditions, warmth and moisture, but also, to a great degree, the result of correct soil maintenance and improvement of its natural properties.

Our agricultural lands are heavily cropped. The proportion of ploughed area in Central Chernozem is over 80 per cent; in the Ukraine 80 per cent; in the Volga-Vyatka, Central Industrial and Volga economic areas 65–70 per cent. It is much higher than in developed capitalist countries. The large proportion of ploughed land is undesirable, especially in the arid steppe zones, bearing in mind the reduction of yield from soils if timely measures for amelioration of damage are not taken.

The arable area has not expanded during the last few years. At the same time the country's population has increased. In 1960 there were 1.04 hectares of arable land per capita; in 1983 the figure was 0.83 hectares. This fact emphasises the need for better utilisation of arable land.

There are quite a number of chernozemic soils in our country having, as is known, highly desirable natural properties. The belt containing these soils extends from Moldavia, South-Western and Southern Ukraine through the North Caucasus, the central part of the Volga area, partly the South Urals, Northern Kazakhstan and some areas of Western Siberia. To the south there are the chestnut soils of Kazakhstan, and to the north the semipodzol and sylvogenic soils of the European part of the USSR, namely, Western Siberia, where they alternate with swamps and then extend into Eastern Siberia. The thickness of the chernozem soil profile, especially in the Ukraine and the Central Chernozem area is 0.4–1.2 metres.

The vast expanses of chernozem soils in our country constitute a most valuable natural asset and they are to be preserved. Soil fertility depends heavily on the presence of sufficient productive top soil, that is, one with enough humus (organic matter). The humus level in soils should be about 2.5–3.0 per cent, and in the basic agricultural regions of the USSR it is estimated to be 30 to 60 tons per hectare. One of the most vital requirements of rational management is to prevent the reduction of the humus layer and, therefore, of the level of crop yield. Especially undesirable is the diminishing of the humus layer in Kazakhstan, on former virgin lands where this level is thin. To recreate humus, organic fertilisers (manure) should be applied in quantities of up to 6–10 tons per hectare; in Central Asia 15 tons. There must be fuller use of existing opportunities for producing organic fertilisers. For example, major cattle breeding enterprises, along with collective and state farms, could organise the processing of their refuse, its storage, transportation to the fields and dunging, which could greatly increase crop yield and cover all the expenses in an acceptable time period as well as doing away with pollution of the environment.

2.1 Application of Science and Technology

The intensification of agricultural land use requires wide application of scientific and technical innovations so that a greater output can be achieved with less input of labour, materials and equipment. Amelioration, fertilisation, erosion control and other components of modern field management are necessary.

'Amelioration' is a radical improvement of land with the aim of increasing the economic fertility of soils. It consists of undertaking hydrotechnical, cultural/technical and agro-technical measures, first on arable lands, but also on haylands and pastures.

2.2 Irrigation and Drainage

Irrigation and drainage are of great importance to the increase of efficiency of agricultural lands. 'Amelioration' makes it possible to overcome natural shortcomings of soils, first on the vast expanses of semi-arid and arid zones where temperatures are conducive to the production of heat-loving crops like cotton and paddy, but where moisture is in acute demand. The area of irrigated land reached 19 million hectares in 1983, while that of drained land was estimated at 18 million hectares. Capital investment in irrigation amounts to 3000–7000 roubles per hectare, while drainage expenditure amounts to 500–1000 roubles per hectare. These costs are recovered in acceptable time periods from additional agricultural production. Irrigation was largely responsible for the increase of average cotton yields from 16.6 metric centners per hectare in 1960 to 31.7 metric centners per hectare in 1980 (28.9 in 1983). Average rice yields rose from 19.3 to 41.9 centners per hectare. Crop yields have increased much more on ameliorated lands, on irrigated lands especially, than in the country at large.

The October 1984 Plenary Meeting of the Central Committee of the CPSU adopted a long-term programme of amelioration, increasing the efficiency of ameliorated land utilisation to provide for a steady increase in the country's food supply. The Plenary Meeting outlined the goal of putting large production zones for farm produce (grain, fodder, vegetables) on an industrial footing. In accordance with this long-term programme, the total area of irrigated land is to increase to 30–32 million hectares, and that of drained lands to 19–21 million hectares; an increase from 1983 of 60 per cent and 11 per cent respectively. Grain production on ameliorated lands would reach 32 million tons by 1990 and 55–60 million tons by the year 2000, including 18–20 million tons of corn, while fodder production would be at an estimated 80 million tons in 1990 and 115–120 million tons in 2000 (evaluated in fodder units).

Production of alfalfa and other legume crops, as well as vegetables, early potatoes and cotton, is expected to increase substantially. The major irrigation project will be in the southern regions of the country where the return on capital investment is likely to be the greatest.

In perspective, amelioration is expected to develop further. Amelioration suggests not only irrigation and drainage, but implies a variety of other measures to intensify agricultural production, accomplishing the transfer from mere adaptation to natural conditions to the creation of an advanced technology-based scientific system of agricultural management and the eradication of dependence on the uncertainties of the weather. Technically efficient procedures, innovative methods of cultivation, erosion prevention and inventory shrinkage control are all part of the package.

The planned yield is at present obtained on only one-third of irrigated lands. In many cases it is very low. On average over 1.5 million hectares of irrigated lands have not been cultivated annually. Many irrigated lands fail to receive enough fertiliser. Use of fertiliser averages 250 kg per hectare, or 25–30 per cent less than required.

It is necessary to increase the efficiency of land reclamation. One of the planned aims is to increase the relative efficiency of irrigation systems. On average it is a mere 0.5, in some places even 0.3 and less, due to water leakage and evaporation. Greater concern is required in the deployment of amelioration systems and in the maintenance of equipment used in watering. There must be a more energetic shift from surface irrigation to modern methods such as sprinkler systems and subsoil drip irrigation, promoting efficiency and water conservation. 'Fregate' and 'Kuban' sprinkling machines are still expensive, but their cost could be reduced with increased large-scale production.

The Plenary Meeting of the Central Committee of the CPSU on 23 October 1984 emphasised that irrigated and drained lands should be provided with everything needed: fertilisers, technology, chemicals for plant protection, and all other material and technical resources, including those for maintenance.

Comprehensive feasibility procedures are necessary in arranging drainage of excessively wet soils. Some swamps are important as riverheads and their drainage has an unfavourable influence on the hydrology of the surrounding territory. Some kinds of bog vegetation, such as cranberries and cloudberries, are quite valuable.

2.3 Fertilisers and Pesticides

The application of fertilisers, pesticides and lime, coupled with irrigation and drainage, is a major component in the scientific and technical progress of agriculture. In 1984, 23 million tons of fertiliser were supplied to the agricultural sector (evaluated at 100 per cent of ingredients of 103 kg per hectare) – twice as much as in 1970. The average wholesale price of fertiliser is 180 roubles per ton, that is, one hectare of land receives fertiliser costing 18 roubles (without transport costs). The use of fertiliser contributes to a 30 per cent or more increase in grain, cotton and sugar-beet harvests. It also accounts for a 15–20 per cent increase in the quantity of potatoes and vegetables produced. Fertiliser application is required in appropriate proportions for varying soils. The lack of phosphoric fertilisers is tangible. More effective use of mineral fertilisers on non-calcareous soils would require lime application. The ration of lime is up to 8 tons per hectare, with the price at 6–8 roubles per ton. A notable upswing in the production and application of pesticides is also needed. Transportation, storage, and application of fertilisers and other chemicals have been improved, though there have been losses, shortcomings and misapplications. These shortcomings could easily be eliminated by the farms themselves. What is needed is an increase in the supply of equipment, fertiliser broadcasters and other machinery for fertiliser and lime application. Both excessive and insufficient application of fertiliser is undesirable. Too much fertiliser does not add to crop yield, and washing away of excessively applied fertilisers by rain and irrigation flows contaminates rivers and has a negative impact on water quality and fish.

2.4 Crop Rotation

Hand in hand with fertiliser application has come the great importance of well-managed crop rotation, scientifically verified and proved by practice, for the preservation of soil fertility and the promotion of agricultural efficiency; diversification of grain, beans, alfalfa and other crops depending on conditions in a particular zone. Monoculture is not permissible. With correct crop rotation, yields could increase 25–30 per cent and even more with fertiliser application. On the other hand, disregard for the rules of land utilisation and overcropping tend to decrease fertility and destroy soils, putting on a semblance of intensification for a short time only.

A careful treatment of soil as a basic means of production in agriculture requires the application of modern methods of cultivation with due regard to the peculiarities of the soils. Ploughing laterally and without a mould-board, preserving stubble and root residues, loosening and other methods of cultivation depending on the nature and structure of the soils, should be applied on a greater scale. All this requires sufficient supplies of agricultural machinery and equipment.

Protection of soils from wind and water erosion is also required.

2.5   Overcoming Erosion

The area of agricultural land subject to erosion is large, amounting to 100 million hectares, including 50 million hectares of arable land.

More than 50 per cent of the USSR's land is subject to water erosion and up to 45 per cent to wind erosion. Gullies cover over 5 million hectares. According to some estimates, annual losses caused by erosion account for 8–10 per cent of the gross agricultural output.

As far back as 1967 the Central Committee of the CPSU and the USSR Council of Ministers adopted the resolution on 'Certain measures to protect soil from wind and water erosion'. There have been extensive efforts to create forest strips and to build other anti-erosion structures. Banking, countour cultivation and ploughing without a mould-board have been expanding. Strip arrangement of crops and fallows has also been used. Anti-erosion expenses are covered in due time, but the scope of such efforts must be extended. A package of measures to protect soils from water and wind erosion and to control surface discharge should be carried out across the larger part of the agricultural land, including not only arable land but also haylands and pastures.

2.6   Avoiding Industrial and Urban Pollution

It is essential to safeguard lands situated close to industrial centres, cities and roads with heavy traffic from contamination from sulphur oxides and other gases, benzopyrene, lead and other heavy metals. Soil contamination has an extremely negative effect on yield, to say nothing of possible penetration of hazardous substances into plants – potatoes, sunflower, grain. Hence the great importance of limiting dust and gas exhaust emanating from industry, transport and towns.

2.7   Avoiding Overuse of Land

The excessive usage of fields, hayland and pasture is inadmissible. The largest areas of native pasture are in Kazakhstan and Central Asia.

They cover 260 million hectares, or four-fifths of the entire area of natural pasture in the USSR. But the fertility of this pasture is very low, in some areas 1–2 metric centners of dry matter per hectare, the average not exceeding 6–7 metric centners. They should receive attention with the aim of preventing heavy grazing and further deterioration. Intensification of grassland farming has been underway, bringing cattle-breeding locations with pasture carrying capacities by zones into proper correlation. It is also being done to ensure the further increase of pasture fertility.

The development of livestock breeding is based not only on grain and fodder yields, but also on hay yields. The area of native haylands has been shrinking and now accounts for 35 million hectares. The larger part of the hay yield is made up of perennial grass, whose yield could be increased. The CPSU Central Committee Plenary Meeting of October 1984 emphasised as urgent the necessity of putting native forage production areas in order. The areas are large, and a major source of natural fodder. It is most important to increase fodder yield (corn, barley, oats, soy beans, etc.) for livestock breeding.

3   LOSS OF LAND FOR NON-AGRICULTURAL USES

Considerable parts of agricultural land are withdrawn annually to satisfy the needs of industry, transportation, towns, etc. It is vital to assess the economic expediency of land withdraw͘. In the first place, if need be, withdrawal should proceed with land unsuited to agriculture and the withdrawal of land from agriculture for non-agricultural use should be restricted when that land is particularly attractive to agriculture and requires little capital investment for crop production. Despite recent reductions, the total area of land transferred annually to the non-agricultural sector has reached one million hectares, 5 per cent of which is arable land and 17 per cent other farm lands.

During the last few years large areas of excellent land, including fertile flood-plain land, have been turned into reservoirs for hydro-electric power stations. Hydro-electric stations, unlike thermal stations, require higher capital investment but produce electricity at little current cost and with a small labour force. They do not pollute the atmosphere as thermal power stations do with emissions of sulphur dioxide, dust and heat. But reservoirs may flood valuable agricultural and forested lands, especially in plains. It is wrong to assess economic losses due to the withdrawal of these lands only in terms of the costs involved in providing land and accommodation at new locations. The compensation might satisfy the owners of the flooded areas but it will not compensate the national economy for the loss of farms and forests. During the last few years the construction of hydro-electric stations on rivers flowing in the plains has been reduced. The total area of major artificial reservoirs amounts to tens of thousands of square kilometres.

Agricultural land is also withdrawn due to the development of opencast mining. In such cases the topsoil should be preserved. According to published data, approximately 75 per cent of disturbed soils will be reclaimed.

Reclamation of dumps by planting trees has been done in Estonia in the opencast mining area, as well as in the Moscow coal basin, the Ukraine, Georgia (Chiatura), Siberia and the Far East. Forests are very important in the preservation of water and land resources, for the improvement of the environment and for providing healthier conditions of life. Forest strips and other protective plantings safeguard fields, gullies and sandstone lands, protecting them from hot dry winds and from wind and water erosion.

Reservoir construction takes place on disturbed lands, along with the construction of recreational sites. This type of work has a key place in the vicinity of Moscow, in Estonia, Ukraine, Byelorussia and Moldavia.

Some agricultural land is allotted for highway and road construction, as mentioned above, which is necessary for the country at large and for agriculture itself. The improvement of transport services and facilities to meet growing agricultural needs would require about one million kilometres of solid-surfaced roads. Some motorways would make use of the layout of existing country roads which would be widened, lined with side ditches and furnished with road maintenance facilities, artificial structures, traffic signs etc.

It is not advisable for agricultural lands to share neighbourhoods with dumps around cities. Annual town refuse quantities amount to 200–500 kilograms per person. Practice has proved the expediency of screening out metals, tyres, glass, paper and other waste, and of the incineration of organic elements, which helps to get rid of litter, using it as fuel.

4 OPTIMAL UTILISATION AND VALUATION PROBLEMS

Rational land utilisation within the framework of an integral agricultural complex would require comparative economic evaluations of all elements of agricultural production. Unfortunately such calculations turn out to be incomplete, since the land, as the basic means of production in agriculture, and other natural resources are unpriced. The price of land is, naturally, not intended to turn it into some commodity to be bought and sold. As people's property, it is not and cannot be a commodity. But the absence of land rating distorts economic calculations of its effective utilisation and of the returns from upgrading, known to require a great deal of labour.

Land rating for comparative economic evaluation, making trade-off against other costs, is possible with due account of a differential rent which could be calculated on the basis of quality of a site and its location. If the differential rent (R) is known, then land price (S) would be $\frac{R}{E_n}$ where E_n is the standard effectiveness ratio.

According to approximate land ratings worked out by researchers, the overall cost of one hectare of agricultural land in the 1960s was 300 roubles, fluctuating from 110–120 roubles in Kazakhstan and Yakutia to 1400–1800 roubles in Krasnodar territory and Moldavia. The average arable land rating was about 700 roubles. In the reports, published recently, these ratings have increased. By the end of the 1970s the average estimate of one hectare of agricultural land was 400–450 roubles and that of arable land 950–1000 roubles.

These ratings seem to be understated. If we assume that the net product per hectare of agricultural land was about 200 roubles in the mid-1980s then, within the next two to two and a half years, the value of the net product per hectare is bound to be equivalent to its rating. However, in agriculture, according to the Methods of Evaluation of Capital Investments Efficiency (3rd edn, 1980) the standard period for the return of capital investment is limited to 14 years (efficiency standard 0.07).

With an average rating of 450 roubles per hectare of agricultural land, its total value in the country would be 272 billion roubles, which is roughly equal to all other production funds. The national assets of the USSR, without the value of land, mineral resources and forests, were estimated at 3.4 trillion roubles at the end of 1984. Therefore the value of agricultural land as a percentage of national assets would be 8.4 per cent. For the sake of comparison it should be noted that the value of land used by US farms was 692 billion dollars in 1982, or about 8 per cent of national wealth.

The urban land of the USSR should be rated higher than agricultural land, estimating it at tens and hundreds of thousands of roubles per hectare.

A large proportion of the USSR agricultural land's value is that of arable land. With the average cost assumed at 1000 roubles per hectare, the total value of arable land would be 227 billion roubles.

Land could have higher value rating if its agricultural production increased. That depends on the quality of land, its fertility and the quality of agricultural management. Land improvement and amelioration and conversion to innovative methods of soil cultivation are necessary. Better machinery should be introduced, its maintenance and repair improved and its idle time due to malfunctioning and failures eradicated. In the long run, all these efforts would be aimed at the intensification of land utilisation. The supply of spare parts should be on a larger scale. Collective and state farms are expected to improve conditions for maintenance and storage of tractors, harvesters and other agricultural machinery.

The Congresses of the CPSU and Plenary Meetings of the CPSU Central Committee have emphasised the necessity of eliminating losses of agricultural production during its transportation, storage and initial processing because of lack of roads, storage facilities, lift conveyors, refrigerators and the capacities of processing enterprises. Better supply of our country's food depends greatly on the elimination of losses of farm produce. In 1976–80 the loss of 1 per cent of harvested grain amounted on average to 2 million tons of grain annually. Because of a disregard of optimal harvesting time, as well as losses during harvesting and transportation, the total amount of losses is very impressive. Improvement of country roads and storage facilities would help to eliminate a considerable part of these losses, ensuring an 8–9 per cent increase in the total annual output.

The completion of the Agricultural Land Cadastre as soon as possible would have an enormous impact on rational land use. This project has already been completed in some Republics and regions of the USSR.

5 CONCLUSION

A justifiable choice of measures aimed at safeguarding land resources, including virgin land utilisation, reduction of agricultural land conversion to other purposes, reclamation of disturbed land, will greatly depend on making use of the data accumulated in the Cadastre. These data reflect the quantitative and qualitative characteristics of lands, that is, the topography, soil, vegetation, erosion liability, as well as soil rating and economic land rating. Based on these data, it is possible to ascertain when fertilisers should be applied (phosphoric, potassic or nitrogenous), which elements are lacking in the soil, whether lime application is required, and which amelioration techniques would be most suitable. Such action would improve soil quality dramatically and increase the level of crop yield. Economic evaluation would show how soon the required investment is to be returned from increased productivity.

The perspectives of further agricultural development have been highlighted in the Food Programme of the USSR and in the Guidelines for the Economic and Social Development of the USSR for 1986–90 and for the period ending in 2000. The main task of the agro-industrial complex is to achieve stable agricultural production so that the country will be provided with food and agricultural raw materials. High ultimate results should be obtained by dovetailing the activities of all parts of the integral agro-industrial complex, increasing the quality of production, eliminating losses, applying large-scale industrial, waste-free technologies and improving production management, transportation, processing and storage. Concrete levels of crop and livestock production have been specified. Realisation of the tasks envisaged under the Food Programme and the Long-term Programme of Amelioration, Irrigation and Drainage has been stipulated along with the fulfilment of cultural/technical goals and improvement of irrigation systems. The task of tangible upgrading and scientific substantiation of the rational redistribution of water resources has been set forth.

Discussion on Part IV

PAPER BY ALADAR SIPOS

'Socialist Technically Oriented Production Systems'

Professor G. S. Bhalla, the lead discussant for Professor Sipos's paper, said the paper systematically outlined changes that had taken place in Hungarian agriculture. There were three phases in this continuum – the 'mistakes' of the past, when agriculture was the source of 'surplus' for industrialisation; the policies initiated after 1956 which stressed the role of both incentives (e.g., prices) and technology; and finally, the current policies stressing the role of modernisation and investment in agriculture.

He noted that Sipos had properly stressed the role of agriculture as an integrated economic activity – that is, agriculture itself became industrialised in the process of economic development (e.g., development of production of meat, milk, etc.). However, in its most recent stage of modernisation, the problem of exports was a serious one. The dilemma was how to maintain the competitiveness of Hungarian agricultural products in Western markets.

In questions and comments following Professor Bhalla's presentation, it was noted that the successful performance of Hungarian agriculture had positive lessons for Poland in showing how there could be balanced development of agriculture and of industry. Competitiveness on the world market, however, no longer depended on quality or the efficiency of production but on the fluctuation of exchange rates. This posed a serious problem for agricultural exports.

Questions were then raised concerning the role of agricultural pricing policy in Hungary; whether the extent and efficiency of mechanisation on small farms was similar to that on large farms; the incentive structure in agriculture and contractual arrangements (who contracts with whom); the reasons for so-called 'overproduction' in Hungarian agriculture; what types of incentives would be necessary in the future (e.g., would subsidies be necessary, as in the USA?); the percentage of private and co-operative farms; and the ecological effects of the mechanisation of Hungarian agriculture.

In response, Professor Sipos replied that the direct planning system

230

in agriculture was abolished in 1956. This was a very good step because it stipulated production both on co-operative and state farms and on private farms. Secondly, it provided impetus to reform later in 1968 – in both agriculture and industry. In Hungary, there was no quota system. Each state farm and co-operative worked out its own plan.

The market in Hungary consisted of three sectors – the state, the co-operative, and the private market. The co-operative or state farms had the right to sell to the state, to process the product, or to sell the product in the private market.

Farms had the right to create associations or joint ventures. Every state and co-operative farm was independent and there was no pre-scription on the share of product sold to the state.

There were problems for the economy. One-third of Hungary's food production (processed and unprocessed) was exported. About 50 per cent of the food exports went to Comecon countries with the remainder to developing or developed countries. There were several difficulties with the world market. First, the traditional market for Hungary was Western Europe, but within the European Economic Community (EEC) there was overproduction of agricultural commodities. Secondly, there was a trade war between the EEC and the USA involving agricultural commodities. This was a crucial problem for the development of Hungarian agriculture. Hungary needed to learn to adapt to this adverse world economic environment. One element in the programme which dealt with the situation was to reduce energy consumption in agricultural production. Energy was used for drying agricultural products (e.g., corn). Twenty years ago, when the price of oil had been low, a great deal of energy was used. In the Five-Year-Plan, new methods to reduce energy consumption on state farms and co-operative farms in the drying of grain had been developed. Though oil consumption was lower now, this was not enough. Earlier, Hungarian wheat prices were lower than world prices. The price of wheat on the international market had been US $200 and was now US $80. Formerly, it was not necessary to subsidise grain exports from Hungary. Grain exports had been very profitable, but now that was not so. In Hungary, an impressive growth rate in agriculture had been achieved. Now it was necessary to increase efficiency and improve the quality of production. There were many problems in this field. Hungarian industry was not fully developed. In particular, the packaging of food was not as attractively done as in the West.

In regard to the technological problems of agriculture, it was essential to try to import machinery from different countries and not just from Comecon countries. This was not an easy task. The price of machinery had been increased and oil receipts had fallen.

He concluded by saying that socialism needed an efficient economic mechanism.

PAPER BY LUO YUANZHENG

'China's Economic Structural Reform and Agricultural Development'

Questions and comments evoked by Professor Luo's paper concerned the fact that the paper was not comprehensive in that the strategy of rural development began as far back as 1949 and was based on early land reforms, and the paper dealt only with the reforms after 1979; whether increased incomes from agriculture would be a threat to population policy in China; how the author could assert that identical development policies were followed in capitalist and socialist countries; the need to spell out the characteristics of reforms of institutional structures in China; whether industry had been able to absorb the labour migrating from rural areas; whether the granting of increased incentives to agriculture and permitting private hiring of labour had led to an increased burden on the consumer, on the one hand, and the exploitation of labour on the other; the policies with regard to wage labour; the guiding principles behind the price reforms; the policies of the communes in the future; the inherence of rural industrialisation taking place in China; and whether there was a conflict between socialist ideology and the anti-egalitarianism which China was experiencing. Since the spectacular success in agriculture was seemingly due to organisational changes, better management, and increased incentives while technical factors obviously did not play an important role, what were the prospects for the future? Were there adequate resources for future growth in productivity? What direction would agricultural development take? There was objection to the concept of the existence of one economic law governing rural development. There was seemingly no one general pattern of development of agriculture and industry common to both socialist and advanced capitalistic systems.

Finally, referring to the Hungarian experience, it was averred that agricultural and rural development were not synonymous. Slow urban development took place even in the Eastern periphery of Europe and the tertiary development of rural areas was very important. In Hungary, about one-quarter of the work force was in 'rural factories'. Hence the relevance of the western experience might not be very useful for China and the strategy of rural industrialisation was an interesting aspect of Chinese strategy.

Professor Luo replied that agrarian policies after 1949 restricted the initiative of the peasantry. There were low procurement prices for agricultural products and a lack of availability of essential consumer items such as bicycles and radios. In 1979 reforms were initiated to increase output and productivity through greater use of the market mechanism and reliance on objective economic laws. The resulting increase in agricultural incomes found reflection in the fact that Chinese peasants today could buy TVs, cars, refrigerators, and watches – i.e., consumer durables and equipment for repairs, and other items.

Thus, the role of incentives was extremely important. Secondly, the government's economic policy was to encourage rural industrialisation and not simply rural migration into the cities.

On the question of inequality, he pointed to the emergence of rich peasants in certain parts of China as being encouraged. Inequality, he indicated, was not a problem. 'Rich and poor were temporary phenomena'. The rich showed others in the villages what prospects could be. Hence, surplus labour would be absorbed. Enterprise was being encouraged by local authorities and banks. Regarding links between the rural areas and cities – contracts linked the two. For example, if exporters in Shanghai could not fulfil a contract, they could subcontract to a rural firm. As to the payment of wages, only urban workers were paid wages – family workers redistributed the family income.

Turning to the question of population, he said that China had been forced to control population growth but did not control population growth in minority communities, especially in rural areas.

Regarding the use of markets, he said this was not capitalism because peasants could not own land. This was a responsibility system to increase efficiency which had to be encouraged, not through force (as in the 1960s) but by the use of economic instruments – prices, improved organisation and management, and information – in order to help the countryside to modernise. Earlier co-operatives existed, but they had not been entrusted with the task of greater responsibility – hence the emphasis on the new policies to increase productivity.

PAPER BY TIGRAN KHACHATUROV

'Intensification of Land Utilisation'

Questions raised in the general discussion concerned how agriculture would be affected, given the economic strategy of the 27th Congress of the Communist Party of the Soviet Union which envisaged a redistribution of capital investments in favour of industry; the main problems in evaluating soil and agricultural assets: the decentralisation of agricultural economic activities; whether an evaluation of the national utilisation of land could be done at the micro level; reasons for the better performance of agriculture in other countries (were they related to incentives?); measures considered regarding incentives in the 27th Congress; whether there were food shortages in the USSR; the characteristics of agro-based industrialisation; the characteristics of irrigation measures; and finally, whether the lag in agricultural development (compared to that in industry) was deliberate or due to errors in planning.

Academician Khachaturov replied that, in the USSR, there was demographic pressure requiring increased agricultural production and no possibility of increasing the sown area. Hence there was a need for further improvements in land use.

Results of large investments in agriculture were disappointing because of poor management and the poor quality of equipment. Improvements in the quality of the soil required investments amounting to 1000 roubles per hectare, but corresponding investments in industry were much higher.

As for the decentralisation of economic activity, conditions were very different in different parts of the USSR so no simple measures could be recommended.

Evaluating the soil at the micro level, he opined, was not of much help.

Turning to the question of incentives and (again) performance, the need for better management and not simply more investment in agriculture was reiterated. Some proposals were being considered for giving increasing incentives to individual farmers. There had been food shortages because of the higher rates of growth of output of industry as compared to agriculture, but there was no hunger. Demands of the population, however, especially for high-quality products, were quite often not met; hence the need for increasing agricultural output faster than that of industry. There were losses in agriculture because of the lack of infrastructure. Regarding the balance between raw material and food production, he averred that balance between different sectors of the economy was the more important concern. Raw materials were a requisite because of the policy of industrialisation, but increasing efficiency in the production and use of raw materials was still a problem. Finally, he referred to N.I. Ryzhkov's speech to the 27th Congress regarding the future development of agro-industrial complexes. The goal laid out in the State Food Programme for the period 1986–2000 was the attainment of complete self-sufficiency in food and in raw materials originating in the agricultural sector.

Index

Adelman, I., vii, xiii, xv, xviii–xxi,
  20, 24, 29, 76–7, 81, 82, 177
Adiseshaiah, M. S., xiv
adjustment
  capital stock, 152–8
  external cost, 157–8
  labour force, 145–51
  policy, 42
Agarwala, A., 96
agrarian reform, see land, tenure
agriculture
  collectivised, 186, 191–3, 198–202,
    204, 231, 233
  in development process, xix–xxi,
    81–96, 110–35, 202–8, 216–29,
    230–3
  diversification, 104–6, 137–9, 208
  dry-land, 97–101
  employment, xix, 64–6, 68, 116
  exports, xix–xx, 82, 203, 209,
    230–1
  peasant, xix, 63, 94, 97–9, 104–8,
    110–11, 138, 161–78, 190,
    197–201, 211–15, 233
  prices, 199, 208–9
  productivity, 81–5, 116–17, 130–1,
    193, 203
  subsistence, xix–xx, 212
  technology, 94–5, 130, 190–3,
    203–8, 222–6, 230–2
Ahluwaliah, M. S., xiv
Ahmed, R., 160
Aiyaswammi, Dr, xvi
Alma Ata Conference (WHO and
  Unicef), 33, 34
altruism, 6, 9
Argentina, xxi, 143–60, 179–80
Arrow, K. J., vii, ix, x, xiii, 20, 177
Aspremont, C.d', 20
Awasthi, D. S., xiv
Axelrod, R., 5

Bacha, E. L., ix
Bairoch, P., 81

balance of payments, 11, 13, 14, 86,
  90
banking system, international, 3,
  12–14
Barbeiri, J., 120–1, 123
Barbosa, F. de Holanda, 179
Barco, V. (President of Colombia),
  39
Bardhan, B., 113
basic needs, 21–2, 24, 28–30
Bell, C., xv, xxi, 161–78, 180–1
Bentzel, R., ix
Berlin, I. (Sir Isaiah), 21, 30
Berrian, D., 68
Betancur, B. (President of
  Colombia), 38–9
Bhalla, G. S., 230
Bhatt, M., xiv
Binswanger, H. P., xv, xxi, 110–35,
  139–40, 173–4, 177
Bliss, C. J., 162
Bogomolov, O. T., ix
Borner, S., ix
Bose, A. B., 35
Boulding, K., 5–6
Bowers, A., 133
Brahmananda, P. R., vii, ix, xiii, xiv
Brandt, W. (Chancellor, Federal
  Republic of Germany), 7
Brandt Commission, 7
Bryant, R., 10
Burkina Faso, 39, 40
Butler, J., 9

cadastral survey, 228–9
Canada, 217
Canara Bank, xi
capital assets, 46, 151
cartelisation, 13
caste system, 24
Cavallo, D., xv, xxi, 143–60, 179–80
Center for Disease Control, Atlanta,
  40
Central America, Kissinger Report,

Central Bank, 12
Chakravarty, S., vii, xii, xiii, xiv
Chandrakant, M. D., 104
Chenery, H., 90
Child Survival Revolution, Turkey, 39
China, xxi, 35, 90, 211–15, 232–3
Cipolla, C., 95
Coase's theorem, 4–5, 72
Colombia, 38–9
Comecon, *see* Council for Mutual Economic Assistance
Communist Party, China, 212
Communist Party of the Soviet Union, 216, 221, 222, 224, 225, 228, 234
compensation principle, 5, 72, 95
competition, 206, 230
    see also market
contracts, 161–78, 180–1, 199, 215, 230, 233
Cooper, R. N., 4
Cornell University, 68
Cornia, G., 36
Council for Mutual Economic Assistance (CMEA), 231–2
Csikós-Nagy, B., vii, ix, xiii, xv
Czechoslovakia, xxi, 185–96

Dahyia, Bhagwan, 78
Dantwala, M. L., 128
Dasgupta, A. K., 18
Dasgupta, P., xv, xviii, 18–31, 74–6, 136
DCM Ltd, xii
Deane, P., ix
Defourny, J., 51, 63, 69
democracy, 4, 9, 106–8, 200–1
Deshpande, R. S., 108
development
    aid, 9–11, 13, 72
    history, xix–xxi, 81
    and income, 27–9
    rural, 97–109, 110–35, 137–40, 143
disarmament, 73
Dobb, M., 81
Domenech, R., 159
Dorner, P., 81
dual economy, xix–xx, 82, 181

Dubey, M., xiv

Edgeworth, F. Y., 73
education, xx, 22, 147, 179, 212
efficiency, 5, 26–30, 75–6, 95, 176
Eicher, C., 96
Eisner, R., 151, 152
elasticity
    demand, 83–5, 87–93, 95, 112, 120–1, 124–5, 129, 131, 143–4
    employment, 86–94
    supply, 91, 120–1, 124, 131–2, 159
Ellis, H. S., x
employment
    agriculture, xix, 64–6, 116, 131–2, 174–5
    choice, 147–51
    creation, 23–4, 101–4, 213–14, 215
    industrial, 82–5, 187
    multiplier, 139
    rural, 98–9, 111, 186–7
    by occupation, 213–15
    as social indicator, 43
entitlement theory, 9–10, 22–30, 75, 137, 140
Epstein, L. G., 148
equity, 8–9, 19, 26–30, 45–71, 68, 72–6, 81–96, 99, 136–7, 197
erosion, 224, 226
European Economic Community, 231
Evenson, R. E., 113
Export Import Bank of India, xii
exports, xix–xx, 13, 118–25, 209

Falcon, W. P., 124
Federation of Indian Chambers of Commerce and Industry, xii
Fei, J., 81, 82
Fields, G., 27
Fitoussi, J.-P., x
food
    consumption, 29, 85, 143–4, 203
    imports, xx, 86, 90
    insufficiency, 19, 21–2, 24
    packaging, 231
    price, xxi, 74, 82, 86, 93, 95, 111, 112–13, 125–30
    production, xx, 201, 209

supply, 43, 74, 77, 193–4, 211–12, 229, 234
and work programmes, 138
Ford Foundation, xi
Foster, J., 46
Frisch, R., 90, 91

Garton Ash, T., 16
General Agreement on Tariffs and Trade, 16
Gevers, L., 20
Ghandi, I. (Prime Minister of India), 40
Ghosh, A., xiv
Gorbachev, M. S., 216
Gould, J. P., 151
government
  expenditure, 46–67
  information, 25
  intervention, 97–109, 137–40, 198–209, 212
  policy, xxi, 5, 36, 42–3, 145, 158, 176
Grant, J. P., xv, xviii, 32–44, 76–7
Green Revolution, 97, 116–17, 130–1, 140
Greer, J., 46
Group of Five, Group of Seven, 8
growth
  agriculture-led, 81–96, 136–40
  balanced, 136, 214–15
  and demand, 35–6, 136, 139
  and equity, 8, 74
  and exports, xix–xx, 13, 118–25
  and health, 35–6
  industry-led, 136
  objectives, xviii
  and sector proportions, 143–60
  and time, 27–8
Guha, A., 20

Haberler, G., x
Hahn, F. H., 177
Hajela, P. D., xiv
Hayami, Y., 81, 128
Hayek, F., 23
Haykin, S., 124
Hazell, P., 131
health

and alcohol, 40
care, 22, 33–40, 211
child, xviii, 32–44, 76–7, 136
economics, 32–5, 41–3
and income, 32–8, 76–7
indicators, 29, 32–44
non-market care, 76–7
rural, 34, 188, 190
and smoking, 33, 34, 40
Hillebrandt, P. M., x
Hirschman, A. O., 37, 82
Holanda Barbosa, F. de, 179
Holland, *see* Netherlands
housing, *see* infrastructure
human resources, 14, 37, 46, 144
Hume, D., 16
Hungary, xxi, 197–210, 230–3

import substitution, 82, 117, 136
incentives, 28
income distribution
  and government policy, 5, 7, 48–60, 78
  and growth, xviii–xxi, 29
  intersectoral, 94
  and rationing, 25–8
  rural, 114–22, 125–30, 132, 136–7, 139–40
  and social justice, 68
  statistics, 43
  and structural change, 81–5
  and utility, 19
  and vulnerable groups, 32
India, 35, 78, 90, 97–109, 114, 120–1, 123–5, 130–2, 137–9, 162, 174–7, 179, 180, 181
Indian Council for Cultural Relations, xii
Indian Council of Social Science Research, xi
Indian Economic Association, vii, xi, xii
Indonesia, 45, 65, 68
Industrial Credit and Investment Corporation of India, xi
Industrial Development Bank of India, xi
Industrial Finance Corporation of India, xi

Industrial Reconstruction Bank of
India, xi
industrialisation
and agriculture, xx–xxi, 186–93,
202–8, 230–3, 234–5
rural, 181, 213–15
and structural change, 81
inequality
and development, 99, 110–35, 136
and government, 7, 9, 12
and health, 33–5, 43
income, 19
and land tenure, 197, 232–3
and market forces, 21
and planning, 46–62, 72–6
and utility, 20–30
inflation, 4, 12–13, 83
infrastructure, xx, 26, 104, 122, 145,
174–6, 186, 200, 211, 214,
220–8, 234–5
Institute of Applied Manpower
Research, xii
Institute for Social and Economic
Change, 97, 98–9
Institute of Social Studies, The
Hague, 68
insurance, xxi, 161–4, 201
Integrated Rural Development
Programme, Karnataka, 104–6
International Development Research
Centre, xi
International Economic Association,
ix–x
International Monetary Fund, 43
International Social Science Council,
xii
international trade, xix–xx, 4–5,
7–13, 72–4, 82, 90–5, 117,
118–25, 136, 203, 209
investment
agriculture, 114, 139, 204–9, 234–5
international trust, 13
intersectoral allocation, 151–8
job-creating, 101–4, 213–14, 215
rural, 221–2
irrigation, *see* infrastructure
Ishikawa, S., xiii
Islam, N., vii, xiii

Jalan, B., xiv
Janvry, A. de, xv, xx, 67, 81–96,
136–7, 180
Japan, 13–14, 81, 145
Jaynes, G. D., 177
Jeniček, V., xv, xxi, 185–96
Johnston, B., xiii, 81, 136
Jolly, R., xv, xviii, 32–44, 76–7
Jorgensen, D., 81, 82

Kanbur, S. M. R., 49–50, 54, 59, 68,
69
Kant, I., 4
Karnataka governmental support
for Delhi Congress, xi
rural development, 97–109, 137–9
Kaser, M., x
Kenya, 90
Kerala
governmental support for Delhi
Congress, xi
infant mortality rate, 35
Keynes, J. M., 18, 29
Khachaturov, T. S., x, xv, xxi,
216–29, 234–5
Khan, H. A., 55, 65, 68, 70
Khusro, A. M., xiv
Kilby, P., 81
Kindleberger, C. P., 3
Kissinger, H., 6
Korea, Republic, 81
Krishna, R., 113
kulaks, 200–1
Kumar, G., 136
Kuznets, S., 28
Kuznets curve, 28

labour
intensity, xviii
intersectoral distribution, 145–51
participation, 146, 158, 186–7
productivity, xviii–xxi, 193, 211–15
Lakdawala, D. T., xiv
land
constraint, 214
productivity, 87–90, 217–29
reclamation, 222
tenure, xix–xxi, 54, 76, 81, 100–1,

110, 136–8, 145–8, 161–78,
180–1, 197–202, 232–3
use, 86, 93, 132, 180, 186, 216–29,
234–5
valuation, 155, 227–8
Lane, S., vii, xvi, xviii–xxi, 74
leisure, 19, 146–51
Lele, U., 81, 82, 86
Lewis, A., 81
liberalisation, 7, 10, 123–5
Lindahl, E., x
linkage
consumption, 124–5
income, 116–17
intersectoral, xix–xx, 37, 51,
82–95, 191–3, 201–2, 233
market, 137
Lipton, M., 5
Lluch, C., 90
Lorenz redistribution, 29, 30
Lucas, R E., 151, 152
Lundberg, E., x
Luo, Y., x, xv, xxi, 211–15, 232–3

Machlup, F., x
Madaiah, M., xiv
Madhya Pradesh, governmental
support for Delhi Congress, xi
Malaysia, 174–7
Malinvaud, E., x
Malthus, R., 18
Mandal Panchayats, 102
Marglin, S., 24, 28
markets
agricultural, 82, 94–5, 105–8,
113–117, 132–3, 162–3, 173–4,
176–7, 186–7, 231, 233
access, xx, 6
financial, xxi, 12–14, 73, 161,
171–7, 180
international, 3–4, 124–7
labour, 21
tenancies, xxi, 161–78
Marshall Plan, 14–15
Marx, K., 199
Mathur, G., xiv
Mathur, M. V., xiv
Matthews, R. C. O., 17

Maunder, A., 160
Mehrota, S., xvi
Mellor, J., 81, 82, 86, 131, 133, 136,
160
migration, 73, 82, 83, 131, 146–8,
159, 179–80, 215, 232–3
minimum subsistence, 18–30
Monke, E. A., 124
Mundlak, Y., viii, xv, xxi, 133,
143–60, 179–80
Murthy, G. V. S. N, xvi
Mussa, U., 152
Myrdal, G., 6

Nadkarni, M. V., 108
Narain, I., xiv
Narayana, D. L., xiv
Narula, D. D., xiv
National Bank for Agriculture and
Rural Development (India), xi
National Child Survival and
Development Plan, 39
natural resources, 4, 215, 216–19, 227
natural rights, 20–1
Netherlands, 9
Newbery, D. M. G., 162–3, 177
North-South co-operation, 14
Norway, 9
Nozick, R., 23
nutrition, 21–2, 24, 34
see also food

Ohkawa, K., 81
Olson, M., 3, 5, 8, 16
Organisation for Economic
Co-operation and Development
(OECD), 7, 13
Organisation for European
Economic Co-operation
(OEEC), 15
Otsuka, K., 128
Overseas Development Council, 7

Pakistan, 90
Pal, R., 133
Panchamukhi, P. R., xvi
Panchamukhi, V. R., vii, xii, xiv
Papi, G. U., x

Parthasarathy, V. S., 108
Pasinetti, L., x
paternalism, 23
Patinkin, D., x
Pfeffermann, G., 36
Phelps, E. S., 72–3
Philippines, 180
Pischke, J. D. von, 176
planning
  central, 199–200, 212–15, 217,
    230–5
  consumption, 193–6
  local, 97
  structural path analysis, 45, 62–8
  time horizon, 78
pluralism, 22–30
Poland, 230
pollution, 4, 33, 224, 225
population
  control, 132, 212, 215, 233
  growth, 19, 220, 232
  mortality, 32
  occupation, 186–7
  settlement distribution, 185–6,
    211–15, 216–17, 226
  urbanisation, 83, 185–7
positive rights, 20–30, 76
poverty
  alleviation, 45–71, 76, 94, 129,
    181, 211–12
  aversion, 45, 46–7, 52–68
  frictional, xviii
  measurement, 46, 78
  reduction, 10, 78, 99, 103, 105,
    108, 110–35, 137–9
  structural, xviii–xxi, 28–30, 72–4
Powell, A., 90
Prabhu, K. S., xvi
Prasad, K., xiv
Prescott, E. C., 152
price
  agriculture, 81, 118–25, 139–40,
    144, 199, 208–9, 230
  fertiliser, 122–3
  food, 82, 86, 111, 112–13, 125–30
  oil, 14
  policy, 81
  and rationing, 25
Primary Health Care, 34

productivity
  agriculture, 81–5, 116–17, 130–1,
    193, 203
  capital, 157
  labour, xviii–xxi, 193, 211–15
  land, 87–90, 217–29
project evaluation, 24
protection
  agriculture, 113, 231
  competition, 4
  and equity, 7–8
  and liberalisation, 10
public goods, 3, 7–8, 74
Punjab Haryana and Delhi (PDH)
  Chambers of Commerce and
  Industry, xii
Punjab National Bank, xi
Pyatt, G., 51

Quizon, J. B., xv, xxi, 110–35,
  139–40

Rangarajan, C., xiv
Ranis, G., 81, 82
Rao, D. S. G., 108
Rao, V. M., xv, xx–xxi, 97–109,
  137–9
Rath, B., 138
rationing, 25, 111, 125–9, 132
Rawls, J., 26–7, 30, 72–3
Ray, D., 22, 29, 30
Reid, J. D., 177
Renborg, U., 160
rent, 66, 93, 95, 112, 132, 161–78,
  180, 200, 227
Research and Information System
  for Non-aligned and Other
  Developing Countries, xi
Reserve Bank of India, xi
Ricardo, D., 18, 19
risk, xxi, 147, 161–7, 168, 175, 179,
  180, 217, 218
Robinson, E. A. G. (Sir Austin), x,
  109
Robinson, S., 70, 90
Roell, A., 131
Rojo, L. A., ix
Rosenzweig, M. R., 113, 173–4, 177
Rosovsky, H., 81

Round, J. I., 51
Rural Landless Employment
    Guarantee Programme,
    Karnataka, 102–3
Ruttan, V., 81
Ryzhkov, N. I., 235

Sadoulet, E., xv, xx, 81–96, 136–7
Samuelson, P. A., x
sanctions
    contractual, 72
    international, 3–4
Sargent, T. J., 157
saving, 13, 28, 114, 152–8
Scandizzo, P. L., 139
Scheinkman, J. A., 159
Schiff, M., 128
self-interest, 3–10
Sen, A. K., viii, ix, xv, 20, 23, 24, 28,
    29, 30
Sen, R. K., xvi
Sengupta, N. K., xiv
Shanmugasundaram, Professor, xiv
sharecropping, 161–78, 181, 200
Shiraishi, T., x
Siamwalla, A., 124
Singh, M., xii, xiv
Singh, N., 177
Singh, S., 96
Sinha, R. K., xiv
Sipos, A., xv, xxi, 197–210, 230–2
Smith, A., 4
social accounting matrix, 45, 50–68,
    78
social choice, 18–31
social conditioning, 24
social indicators, 20, 30, 32–44
social justice
    and development, xviii, 18–31,
        74–6
    and international co-operation,
        3–17, 72–4
    and land tenure, 171–2, 179, 197
    planning techniques, 45–71, 78
social security, 188, 190, 201
South Asian Association for
    Regional Cooperation, 41
South Korea, *see* Korea, Republic

Soviet Union, *see* Union of Soviet
    Socialist Republics
Sri Lanka, 34–5, 90
State Bank of India, xi
Stern, N. H., 162
Steward, F., 36
Stiglitz, J. E., 166, 177
Streeten, P., xv, xviii, 3–17, 22, 24,
    29, 72–4
Strotz, R. H., 151, 152
Subbarao, K., 128
Subramanian, S., 67
subsidies, 117, 125–30, 132, 230–1
Sudan, 90
Sussangkarn, C., 175
Sweden, 9
Sylos-Labini, P., xiii
Syrquin, M., 90

Taiwan, 81
Tata Group of Industries, xi
taxation
    agriculture, 179
    avoidance, 155
    excise, 125–8
    incidence, 95, 129–30
    land, 127, 129–30
    as policy instrument, 7, 198,
        199–200
Taylor, L., 113
technology, agricultural, 82–90,
    94–5, 144, 190–3, 203–8, 222–6,
    230–2
terms of trade, intersectoral, 116
Thimmaiah, G., 108
Thorbecke, E., xv, xviii, 45–71, 78
Toddaro, M. P., 147
Tradeway, A. B., 151
transport, *see* infrastructure
Tsuru, S., x
Turkey, 39, 77
two-gap analysis, 90

unemployment, 12, 74–6, 86, 93,
    149–51, 179, 211–13
Union of Soviet Socialist Republics,
    xxi, 81, 216–29, 234–5
United Arab Emirates, 35
United Nations, 15

United Nations Educational,
  Scientific and Cultural
  Organization (UNESCO), x, xii
United Nations Office on Smoking
  and Health, 33
United States of America, 5, 6, 15,
  33, 35, 40, 145, 217, 231
urbanisation, 83, 185–7, 198, 211–14
Urquidi, V. L., x
utilitarianism, 9–10, 18–30, 72
Uttar Pradesh
  governmental support for Delhi
    Congress, x
  rural development, 138

Varma, R., xvi
Vivekananda, M., 103

Vyas, A., xvi
Vyasulu, V., xvi

wages, 147–51, 163–71
Weitzman, M. L., 20
welfare, 20–30, 73, 74–6
Wharton, C., 96
Williams, R., 90
Williamson, J. G., vii
Witt, L., 96
World Bank, 43, 90
World Employment Programme, 43

Yang, M. C., 133

Zusman, P., 166